The Era of High-Speed Growth

The Era of High-Speed Growth

Notes on the Postwar Japanese Economy

Yutaka Kosai

translated by

Jacqueline Kaminski

UNIVERSITY OF TOKYO PRESS

Translation and publication of this volume were assisted by grants from the Ministry of Education, Science and Culture, Japan, and The Japan Foundation.

Translated from the original Japanese edition: *Kōdo seichō no jidai: Gendai Nihon keizai shi nōto* (Tokyo: Nihon Hyōronsha, 1981).

Copyright by University of Tokyo Press, 1986
ISBN 0-86008-341-1
Japan ISBN 4-13-047027-2 (UTP 47274)

Printed in Japan

Contents

List of Tables   vii
List of Figures   x
Preface   xi
Preface to the English Edition   xiii

Prologue: The Course of Rapid Growth   3

Part I. Reconstruction

1. Occupation and Reform: The Beginnings of   15
   Postwar Democracy
2. Recovery and Inflation   33
3. The Dodge Plan and the Korean War   53
4. The Special Procurement Boom: Economic Outcome   69
   of the Korean War
5. The Bases for Economic Growth   79

Part II. Growth

6. The Beginning of Rapid Growth   95
7. The Technological Revolution and Its Impact   111
8. Income Doubling and Trade Liberalization   127
9. An Interlude in Rapid Growth   143
10. The Economic Superpower   157

Part III. The Changeover

11. From Yen Revaluation to Oil Crisis   173
12. Reaching for Steady Growth   189

Epilogue: Looking Back on the Rapid-Growth Era   201

Bibliography   213
Index   217

List of Tables

P–1.	Summary of Reconstruction and Growth	4
P–2.	Growth Rates, Investment Rates, and Capital Coefficients for Each Five-Year Period	5
P–3.	Labor Productivity	7
P–4.	Analysis of the Primary Growth Factors	8
P–5.	Annual Increase in Gross Expenditure, by Demand Item	9
P–6.	Income Distribution and Savings	10
1–1.	Results of the Land Reform	21
1–2.	The Relative Decline in Farm Rents	21
1–3.	Number of Farm Households by Amount of Land under Cultivation	22
1–4.	Prewar Labor and Farm Tenancy Disputes	22
1–5.	Major Applications of the 1947 Measures for the Elimination of Excessive Concentration of Economic Power	25
1–6.	The Decline in Industry Concentration Ratios	26
1–7.	Labor Union Growth, 1945–49	28
2–1.	Shifts in Key Economic Indicators, 1945–49	34
2–2.	A Rendering of Accounts for the National Economy	35
2–3.	Damage to the National Wealth Due to the Pacific War	38
2–4.	Productive Capacity at the Time of the Defeat	39
2–5.	Population and the Number Employed, by Industry	40
2–6.	Trends in Imports of Key Products	40
2–7.	The Stagnation of Production during the Latter Half of 1946	42
2–8.	Postwar Activities of the Reconstruction Finance Bank	45

2–9.	Changes in the System of Controlled Prices	46
2–10.	The Status of Price-Differential Subsidies	46
2–11.	Price Changes, 1946–49	48
3–1.	The Revival of Production and the Blunting of Inflation	56
3–2.	Economic Recovery Plan, First Draft	57
3–3.	The Dodge Super-Balanced Budget (FY 1949)	61
3–4.	Progress under the Dodge Plan	63
3–5.	Influence of the Dodge Plan and the Korean War	66
4–1.	Price Increases during the Korean War (1949 as base year)	71
4–2.	Fluctuation in the Balance of Payments	72
4–3.	Principal Export Items	73
4–4.	Changes in Economic Indexes, 1946–53	75
4–5.	Wage Differentials in Manufacturing Industries, by Scale of Operation	77
5–1.	Results of Plant and Equipment Investment under the First Iron and Steel Rationalization Plan	81
5–2.	Plant and Equipment Investment by the 18 Major Firms in the Coal Mining Industry	83
5–3.	The Electric Power Development Plan	83
5–4.	Effects of Rationalization Investments	84
5–5.	Industrial Capital Supply Conditions	90
5–6.	Conditions for Capital Accumulation	91
5–7.	The Pattern of Growth in the Postwar Reconstruction Period	92
6–1.	Changes in Gross National Expenditure	97
6–2.	Changes in Economic Indicators	101
6–3.	Dating of Business Cycles	107
6–4.	Capital Stock and Plant & Equipment Investment	108
7–1.	Capital Formation in the Rapid-Growth Period	112
7–2.	Plant and Equipment Investment under the Second Iron and Steel Rationalization Plan	115
7–3.	Sales Growth Rates and Financing Patterns, 1955–63	124
7–4.	Population Increases, by Region, from 1955 to 1960	125
8–1.	The Income Doubling Plan and Results Achieved	130
8–2.	Time Schedules for the Liberalization Plan	134
8–3.	Changes in the Rate of Import Liberalization	136
8–4.	Adjustments in Economic Growth and the Capital Stock	139
8–5.	Labor Supply and Demand, and Price Trends	140

9–1.	Composition and Rate of Growth of Gross National Expenditure	144
9–2.	Financial Trends in the First Half of the 1960s	145
9–3.	Distribution of Firms by Rate of Growth	150
9–4.	Business Conditions of Retail Firms	151
10–1.	Main Economic Indicators for the Latter Half of the 1960s	158
10–2.	Fiscal and Monetary Indicators for the Latter Half of the 1960s	159
10–3.	Fluctuations in Real Gross National Expenditure	161
10–4.	Changes in the Composition of Exports and Imports	165
10–5.	Particulars of the Liberalization of Capital	166
11–1.	Multinational Exchange Rate Adjustments (end of 1971)	174
11–2.	Changes in the International Balance of Payments	177
11–3.	Changes in Fiscal Policies	182
11–4.	The Advance of Inflation	185
12–1.	Government Intervention in the Prices of Individual Commodities	190
12–2.	Money, Price, and Output Trends (by comparison with the previous recession period)	192
12–3.	Nominal and Real Price Changes in the Period of Inflation	193
12–4.	Changes in Key Economic Indicators, 1975–78	194

List of Figures

P–1.   Plant and Equipment Investment and Personal Savings   10

6–1.   Prices, Output, and Inventory-Sales Ratios   103

7–1.   The Scaling-Up of Steam-Powered Generators   117

7–2.   Shifts in Purchasing of Key Consumer Durable   122
       Goods

Preface

This book is one viewer's history of the contemporary Japanese economy, from 1945 until the early 1980s. I have attempted to clarify the correspondence between (1) macro and micro, (2) the real and the financial aspects of the economy, (3) data and explanation, (4) "illustrations" and analysis, and so on, and in each instance to strike a balance between the two. Through my professional work as an economist, I am most familiar with the figures on the macro economy from the National Economic Accounts, and a primary concern of this book has been to present the substance in this form. Furthermore, attention to both the real and the financial aspects of the economy reinforced my conviction that Japan's rapid growth was promoted in unexpectedly close accordance with the game rules of classical capitalism.

A balance between data and explanation, "illustration" and analysis, is associated with a style more narrative than analytical. No specialist at historical narrative, I generally set ease of reading as the standard to strive for. Basic documents and summary statistics are interspersed with the text and arranged as conveniently as possible in order to give immediacy to the narrative. Historical writing entirely in analytical language breeds tediousness, and the abuse of metaphors laden with value judgments should also be avoided.

The writing of this book was occasioned near the end of 1977 by the urgings of Hayashi Yasunori, then editor-in-chief of *Keizai seminā* [Seminar on the Economy], to run a serial history of the contemporary Japanese economy in his journal. These articles were carried monthly from April 1978 to March 1979 under the title "The Course Taken by the Japanese Economy." During that time I received encouragement from Mr. Hayashi's successor, editor-in-chief Horioka Haruo, and from Moriya Katsumi. When these materials were gathered together into a book, I became once again, as with my previous book, much indebted to Tanaka Toshiro. In addition, at that point I rewrote the prologue and epilogue and added a number of touches in several other parts.

At the beginning of 1978, after having agreed to write the series of articles, I was appointed chief of the Price Bureau's Price Adjustment Division at the Economic Planning Agency. This put me on the front lines of price administration matters such as negotiations with each ministry over the setting of public utility rates. It also curtailed my free time, and more than once I found myself drafting an article beginning on a Saturday night and somehow or other polishing it off sometime Sunday. But, despite the pressure of time, I am grateful for the opportunity of writing the articles. The process contributed to my own sense of self-worth at the time, and it enriched my life. I would like to express my appreciation to my superior in the Price Bureau at that time and to all my colleagues, who kindly guided and assisted me in my capacity as a public servant.

I was greatly benefited by the guidance of a number of teachers and senior colleagues, including Shinohara Miyohei, Nakamura Takafusa, Sakisaka Masao, Kanamori Hisao, Shimada Katsumi, and Uchino Tatsurō, and was privileged to have their participation on any number of occasions in retrospective examinations of the Japanese economy's movement through time since World War II. The work done at that time has both directly and indirectly provided the basis for this book. For this I must express my gratitude to each of the individuals involved. Needless to say, however, any errors included in this book are my responsibility alone.

Finally, on a personal note, I would like to call to mind the memory of my deceased father, immersed as he was in his hobby of ancient literature; and I would like, as well, to see my family, which has long shared in my joys and sorrows, take pleasure with me in the publication of this book.

February 1981   YUTAKA KOSAI

Preface to the English Edition

It is my great pleasure that my book, *Kōdo seichō no jidai*, has been translated into English. I hope that it will have something to say to readers outside Japan about the postwar Japanese economy and its political and social setting.

The original Japanese edition, which was published in 1981, was written for readers who, as the author's contemporaries, had had more or less the same experiences. Some explanatory notes have been inserted where references were thought to be a bit difficult for non-Japanese readers to comprehend easily. For example, Marxist views on economic growth are frequently referred to in the first half of the book: this is because theoretical Marxism was an important force among Japanese intellectuals and economists in the 1950s and 1960s (although its influence has rapidly declined since that time); without knowing this fact, which Japanese take for granted, readers will be unable to understand why Marxist views are referred to with such frequency in a discussion of growth in a capitalist economy.

Some of the statistical data quoted in this book have been revised; however, in most cases I decided it would be preferable not to employ revised figures, so that White Papers, reports, and other documents are accompanied by the statistics on the basis of which they were compiled. In a few cases, more recent figures have been added for purposes of comparison. Documents on the Japanese economy issued by the Occupation authorities and other overseas source materials are quoted in the original English wherever the original version was available to the author or translator. In a few cases, where searching failed to turn up original documents or reports, quotations are retranslated from Japanese or paraphrased. In spite of all these difficulties, I hope this book will add to understanding of the Japanese economy and its rapid growth beginning in 1955.

I am indebted to many people who worked toward the publication of both the English and Japanese editions of this book. In particular, I would like to express my deep appreciation to the translator, Jacqueline Kaminski, and to Director Kazuo Ishii and editor Susan Schmidt of the University of Tokyo Press.

September 1985   YUTAKA KOSAI

The translator would particularly like to thank Yoshifumi Miyagi and Nobuhiko Tsuzuki for their patient and painstaking assistance in illuminating obscurities and dispelling befuddlements that arose at many a turn in the preparation of this translation.

JACQUELINE KAMINSKI

The Era of High-Speed Growth

Prologue: The Course of Rapid Growth

Between 1945 and 1970 the Japanese economy achieved what is rare both historically and by international comparative standards: growth at the high annual rate of nearly ten percent. This book takes a retrospective look at historical events during that period. In this section, I will give an overview and then set out a number of macroeconomic statistics that will give quantitative specificity to our subject. In conclusion, I will raise several issues which warrant investigation.

The postwar Japanese economy may be roughly divided into three periods: the recovery from 1945 to 1955, the ensuing period of rapid growth ending about 1970, and the adjustment period of the 1970s and early 1980s, characterized by a general movement toward stable growth.

During the recovery, economic growth was high but the standard of living was low, and international payments deficits, unemployment, and inflation afflicted the economy. In the rapid-growth period that followed, the growth rate began to rise and the living standard turned upward as well; international accounts shifted into balance, full employment was achieved, and price increases were mild compared to those of the immediate postwar years. Supporting this period's high growth was the technological revolution proceeding in a wide range of fields, aimed at catching up with the advanced countries and driven by firms' ardent desire to compete.

This rapid growth was bound to come to an end sooner or later. However, what actually succeeded rapid growth was a process whereby growth was sharply reduced. This process was initiated by the series of shocks consisting of the revaluation of the yen, inflation, the oil crisis, and so on, that occurred at the beginning of the 1970s. Plagued by the trilemma of rising prices, unemployment, and international payments imbalances virtually throughout the 1970s, the Japanese economy, with its lowered rate of growth, was compelled to adapt to a new (and lower) growth path.

3

Table 9–1. Summary of Reconstruction and Growth

	Reconstruction Period		Rapid Growth Period		Adjustment Period		Stable Growth Period	
	1946–50	1951–55	1956–60	1961–65	1966–70	1971–75	1974–80	1981–85
Economic Growth Rate (%)	9.4	10.9	8.7	9.7	12.2	5.1	5.1	4.4
Rate of Price Increase (CPI, %)	44.4	6.3	1.5	6.1	5.4	11.5	6.4	2.7
Unemployment Rate (%)	1.0	1.7	2.0	1.3	1.2	1.4	2.1	2.5
Balance of Payments ($ millions)								
Current Balance	634	524	115	−1,358	6,201	6,912	1,933	25,222
Trade Balance	−939	−1,963	468	1,955	13,626	26,990	11,268	35,388
Growth Conditions	Reconstruction	Independence	Technological Revolution, Modernization		Emergence of Superpower	Yen Revaluation, Oil Crisis	Adjustment	Stable Growth
Prices	Postwar Inflation	Inflationary Disturbances	Stability	Productivity Differential Inflation	Import Inflation	Hyper-inflation	Effort to Stabilize	Stability
Labor Supply	Over-supply	Over-supply	Over-supply	Short-age	Short-age	Over-supply	Equilibrium	Equilibrium
Balance of Payments	Deficit	Deficit	Equilibrium	Equilibrium	Surplus	Fluctuating	Fluctuating	Surplus

Source: From Kokumin shotoku tōkei [National Income Statistics]. Figures for 1981–85 are based on the quarterly forecast of the Japan Economic Research Center, July 1985.

Note: For the 1946–50 period, the first year for which data are available varies; the figures in column 1 are averages for 1946–1950 in some cases and for 1947–1950 in others.

Table P–1 presents an overview of the above process broken down by five-year intervals.

Capital Coefficients and Investment Ratios

According to the Harrod-Domar model, the economic growth rate G breaks down into two factors, the capital coefficient c and the investment ratio s. The relationship among the three is expressed by the equation $G\,c = s$.

Following this equation, let us compare the growth rates, capital coefficients, and investment ratios for each five-year interval in the postwar period (Table P–2). The striking fact is that the marginal capital coefficient for the reconstruction period is conspicuously low, and for this reason the resulting investment ratio is also small. The large capital stock inherited from the prewar and wartime years made very rapid economic growth during reconstruction possible without new investment, if only increased imports of raw materials could be arranged.

The marginal capital coefficient for the period of rapid growth in the 1960s showed an increase over the reconstruction period but remained low (2 or below) by international standards. This reflected the fact that the rate of technological advance was high during this period. Although the capital coefficient was relatively low, the high rate of economic growth inevitably led to a sharp increase in the investment ratio relative

Table P–2. Growth Rates, Investment Rates, and Capital Coefficients for Each Five-year Period

	1945–50	1950–55	1955–60	1960–65	1965–70	1970–75	1975–80
Economic Growth Rate	9.4	10.9	8.7	9.7	12.2	5.1	5.6
Investment Rate A	9.3	7.9	11.4	14.8	18.1	18.2	17.1
Investment Rate B	8.3	10.8	16.5	18.5	18.5	17.8	14.7
Capital Coefficient	1.0	0.7	1.3	1.5	1.5	3.6	3.1
Relative Price	0.89	1.37	1.45	1.25	1.02	0.98	0.86

Notes: Investment Rate A: Private plant and equipment investment ÷ GNP.
For 1945–50, (Investment in private housing + Private plant & equipment) × 2/3, in real prices (1970 prices).
B: Same as above, in nominal prices.
Capital Coefficient = Investment rate A ÷ Economic growth rate.
Relative Price = Investment rate B ÷ Investment rate A
= Investment deflator ÷ GNP deflator.

to that of the reconstruction period. What made possible such a rapid increase in the investment ratio? How did firms and households manage in response to it? This question is the greatest key to solving the riddle of rapid growth.

In the 1970s, the growth rate declined and the investment ratio likewise sagged. On the other side of the coin, the marginal capital coefficient rose markedly. This reflects the decline in plant operating rates during this period, but at the same time such factors as the increase in the relative importance of replacement investment which accompanied the decline in the growth rate and expanded investment in energy conservation were also influential. Japan's marginal capital coefficients approached those of West Germany and the United States during this period.

The reconstruction period was characterized by a high growth rate and a low investment ratio. The period of rapid growth was distinguished by a high growth rate, a high investment ratio, and, in addition, a comparatively low capital coefficient. A major issue in modern Japanese economic history is the elucidation of the conditions which made possible such a growth pattern, not only at the macro level but descending all the way down to concrete behavior at the micro level.

Productivity Increases and Changes in Industrial Structure

The economic growth rate in terms of labor inputs can be broken down into the rate of increase in the labor force plus the rate of increase in productivity. Table P–3 compares the rates of increase in employment and in productivity from this point of view. The rate of productivity increase during the period of rapid growth tends to be rising. Moreover, employment increases in this period are high at around 2 %. Labor supply was abundant. Furthermore, a portion of productivity increases was supported by the sharply rising capital equipment ratio.

Changes in the industrial structure also contributed to productivity increases. If one separates industry into manufacturing and non-manufacturing sectors, it can be seen that the productivity of manufacturing industries led the way in the upward climb. The gradually rising share of these manufacturing industries during the rapid growth process reinforced the impact of increases in manufacturing productivity on overall productivity increases. The labor force shift out of the non-industrial sector and into industry also had the effect of increasing average productivity.

In calculating such structural changes one encounters such problems as the fact that results differ according to the method used to categorize

Table P–3. Labor Productivity

(%)

	1945–50	1950–55	1955–60	1960–65	1965–70	1970–75	1975–80
Real Growth Rate	9.4	10.9	8.7	9.7	12.2	5.1	5.6
Percent Increase in Employment	2.3	2.7	2.2	1.7	1.8	0.4	1.2
Increase in Productivity	7.1	8.2	6.5	8.0	10.4	4.7	4.4
		(24.2)	(25.4)	(29.7)	(29.7)	(27.6)	(26.1)
Manufacturing Industries	—	12.0	9.6	7.9	12.3	2.0	7.0
Other	—	7.0	5.5	8.1	9.7	5.6	3.5
Contribution Rate of Manufacturing Industries	—	35.4	37.5	29.3	35.1	11.7	41.5
Relative Productivity of Manufacturing Industries at Beginning of Period	—	1.55	1.35	1.34	1.16	1.17	1.05
Employed Persons' Shift Point	—	1.6	4.2	2.3	1.7	−0.9	−1.7
Contribution Rate Due to Shift	—	0.9	1.5	0.8	0.3	−0.2	−0.1

Notes: (1) Productivity increase in manufacturing industries = Expansion in mining and manufacturing output − Increase in the number employed in manufacturing.

Data on employment in manufacturing industries are from the national census to 1975, from labor force surveys for the most recent period; figures for fiscal 1980 are September data.

(2) Parentheses indicate manufacturing industry weights. Based on national income weights by industry at the mid-point of each period. Data for the most recent period were linked with the new SNA statistics in 1975.

(3) Relative productivity was obtained by dividing the weights in item (2) above by the distribution ratios in the national census.

(4) Employed persons' shift point is the degree of change in the distribution ratio in the national census (percent shift).

(5) Contribution rate due to shift is (relative productivity − 1) × shift point.

sectors of the economy, the fact that growth and structural change cannot be readily demarcated in any simple way, etc. However, Table P–3 serves the useful purpose of keeping one mindful that swift changes in industrial structure were considered to be a condition for rapid growth.

The Expansion of Demand

In the preceding sections we examined economic growth in terms of capital and in terms of labor. In this section we will present a summary treatment of "growth accounting" using a simple series of data (Table P–4). In addition to capital stock and the number of employed, this table also includes hours of work, quality of capital (vintage), and quality of labor (years of education).

In growth accounting the value "capital's share × increase in capital stock + labor's share × increase in labor inputs" is calculated, and the difference between this and the growth rate is considered to be the neutral rate of technological advance. The results of these calculations are in practice strongly dominated by the values of the capital and labor shares. Here, the share of capital was calculated at 0.3, and that of labor as 0.7.

Thus it is clear that technical progress and the rapid accumulation of capital supported rapid growth.

Analysis of the Principal Growth Factors

Next, let us look at the growth pattern from the demand side. During the reconstruction period consumption expanded swiftly along with exports. In contrast, plant and equipment investment increased rapidly as we moved into the period of rapid growth. One can discern at five-year intervals, however, the peaks and troughs of waves in the rate of this increase in plant and equipment investment (a medium-term cycle

Table P–4.   Analysis of the Primary Growth Factors

	1955–60	1960–65	1965–70	1970–75	1975–79	1955–70	1970–79
Growth Rate	8.7	9.7	12.2	5.1	5.9	10.2	5.4
Labor Force	2.4	0.8	1.3	−0.3	1.5	1.5	0.6
Employed Persons	2.2	1.7	1.8	0.4	1.2	1.9	0.8
Working Hours	0.8	−1.0	−0.5	−1.7	0.7	−0.3	−0.6
Quality of Work	0.4	0.4	0.6	0.9	0.2	0.5	0.6
Capital	4.0	5.3	5.4	3.7	1.9	4.8	2.9
Capital Stock	7.4	11.2	12.7	11.1	6.4	10.4	9.1
Quality of Capital	5.9	6.5	5.4	1.2	0.0	5.7	0.7
Independent Technological Progress	2.3	2.4	5.5	1.7	2.5	3.9	1.9

Source: Kosai and Toshida, 1981.

Note: Assumes a distribution ratio of labor 7: capital 3.

Table P–5. Annual Increase in Gross Expenditure, by Demand Item

(%)

	1945–50	1950–55	1955–60	1960–65	1965–70	1970–75	1975–79
Private Final Consumption	10.2	9.9	7.7	8.3	9.7	6.0	4.9
Private Housing	1.9	15.9	14.5	17.4	13.7	6.2	1.8
Private Plant & Equipment		8.6	22.6	8.7	22.8	0.9	7.3
Government Final Consumption	13.4	2.4	2.9	7.1	5.1	5.6	4.2
Public Capital Formation	−9.2	23.3	13.8	16.0	10.8	6.7	7.7
Exports, etc.	99.5	13.9	12.3	14.9	15.7	11.8	10.3
(*less*) *Imports, etc.*	*25.1*	*18.1*	*16.9*	*12.5*	*16.6*	*6.8*	*9.5*
Gross National Output	9.4	10.9	8.7	9.7	12.2	5.1	5.9

Source: From "Kokumin shotoku tōkei" [National Income Statistics].

of ten years). In the rapid-growth period public capital formation and housing investment displayed precisely countercyclical fluctuations. Consumption and exports during this period, just like the overall growth rate, showed a rising trend (Table P–5).

In the early phase of the adjustment period, the expansion was blunted in all sectors, but the slowdown in plant and equipment investment is striking.

Thus we reaffirm that the period of rapid growth differs from the reconstruction and adjustment periods in that it was an era of high growth *and* high levels of investment. In addition, the not just rising but accelerating trend in exports means that, against a backdrop of expanding domestic markets and increasing productivity, the Japanese economy's invasion of world markets was proceeding at a brisk pace.

The Savings Rate and Income Distribution

The obverse of a high level of investment is a high level of saving. During the rapid growth process the personal savings rate rose virtually in parallel with the rate of plant and equipment investment. Figure P–1 plots levels of investment and savings rates in the Japanese economy between 1955 and 1975.

A little thought might suggest that two factors are likely to be the mechanism whereby this investment-saving linkage is effected: (1) high investment produces high profits, raising savings rates; (2) rapid growth produces an unequal distribution of income and raises the savings rate. However, neither of these scenarios is appropriate for the Japanese economy in the rapid-growth period.

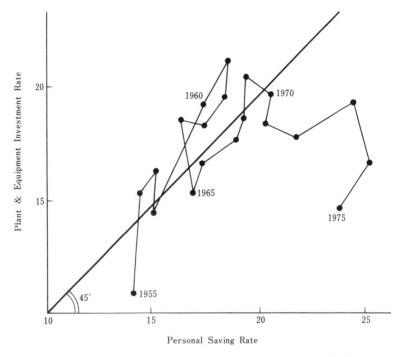

Figure P–1.   Plant and Equipment Investment and Personal Savings
Source: "Kokumin shotoku tōkei" [National Income Statistics].

Table P–6.   Income Distribution and Savings

	1950	1955	1960	1965	1970	1975
Personal Disposable Income/ GNP	71.1	74.0	67.7	68.1	64.2	72.9
Retained Income/GNP	28.9	26.0	32.3	31.9	35.8	27.1
Personal Savings Rate	8.7	13.9	17.4	17.0	20.1	22.2
Retained Savings Rate	83.0	61.2	72.5	70.5	76.5	61.6

(%)

As Table P–6 shows, personal disposable income as a proportion of GNP declined while the GNP proportions of other earned surpluses rose during rapid growth. Yet without an increase in the personal savings rate, and in the absence of a more precipitous change in the distribution of income, a saving and investment balance probably could not have been established.

This rise in the personal savings rate did not accompany a growing inequality in the distribution of personal income. It arose, instead, in the process of equalization. The wage differential which developed in the latter half of the reconstruction period, as the two-tier dual economic structure became more pronounced, shrank somewhat in the process of absorption of the surplus labor force as the economy moved into the rapid-growth period.

Money, Prices, International Payments, and Fiscal Accounts

As shown in Table P–1, both before and after the era of rapid growth there were periods of hyperinflation and of large deficits in the nation's international payments balance and its fiscal accounts.

With the exception of the latter half of the 1960s, during rapid growth the international payments accounts and the national budget were more or less balanced. In this process, while personal savings surpluses and firms' investment surpluses virtually mirrored each other, a growing money supply was provided by increasing the domestic currency—that is, by creating accounts in banks backed by the credit of the Bank of Japan. The goal of financial policy during the era of rapid growth was to maximize the growth rate subject to balance in the international accounts: this was the lowest of ceilings to impose on growth but one which at the same time served to demarcate the upper limit on price increases. From the latter half of the 1960s onward, this balance began breaking down: the balance of payments showed surpluses, and labor shortages appeared. The combined impact of this breakdown and the contemporaneous misguided responses to environmental changes which brought on the disorders of the 1970s accumulated enough force to become the beginning of the end of rapid growth.

The Conclusion of Rapid Growth

At the time of their defeat in the Second World War, the people of Japan were reeling under the strain of starvation and dire poverty. By the end of the rapid-growth era, they had attained affluence. Parliamentary democracy put down roots; and within a framework in which the market mechanism functioned effectively, income became distributed more equally and a distinctive middle-class society rose and flourished. Per-capita income, which had been one-ninth that of the United States in 1950, was 80% in 1978, and could be said to have achieved a par with Western Europe.

There are problems in viewing rapid growth as simply a success story. The drawbacks cannot be long ignored: the destruction of the environment, excessive commercialism, the fragile resource base, and so on. However, there can be no doubt that this was a distinctive era, full of vitality. Rapid growth *per se*, viewed as historical phenomenon, is fascinating. How did it begin; how did it end? From an economist's point of view: how was the expansion of production possible in the midst of low levels of investment and saving during the reconstruction period? What was the pivot upon which this situation turned into the growth period's high levels of investment and saving? How were balance of payments equilibrium and price stability possible during rapid growth? In undertaking a retrospective review of this period, one may approach it from whatever angle one prefers, whether it be human behavior and decisions, the relationship between the faddish and the immutable, or what have you.

Rapid growth has ended, but many of the concerns of today's world have been carried over from the rapid-growth period. It can hardly be thought that tracing the historical course of these events will rob them of their character as contemporary issues.

Let us then, begin our retrospective with the postwar recovery. We will attempt a final recapitulation of the era of high-speed growth in the epilogue.

Reconstruction

1

Occupation and Reform:
The Beginnings of Postwar Democracy

The Potsdam Declaration

On August 15, 1945, Japan accepted the Potsdam Declaration and surrendered to the Allied Powers. Three years and eight months had passed since the attack on Pearl Harbor, eight years since the beginning of the Sino-Japanese War, and fourteen since the "Manchurian Incident." With Japan's surrender, the Second World War came to an end.

The Postdam Declaration which Japan accepted was announced as the result of the Allied summit conference held at Potsdam in July 1945. It included the following stipulations.

There must be eliminated for all time the authority and influence of those who have deceived and misled the people of Japan into embarking on world conquest, for we insist that a new order of peace, security and justice will be impossible until irresponsible militarism is driven from the world. (Paragraph 6)

Until such a new order is established *and* until there is convincing proof that Japan's war-making power is destroyed, points in Japanese territory to be designated by the Allies shall be occupied to secure the achievement of the basic objectives we are here setting forth. (Paragraph 7)

The Japanese Government shall remove all obstacles to the revival and strengthening of democratic tendencies among the Japanese people. Freedom of speech, of religion, and of thought, as well as respect for the fundamental human rights shall be established. (Paragraph 10)

Japan shall be permitted to maintain such industries as will sustain her economy and permit the exaction of just reparations in kind, but not those which would enable her to rearm for war. To this end, access to, as distinguished from control of, raw materials shall be permitted. Eventual Japanese participation in world trade relations shall be permitted. (Paragraph 11)

15

After setting out the above terms, the Declaration added the following:

The alternative for Japan is prompt and utter destruction.

At the time, the Japanese economy was already close to complete collapse, and acceptance of the Potsdam Declaration was the only rational choice. This was particularly so since the Declaration's issuers were backed up by such a glaring difference between their own power and that of the Japanese that it only seemed to give the lie to their claim that "The Japanese shall not be enslaved as a race or destroyed as a nation." In the Japan of that time the defeat was called "the end of the war" and the occupation of the country by force was called "a stationing of troops"; but no matter what the euphemisms, they did not change the basic situation.

As indicated in the Declaration, Japan was occupied by the U.S. Army under Supreme Commander for the Allied Powers (SCAP) General Douglas MacArthur.[1] Since the Occupation army's power was absolute, the demilitarization and democratization policies which were the stated goals of the Potsdam Declaration were, in the event, implemented by force. The Occupation authorities purged, arrested and tried the war leaders, had offending passages in wartime textbooks inked out, forbade the staging of feudal vendetta plays such as *The Forty-seven Ronin* (Chushingura), and freely opened the personal correspondence of individuals who had been selected as examples. General Headquarters (GHQ) approval was required for all major (and sometimes not-so-major) policies. During the Occupation the people were subjected at every opportunity to the preachy proclamations and solemn circumlocutions of General MacArthur, who apparently thought that the Japanese were a nation of 12-year-olds. In a letter written in 1948, for example, the General opined that the economic system which Japan should adopt is "one which embodies the tenets of private capitalism based on the principles of free enterprise competition; and the fact that this is the only ststem which maximally stimulates the development of the basic requirements for human progress, that is, individual ingenuity and individual drive, is clearly demonstrated by long experience."

Not as much of a monolith as it appeared to be, the Occupation had its share of internal strife, disorders, scandals, and intrigues, and more than a few Japanese greased these chinks in the system and wriggled their way through. However, there can be no doubt that, on the whole,

---

[1] The U.S. Initial Post-Surrender Policy for Japan declared that ". . . in the event of any differences of opinion among [the principal Allied powers], the policies of the United States will govern."

the Occupation was at first extremely effective in pursuing its policies of demilitarization and democratization. Even if these policies are seen as originating in the national interests of America itself, with its dominant objective that "Japan will not again become a menace to the United States" (U.S. Initial Post-Surrender Policy for Japan, Sept. 22, 1945), at the same time they were founded on the ideals of American democracy as expressed in such concepts as "the Four Freedoms," and were pressed forward by the missionary fervor of those who were in charge on the scene.[2] As it turned out, this idealism aroused broad sympathy and support among the Japanese people.[3]

The fact is that the fundamental, lasting impact of the occupation of Japan consisted of Japanese-American contact at the grassroots level: it was essentially a cultural affair. The Yankees who appeared in the ruins of the streets after the air raids were youthfully breezy, neatly dressed, and, more than anything else, well fed. To the thronging children, the chocolate they tossed down from their Jeeps tasted captivatingly sweet. The ordinary Japanese had never seen so many foreigners (the Occupation army at one time amounted to 400,000 men). Thus, to the hungry and malnourished Japanese with only the threadbare shirt on his back, the Americans' evident prosperity looked like a reason in itself for Japan's defeat in the war. What had once been the enemy devils overnight became the object of the Japanese people's keen curiosity and envy, and "Come, Come, Everybody,"[4] the theme song of NHK Radio's English conversation program, resounded in the streets.

Thus began the rapid Americanization of Japanese culture. However, if this process had turned out to be nothing more than a one-way demonstration effect of American culture in Japan, a colonial mentality would probably have emerged in the end. That this did not occur is due to the fact that the Japanese people, although defeated in war, nevertheless had "roots" in an independent culture. The ethos which was to sustain the rapid growth of later years was formed in the tension that arose when the traditional studiousness of the Japanese encountered American culture.[5]

[2] As another example of an occupation linked to liberation and reform, Napoleon's conquest of Europe comes to mind. Even the Japanese militarists dreamed of building a paradise in Manchuria. Nor is it strange for idealism to be pursued more zealously in occupied territory than in the homeland.

[3] For example, Ronald Dore points out that the land reform progressed smoothly by virtue of a reforming zeal among the Japanese rank and file (Dore, 1959:148).

[4] Sung to the tune of "Shōjōji no Tanukibayashi" ("The Badgers Whoop It Up at Shōjō Temple"), a children's song from the Meiji era. —Trans.

[5] Such works of literature as "The American School" by Kojima Nobuo (1954) are useful sources on psychological reactions to the Occupation.

Postwar Reforms

The Potsdam Declaration sought the demilitarization and the de-militarization of Japan. The U.S. Initial Post-Surrender Policy for Japan gives a more concrete idea of its substance. Among the clauses concerning the economy are the following:

> The existing economic basis of Japanese military strength must be destroyed and not permitted to revive.
>
> Encouragement shall be given and favor shown to the develop-ment of organizations in labor, industry, and agriculture, organ-ized on a democratic basis. Policies shall be favored which permit a wide distribution of income and of the ownership of the means of production and trade.
>
> Those forms of economic activity, organization and leadership shall be favored that are deemed likely to strengthen the peaceful disposition of the Japanese people, and to make it difficult to com-mand or direct economic activity in support of military ends.
>
> To this end it shall be the policy of the Supreme Commander:
>
> (a) To prohibit the retention in or selection for places of impor-tance in the economic field of individuals who do not direct future Japanese economic effort solely towards peaceful ends; and
>
> (b) To favor a program for the dissolution of the large industrial and banking combinations which have exercised control of a great part of Japan's trade and industry.

Thus, while on the one hand demilitarization and democratization were stressed, a coolly detached attitude with regard to Japan's eco-nomic reconstruction may be detected:

> The Japanese people shall be afforded opportunity to develop for themselves an economy which will permit the peacetime require-ments of the population to be met.
>
> The plight of Japan is the direct outcome of its own behavior, and the Allies will not undertake the burden of repairing the damage.

Of the economic democratization policies implemented by the Oc-cupation, (1) land reform, (2) the dissolution of the zaibatsu, and (3) labor reform will be examined here.

Land Reform

Land reform was not clearly mentioned in the U.S. Initial Post-Surrender Policy for Japan. The first initiative for land reform came from Agriculture Minister Matsumura Kenzō and progressive bureaucrats in the Ministry of Agriculture and Forestry. An amended agricultural adjustment bill which limited the amount of land that could be owned to 5 *chō* (1 *chō* = 2.45 acres or a little less than 1 hectare) and which stipulated that tenant farmers pay their rents in cash was introduced in the 89th Extraordinary Session of the Imperial Diet in the fall of 1945, passed on December 28, and implemented as 1946 began, as the first Agricultural Land Reform.

It was during the course of deliberation on this bill that the Occupation completely reversed its bystander attitude and began to take an active part in land reform. Apparently this change was occasioned by a memorandum on land reform drafted by Robert Fearey which caught the eye of General MacArthur himself and captured his imagination. Ronald Dore conjectures that MacArthur became interested in promoting the land reform as his own personal project either in connection with recollections of the story of the Gracchi in Roman history which he learned at West Point, or out of motives related to his father's involvement with land reform in the Philippines (Dore, 1959:131–32). On December 9, 1949, the Supreme Commander for the Allied Powers (SCAP) administered a severe shock to the Japanese government with the dispatch of a Memorandum Concerning Rural Land Reform, which became popularly known as the Farmers' Liberation Decree:

> In order that the Imperial Japanese Government shall remove economic obstacles to the revival and strengthening of democratic tendencies, establish respect for the dignity of man, and destroy the economic bondage which has enslaved the Japanese farmer to centuries of feudal oppression, the Japanese Imperial Government is directed to take measures to insure that those who till the soil of Japan shall have more equal opportunity to enjoy the fruits of their labor.

The Agricultural Land Reform bill was debated at the Allied Council for Japan (ACJ) by representatives of the Allied Powers. All felt that the Japanese government's bill was not thoroughgoing. The proposals of the English representative, MacMahon Ball, received support and formed the baseline standard for the subsequently implemented Second Agricultural Land Reform. In July of 1946 the Japanese government reached agreement on Proposed Special Measures for the Establishment of Owner–Cultivators and an Amended Land Adjustment Law; after passing the 90th session of the Diet, both were officially

promulgated on October 21, 1946. The land of absentee landlords was
to be completely bought up; the landholdings of resident landlords not
engaged in cultivation were limited to 1 *chō* or less; the holdings of
landed tenants were restricted to 3 *chō* or less; and the land committees,
to which were added tenant-farmer representatives, undertook the
buying up of land from the landlords and its resale to their tenant
farmers. The tenant farmers paid 757 yen per *tan* (1 *tan* = 245 acre) of
rice paddy and 446 yen per *tan* of upland field, while landlords received
in government bonds 978 yen and 577 yen, respectively, per *tan* of the
two kinds of property. This amounted to no more than 7% of the crop
value per *tan* per year. Due to the inflation, government purchases of
land in 1947 and 1948 were "tantamount to confiscation" (Cohen,
1949: 444).

The spirit which supported this drastic land reform, as it resounds in
the above-quoted memorandum, was the sense of a mission to destroy
the feudal fetters of Japanese agriculture. It was believed that in order
to liberate Japanese farmers, "no stone will be left unturned short of
the absolute destruction of such fundamental evils connected with the
land." This approach was reminiscent of Jeffersonian democracy and
the Populist movement. Conceiving of Japan as analogous to China
on the basis of their knowledge of the latter, the adherents of this view
held notions similar to those common among American and European
intellectuals of the day, who emphasized the remaining non-modern
elements in Japan and derived a sense of superiority thereby. This phenomenon moreover meshed with a sense of inferiority among Japanese
intellectuals toward the advanced nations, and it was particularly compatible with the *kōzaha* theory, which saw the roots of Japanese capitalism in the semi-feudal landholding system of Japanese agriculture,
and as a result interpreted the land reform as a democratic revolution
and welcomed the destruction of the *ancien régime*. Proponents of the
rival *rōnōha* theory, which identified the Meiji Restoration of 1868 as
a bourgeois revolution and the origin of Japanese capitalism, received
the land reform comparatively coolly.[6]

In search of the landlords who controlled the rural villages, *Japan
Diary* author Mark Gayn visited the leading households of the village
of Sakata (Gayn, 1948: 60 ff). However, one of the special characteristics of Japan's tenant-farmer system was that hardly any big landlords
existed; instead, there was a profusion of small and medium-scale

[6] A more detailed discussion of the *kōzaha* and *rōnōha* theories on the origins
of Japanese capitalism, as well as profiles of the principal scholars involved in the
intellectual disputation between the two schools of thought, can be found in the
overview of Japanese economic history edited by Sumiya and Taira (1979).

Table 1–1. Results of the Land Reform

(1000s of hectares, %)

Pre-Reform	Agricultural land area	A	5,112		100.0
	Area under tenant farming	B	2,348	B/A	45.9
Land Reform	Bought up by the authorities	C	1,916	C/A	37.5
	Tenant-farmed land	D	1,880	D/B	80.1
	Held by absentee landlords		706		
	Held by resident landowners		868		
Post-Reform	Agricultural land area	E	5,157		100.0
	Area under tenant farming	F	520	F/E	10.1

Source: Ministry of Agriculture and Forestry, Nōchi to kaihō jisseki chōsa [Investigation of the Results of the Agricultural Land Reform].

Note: Pre-reform data are from a survey conducted November 23, 1945; post-reform data are for August 1, 1950.

landlords whose lives were not much different from those of tenant farmers. The number of landlords whose land was bought up in the land reform came to a total of 3.7 million. To that extent MacArthur's conception of the situation was anachronistic. If land had been accumulating in the hands of a noble class, the church, or a czar, how simple the liberation of the rural land probably would have been. (Just as today, if land were being bought up by monopoly capital, the residential land shortage could be solved by expropriation. Today, as of old, the fact that land is held in tiny, widely dispersed plots and the number of landholders is an enormous figure makes the resolution of Japan's land problems difficult.) In view of this, the Occupation's absolute power, its quixotic misapprehension, and its enthusiasum were all the more necessary in implementing the land reform.

In spite of all this, however, the fact that the land reform completely destroyed the tenant farmer system was highly significant (Table 1–1). Farm rents, which had constituted 5% of national income before the war, became negligible afterwards, and farm household incomes grew

Table 1–2. The Relative Decline in Farm Rents

(¥ millions, %)

		1930	1950
National Income	A	11,740	3,361,048
Farm Proprietors' Income	B	939	694,072
Farm Rents	C	623	2,005
C/A		5.3	0.06

Source: Keizai Shingi Cho, "Nihon keizai to kokumin shotoku" [The Japanese Economy and National Income].

(Table 1–2). As a result, farmers' will to work rose, and the basis for a conspicuous rise in agricultural productivity was created.

The land reform should not necessarily be thought of as an antifeudal revolution. From the end of the Tokugawa period through the early decades of the Meiji era, landlords had played an entrepreneurial role as owner-cultivators or gentleman-farmers (Tsuchiya, 1939; Tohata, 1954). After the 1890s, however, they became more and more parasitic. The land reform reduced the income share of these parasitic landlords to zero and, by distributing the land virtually *gratis*, it forced the farmers engaged in cultivation to take up the entrepreneurial role in their former landlords' place.

However, due to the increase in the postwar farm population, the cultivated land area was broken up into still tinier plots (Table 1–3). In addition, since the land reform secured social stability and ended tenant farmer strikes—which before the war had exceeded industrial labor strikes in both number of incidents and number of participants (Table 1–4)—these villages became the backbone of support for the

Table 1–3.　Number of Farm Households by Amount of Land under Cultivation

(1000s of households, %)

	1930		1940		1950	
5 ha. or more	70	(1.2)	76	(1.4)	48	(0.8)
3–5 ha.	128	(2.3)	119	(2.2)	77	(1.2)
2–3 ha.	314	(5.7)	309	(5.7)	208	(3.4)
1–2 ha.	1,217	(22.1)	1,322	(24.5)	1,340	(21.7)
0.5–1 ha.	1,892	(34.2)	1,768	(32.8)	1,973	(31.9)
0.5 ha. or less	1,891	(34.3)	1,796	(33.3)	2,522	(40.8)
Totals	5,511	(100.0)	5,390	(100.0)	6,176	(100.0)

Table 1–4.　Prewar Labor and Farm Tenancy Disputes

(Incidents, 1000s of persons)

	Labor Union Disputes			Tenancy Disputes		
	No. Incidents	Partici- pants	Union Members	No. Incidents	Partici- pants	Union Members
1919	2,388	*335	—	326	—	—
1926	1,260	127	284	2,713	*150	346
1935	1,872	104	408	*6,824	113	242
1941	334	17	—	3,308	32	23

Source: Statistics Division, Economic Planning Agency, "Kihon Nihon keizai tōkei" [Basic Statistics on the Japanese Economy].

Note: * Prewar peak.

conservative political parties. A new postwar middle class developed, with consciences unmarked by the colonies and tenant farm holdings that marked and haunted the prewar intellectual class.

What were the negative effects of the destruction of the landlord system? We have seen above that the landlords were already losing their entrepreneurial role, a portion of which was taken over by the state. Examples are government investment in land improvement and price supports through the Food Control accounts. In exchange for voting for the conservative political party, the farm villagers obtained protectionist agricultural policies. The other functions which the landlord system had fulfilled—that is, supplying the cities and industry with savings and a work force, were compensated for by the higher savings rates in urban worker households and a swift increase in numbers of graduates of institutions of higher education during rapid growth. Apprehensions that landholdings would be further broken up into minute parcels to provide for equal inheritances among heirs were dispelled by the fact that, during rapid growth, the second and third sons of farm families found opportunities to work in the cities.[7]

The land reform provided the foundation for agricultural productivity increases and for stability in the rural villages, and it prepared the way for rapid growth and the development of middle-class society. However, we must not lose sight of the fact that that very success was guaranteed by the subsequent achievement of rapid growth (Tohata, 1954:103–26).

The Breakup of the Zaibatsu

Unlike the land reform, the dissolution of the zaibatsu was included in the Occupation program from the very beginning. We have already quoted a passage from the U.S. Initial Post-Surrender Policy for Japan proposing the breakup of "the large industrial and banking combinations." The aim was, in the words of Corwin D. Edwards, who headed a 1946 study commission on economic reform, to "destroy both the psychological basis and the institutional basis for Japan's military power." At the beginning of the Occupation, America was at the height of a zaibatsu witch hunt.

They are the greatest war potential of Japan. . . . They profited immensely [from militarism.] . . . Unless the Zaibatsu are broken

---

[7] In the case of France, the equalization of land distribution under Napoleon is said to have delayed industrialization, in contrast to enclosure in England, which stimulated it. Land reform *per se* cannot be cited as a condition for industrialization (Gould, 1972: 79–80).

up, the Japanese have little prospect of ever being able to govern themselves as free men. As long as the Zaibatsu survive, Japan will be their Japan. (Pauley Report on reparations policy, 1946)

Japan's industries were controlled by a small number of zaibatsu, which were supported and strengthened by the Japanese government. The concentration of industrial control stimulated the existence of semi-feudal relations between labor and capital, depressed wages, and obstructed the development of labor unions. Moreover, it interfered with the creation of new enterprises by independent businessmen and prevented the rise of a middle class in Japan. Because there has been no such middle class, to this day there does not exist in Japan an economic basis for the individual to be independent, and hence neither did any power develop to oppose the military clique; and for this reason as well, no national feeling of democratic humanitarianism developed as a force opposing military designs on other countries. Furthermore, low wages and the accumulation of profits under the exclusive control of the zaibatsu choked off domestic markets, increased the importance of exports, and thus spurred Japan forward into an imperialistic war. (Corwin D. Edwards, in 1946 report)

This impassioned report is not without a certain quaintness, mixing as it does the romanticization of middle-class society with the flavor of a left-wing official statement.

The dissolution of the zaibatsu began in October of the year of defeat, 1945, with negotiations between the Occupation bureaucrats and the four main zaibatsu for the breakup of the core companies (*honsha*). By mid-month the Yasuda Hōzen Company had resolved to break up; but Mitsubishi's President Iwasaki Koyata, who opposed dissolution to the last, insisting that the zaibatsu did not bear responsibility for the war, finally accepted the demand for dissolution only at the end of that month after heart-to-heart talks with Finance Minister Shibusawa Keizō.

In order to dispose of the stocks of these zaibatsu, a Holding Company Dissolution Commission was formed in April 1946. From then until June 1947, a total of 83 companies were designated holding companies. Of these, 28 were liquidated as holding companies in their zaibatsu groups. The continued existence of another 51 as industrial firms was sanctioned after their stockholdings were transferred away. Singled out as special examples were the general trading companies Mitsui Bussan and Mitsubishi Shoji, which were ordered dissolved immediately by a decree of GHQ on July 3, 1947. This order was extremely stern: it forbade company officers at the level of division chief (*buchō*) and higher to cooperate in forming a new company, and prohibited the hiring of 100 or more company employees by any single employer elsewhere; Mitsui Bussan and Mitsubishi Shoji were dissolved according to the very letter of the law. Why were such measures taken against these two companies alone? Not even the formal history of the Holding Company Dissolution Commission, *The Japanese Zaibatsu and Their Dissolution (Nihon zaibatsu to sono kaitai)*, gives a clear explanation of the situation.

In January of 1947, it was determined that the political Purge Order would be applied to economic circles as well, with the result that 2,200 executives of 250 large companies were purged and barred from public positions. In April of the same year the Antitrust Law was enacted, with the hope that it would prevent a revival of the zaibatsu. In December a Law for the Elimination of Excessive Concentration of Economic Power was passed, and 325 companies (with paid-in capital amounting

Table 1–5. Major Applications of the 1947 Measures for the Elimination of Excessive Concentration of Economic Power

Company	Form of Compliance
Nippon Steel Corp.	Divided into two companies, Yawata Steel and Fuji Steel (currently Shin Nippon Steel Corp.)
Mitsui Mining	Split into Mitsui Mining and Kamioka Mining (later Mitsui Mining & Smelting Co.)
Mitsubishi Mining	Split into Mitsubishi Mining and Taihei Mining (later Mitsubishi Metal Corporation)
Tokyo Shibaura Electric Co.	Disposed of one research institute and 27 out of 43 plants
Hitachi, Ltd.	Disposed of 19 out of 35 plants
Mitsubishi Heavy Industries	Divided into three companies: Eastern, Central, and Western Japan Heavy Industries (currently Mitsubishi Heavy Industries)
Ōji Paper Co.	Split into three companies: Tomakomai (later Ōji), Jujo, and Honshu Paper Companies
Daiken Industries	Split into Kureha Spining, Itoh & Co., and Marubeni
Dainippon Beer	Divided into Nippon Beer and Asahi Breweries

Source: Mochikabu Kaisha Seiri Iinkai (Holding Companies Dissolution Commission), *Nihon zaibatsu to sono kaitai* [The Japanese Zaibatsu and Their Dissolution].

Table 1–6. The Decline in Industry Concentration Ratios

Industry	Market Share	
	1937	1949
Pig iron (3 firms)	94.0	88.8
Cement (3 firms)	63.0	55.3
Pulp (the former Oji Co.)	49.3	39.4
Shipbuilding (Mitsui, Mitsubishi, Sumitomo)	50.7	37.5
Ammonium sulfate (Mitsui, Mitsubishi)	49.0	39.1

Source: Economic Planning Agncy, "Kihon Nihon keizai tōkei" [Basic Statistics on the Japanese Economy].

to 65.9 % of the total for all corporations) were designated as the targets of measures to eliminate excessive concentration. However, during the course of 1948 these designations were withdrawn one after the other, and banks were treated as outside the purview of the law, so that the number of firms to which this law was actually applied came to only 18. However, those 18 companies were all huge enterprises, and these measures for the elimination of concentration completely changed the industrial map for steel, shipbuilding, paper, brewing, and several other industries (Table 1–5).

What did the breakup of the zaibatsu bequeath to the Japanese economy? The degree of concentration in industry decreased (Table 1–6), and intra-industry competition was enlivened as the dissolved firms in a sense prepared the way for a new system of independent firms. Perforce transformed into a more youthful group by the purge, the new generation of managers, promoted from undistinguished "third-rank" positions,[8] became the new captains of industry, preserving their companies in the face of zaibatsu dissolution and aggressive labor movement offensives.[9] Nowhere was the separation of management and ownership more thoroughgoing than in postwar Japan.

The dispersal of the zaibatsu stocks had the effect of making negotiable securities an item for mass acquisition. Moreover, while both the political left and the right attacked the zaibatsu before the war, business in the postwar years was immune to popular criticism for several decades, until about 1970. There is much substance to the

[8] The term "third-rank executive" (*sandō jūyaku*) came into circulation as a result of its use in a popular novel by a Sumitomo employee.

[9] See the series of memoirs of representative contemporary leaders of the financial world published by Nihon Keizai Shimbunsha under the title *Watakushi no rirekisho* (My Personal History). For Nagano Shigeo, Hasegawa Norishige, Suzuki Haruo, and others, the zaibatsu dissolution and the breakups and divestitures under the concentration elimination measures were major turning points in their personal as well as professional lives.

contention that Japan's industrialization in chemicals and heavy industries was driven by the so-called new zaibatsu rather than the old,
and this suggests that the old captains of industry had lost their function
as entrepreneurs and instead tended to behave like conservative finance
capitalists. The breakup of the zaibatsu prepared the way for the
demise of the era dominated by finance capital and for the arrival of
the new industrialism.

After the dissolution a revival of sorts occurred as a "keiretsu-fica-
tion"—movement into industrial groupings—of firms proceeded. The
role which the zaibatsu core companies had once played was coming
to be played by the principal banks. However, in comparison with the
control exerted by the zaibatsu core companies, the banks' control was
weak, and the position of industrial capital relative to prewar days was
remarkably strengthened. From the standpoint of postwar Japan's
flourishing entrepreneurial spirit and high propensity to invest, the
zaibatsu dissolution had a beneficial influence on the economy.

Labor Reforms

On October 11, 1945, General MacArthur called on the Japanese
government to make major reforms for the preservation of human
rights: (1) the enfranchising of women, (2) promotion of labor unions,
(3) liberalization of education in the schools, (4) abolition of any
system as entangles the lives of the masses in fear, and (5) democratization of the Japanese economic structure. On the same day the Labor
Advisory Commission assembled its Advice on Labor Legislation and
Labor Administration in Japan. The labor reforms, which centered
around the recognition and promotion of labor union activities, were
already included in the conception of reform which MacArthur had
enunciated as he addressed the Japanese nation while en route to Japan.
But this occasion was probably the first time the Japanese people gained
a clear understanding of the Occupation's attitude toward labor union
activities.

> While the betterment of the workers and other classes is itself one
> of the best guarantees for preventing a renewed outbreak of mili-
> tarism and invasions in the future, it is also a principal route to
> greater freedom and greater material blessings for the Japanese
> people in general, and without this, their lasting support for dem-
> ocracy cannot be assured. (Report of the Labor Advisory Com-
> mission)

The Labor Union Law, drafted by the Labor Legislation Council

Table 1–7. Labor Union Growth, 1945–49

	1945	1946	1947	1948	1949
No. of Unions	509	17,266	23,323	33,926	34,688
No. of Union Members (1000s)	380	4,926	5,692	6,677	6,655
Rate at which Organized (%)	3.2	41.5	45.3	53.0	55.8
No. of Strikes	—	810	683	913	651
No. of Members Participating in Strikes (1000s)	—	635	295	2,605	1,240

Source: Ministry of Labor, Sengo rōdō keizai shi [History of Postwar Labor Economics], Analytical Section, Table 17.

(Suehiro Itsutaro, Chairman), was promulgated on December 22, 1945, and went into effect in March 1946. Workers' rights to organize, to engage in collective bargaining, and to strike were affirmed in this law. In addition, the Labor Relations Adjustment Act was passed in September 1946, and the Labor Standards Law was enacted on April 7, 1947. These went into effect in September 1947.

In the midst of all this, labor unions were organized at a precipitous rate (Table 1–7). The proportion of workers organized exceeded 50% in 1948, and amid the inflation and severe poverty of that time, disputes and strikes against management also occurred frequently, sometimes resulting in such settlements as Kanto Electric Power's acceptance of the union's demand for a five-fold wage increase. Then, too, there was the episode which occurred when an on-site inspection of the Takarazuka girls' theatre troupe was made in connection with the implementation of the basic labor standards law. The dancers are reputed to have cried with disdain, "We're not workers, we're artists!"

The Occupation's predisposition to support labor union activities ended abruptly with the stop order for the General Strike of February 1, 1947, in which 2,600,000 people were expected to participate. The order was followed by the promulgation of Government Ordinance No. 201, which deprived national civil service employees of the right to strike after July 1948; the Red Purge at the beginning of the Korean War; and the curbing of union activities. On the basis of such events as these, which collectively constitute a major part of what is often termed the "reverse course," a powerful case can be made for the view that the Occupation's labor policies changed from revolutionary to reactionary in a short period of time. This view, however, is as simplistic as the one which cheered the occupiers as liberators. Far closer to the mark is Professor Suzuki Takeo's view that the fostering of labor unions was viewed by the Occupation authorities as within the framework of a democratic society. The union they had in mind, however, was an American-style trade union or industry-wide union organization. The type that arose in postwar Japan was a labor union organized around the enterprise unit, with blue-collar laborers and white-collar workers all lumped together as one within their enterprise unit.

Mixed up together in the postwar labor movement are, along with the image of democratic labor unions from the American Occupation, traditional practices such as enterprise familism, the reactivation of prewar union movement leaders who were imprisoned or blackballed during the war years, the legacy of the wartime Patriotic Industrial Associations (Sangyō Hōkoku Kai), and the equalization of living standards in the general impoverishment that followed defeat. In his autobiography, Arahata Kanson, a rehabilitated socialist from the prewar years, relates how, upon being nominated committee chairman of a certain union, he was surprised to be received with old-style military salutes in a factory with red flags virtually sprouting from the rafters (Arahata, 1965). This incident symbolizes well the real state of affairs in the postwar labor reform. With white- and blue-collar workers in the same unions, it became general practice to pay blue-collar workers on a monthly basis, as was common practice for white-collar jobs. This created an environment whereby, as income levels rose with rapid growth in later years, middle-class consciousness spread rapidly.

The fundamental lasting influence of the Occupation reforms lies at the cultural level, in the meeting of the Japanese and American cultures. The tangible effects, which include the fruits of the subsequent rapid growth, are increasingly visible in the history of the labor reforms as well.

Setting Out Toward Democracy

The crowning achievement of the Occupation policies of demilitarization and democratization was, needless to say, the new constitution, which went into effect in May 1947. The Occupation's Government Section drafted the constitution, and the Japanese government and Diet gave their approval upon receiving this draft. Under this constitution Japan renounces war (Article 9) and prohibits discrimination on the basis of sex or social position (Article 14); the extended family (ie) system with its coerced arranged marriages is broken up (Article 24); the people have the right to maintain the minimum standard of healthful and cultured living (Article 25); the right of workers to organize is recognized (Article 28); and the principle of local autonomy is established (Article 92). Under its new constitution, Japan promised to become the most thoroughly pacifistic and democratic country in the world.

The postwar reform which culminated in the new constitution was a democratization supplied and imposed from without. Its success or failure, however, depended on the response of the Japanese people who were on the receiving end of this effort. What in fact were the Japanese thinking; how were they conducting themselves during the period of chaos following the war? One response to this question is the theory that they were "in a state of abstraction": hard pressed by the sudden switch from militarism to democracy, and by commodity shortages and inflation, the Japanese people had no leisure in which to contemplate regaining their poise and self-possession, but could only act reflexively. Another view holds that it was the upsurge in the sabotage of the ruling classes and the people's democratic struggle against it which characterized this period—that this was the seminal period of postwar democracy, its brightest day, and that since then it has only progressively degenerated and become devoid of substance. Yet another view holds that the characteristic feature of this period was the currying of favor with the occupiers and the opportunistic breaking with tradition that accompanied this process.

However, both the "state of abstraction" theory and the "people's struggle" theory are perhaps a bit too simplistic to capture the reality of postwar democracy at the gutted-ruins stage. The Japanese people attempted in real earnest to make freedom and democracy their own. That aim was all the more revealing of their true feelings, emerging as it did immediately after their experience of militarist oppression and defeat. It would be altogether unjust to say that their efforts were only a matter of response to or desire to ingratiate themselves with the Occupation.

In the disarray of the postwar years, the labor movement intensified, the virtues and vices of the Emperor system were debated, and pulp magazines sang the praises of sexual freedom. By today's standards, however, the framework of traditional ascetic virtues was holding firm. In opposition to strikes against management, the movement to "save the nation by increasing production" arose like a floodtide. Nambara Shigeru, a member of the House of Peers and the then president of Tokyo Imperial University, discussed the possibility of the Emperor's abdication on the floor of the Imperial Diet, but his real purpose was to secure retention of the Emperor system in perpetuity. The bestselling novels of Nagai Kafū and Oda Sakunosuke can only be described as exceedingly discreet by the standards of today's popular novels. When

Iwanami Shoten published a new paperback edition of the Nishida philosophical school's bible, *The Study of Virtue* (*Zen no Kenkyū*), people stood in line all night to buy it. In his last writings the intellectual Kawakami Hajime struck a responsive note among his readers by extolling the blessings of being a small country with a small population; the national ideal at that time was not to be an economic superpower, but to build a "nation of culture"—to be "the Switzerland of the Orient." Diligence, thrift, and group-centeredness, required in the economic environment of the time, were virtues which the Japanese people had acquired in the years prior to and during the war. There was broad agreement within the society on the importance of these values.

In Weimar Germany following World War I, a deep cleavage was evident between politics and economics, between democratism and capitalism. According to John Strachey (1956), it is precisely the confrontation between these two that is our modern fate. In contrast to this is the view that demilitarization and democratization specifically were the points of departure for postwar Japan's economic growth (e.g. Miyazaki, 1977). By avoiding the burden of military spending, Japan was able to concentrate on expanding and modernizing its production capacity. The land reform, the breakup of the zaibatsu, and the legalization of the labor movement stimulated productivity and equalized income distribution.

However, both the confrontation theory of democracy and economic development and the harmony theory are overly simplistic and one-sided. Postwar democracy is not merely a phenomenon of the chaotic period following the war; it also includes its later development and the later idealization of its origins. Thus defined, postwar democracy can be seen as having borne within itself the necessary ingredients for the subsequent development of the Japanese economy and its "cultural contradictions" (to borrow Daniel Bell's term); Japan's modern economic history evolved in the tension between the two. The following factors are the hallmarks of that evolution:

(1) the goal of "catching up," established by the military defeat and the Occupation; i.e., catching up with economic democracy and the high American standard of living;

(2) the change in the elite and the revitalization that took place as a result of postwar reforms such as the land reform and the breakup of the zaibatsu;

(3) traditional morality, particularly group discipline, which survived and was even strengthened in the harsh economic conditions after the war.

To what extent were these factors linked, and to what extent did they interact during the economic recovery? This is one of the themes of the chapters that follow.

2

Recovery and Inflation

The period from Japan's surrender in 1945 until the implementation of the Dodge economic stabilization plan in 1949 was a time of hardship in which the Japanese economy struggled to gain a toehold on reconstruction in the midst of the chaos of defeat.[1]

Economic activity ground nearly to a halt as a result of the defeat, and the nation sank to the depths of privation (Table 2-1). Mining and manufacturing production in 1946 was one-fifth of peak levels and no more than a third of prewar output (average for 1934–36). Eight blast furnaces were in operation in August 1945, but by September 1946 this number had shrunk to a mere three at Yawata. Coal production, which had relied upon the forced labor of prisoners of war or on workers requisitioned from colonial areas, fell sharply with the end of the war, from 1,670,000 tons in August 1945 to 550,000 tons in November of the same year. The rice harvest was the smallest since 1903 (5,870,000 tons). Per capita calorie intake in Tokyo fell to 1,352 calories in May 1946. In 1946 the rice ration declined to 2.1 gō per person per day (about 0.8 U.S. pint or 400 millilitres); moreover, delays and non-delivery of rations occurred continually in the large cities. People scraped by as best they could selling personal belongings for food; the Engel coefficient exceeded 60%. Since rations covered less than 20% of the staples required, the remainder was bought on the back market.

Mass starvation—which, it was feared, might take a toll as high as ten million—was somehow avoided with the Occupation's emergency relief food distribution, but victims of malnutrition and methol poisoning were frequent. Nor is it strange that typhus was rampant, considering the large number of people who had neither changes of clothing

---

[1] On economic conditions during this period, refer to the Economic White Papers (*Keizai hakusho*) published annually since 1947 by the Government of Japan; or Cohen (1949).

Table 2–1.   Shifts in Key Economic Indicators, 1945–49

	Prewar Peak (1934–36)	1945	1946	1947	1948	1949
Real GNP per Capita (1970 prices, ¥1000s)	188	—	104	106	121	127
Mining & Manufacturing Output (1955 = 100)	(44) 98.2	43.2	19.2	23.9	31.1	40.0
Rice Production (10,000 tons)	(33) 1,062	587	921	880	997	938
Textile Supply per Capita (pounds)	(37) 12.67	—	2.11	2.07	2.33	1.91
No. Dwellings per Household	(42) 1.06	—	0.91	0.86	0.87	0.88
Engel Coefficient for Urban Workers (%)	(31) 32.5	—	67.8	63.0	60.4	60.1
Electric Power Generating Capacity (100 millions of kw)	(43) 377	219	303	328	378	415
Passengers Carried by National Railways (JNR) (100 millions)	(44) 31	30	32	33	33	30

Source: Statistics Division, Economic Planning Agency, "Kihon Nihon keizai tōkei" [Basic Statistics on the Japanese Economy]; and Japan Statistical Research Institute, "Nihon keizai tōkei shū" [Collected Statistics on the Japanese Economy].

nor soap or bathing facilities. The populace hovered at the level of bare subsistence.

Amidst all this, the streetcars were still running, although broken windows were replaced with planks and the cars super-crowded with commuters who would even stand on the seats to make more room. Thanks to hydropower, electricity was still supplied, although there were repeated power failures. The railroads and electricity were the lifeline that provided a saving link for the economy and gave people's lives some semblance of normalcy.[2]

The pace of postwar recovery was fairly rapid. One could hardly say that the reconstruction was all smooth sailing: in both 1945 and 1946, the revival of production came to a standstill from time to time. But as 1947 began, efforts to resuscitate production finally became focused; and in 1948 mining and manufacturing output increased 30%, reach-

---

[2] At this time Japan was at a low ebb economically, but it should be kept in mind that many of today's developing nations are at a still lower level in terms of electric power and transportation.

Table 2-2. A Rendering of Accounts for the National Economy
(¥ 100 millions)

Gross National Expenditure (1945 prices)	1934–36	1946	1949
Personal Consumption Expenditure	72,747	45,267	61,690
Private Fixed Investment	12,302	10,814	10,551
Inventory Investment	1,605	2,993	1,994
Government Expenditures	38,489	20,696	22,885
Exports, etc.	15,098	380	2,739
Imports, etc.	12,884	1,611	3,379
Gross National Product	127,357	78,489	103,650
(Nominal Gross National Product)	(178)	(5,016)	(34,201)
Income Distribution (Current Prices)	60	1,198	12,347
Employed Persons' Income (″)	43	2,270	12,866
Individual Proprietors' Income (″)	49	239	909
Corporate Income (″)	8	25	978
For reference:			
Rate of Personal Saving (%)	10.2	− 3.4	− 8.3

Source: "Kokumin shotoku tōkei" [National Income Statistics].

ing nearly half the prewar level. Rice production increased to 9,970,000 tons in 1948, and rations increased to 2.5 *gō* per capita per day in 1947 and 2.7 *gō* (more than 1 pint) in 1948. In 1945 rice deliveries filled only 70% of quotas, even though strong measures were taken to meet the targets. In 1946, it took only until May 20 to meet the rice quota, and in 1947 rice production quotas were filled by March 16. The national income accounts show that income distribution during this period was biased toward individual entrepreneur income, and economic growth was sustained by a revival of personal consumption spending (Table 2-2).

A major factor affecting the economy was the severe inflation in progress during this time. In 1945 wholesale prices rose to as much as three and a half times their prewar levels; in 1949 the increase was 208–fold. With the defeat, provisional military expenditures were accelerated; withdrawals from savings and checking accounts also increased, food supplies were inadequate, hoarding occurred, rationing was disrupted, and so on. By the end of 1945 inflation was intensifying with each passing day.

On February 16, 1946, the government announced an emergency policy for coping with the economic crisis; it provided for maintenance of food supplies, strengthered price controls, and stipulated that hoarding and concealment of goods would be exposed. In addition, a monetary policy was to be implemented based on the Bank of Japan Notes and Deposits Ordinance, the Emergency Financial Measures Ordinance, and the Provisional Law for the Survey of Assets, all of which had originally been conceived with a view to the entire population's attitude of resignation to death in war. Finance Minister Shibusawa Keizō appealed to the people in a radio broadcast as follows:

> The Emergency Financial Measures and the policy concerning Bank of Japan banknote deposits are matters of the deepest and most profound concern in the lives of all of us, young and old, male and female, without exception. As of February 16 that is, as of yesterday, free and unhindered payouts from savings deposit and trust accounts which constitute private people's savings are in principle temporarily prohibited exept for sanctioned payments of extremely limited amounts necessary for living expenses, such as ￥300 to a household head, ￥100 to others. Moreover, notes with a face value of ten yen or higher, which everyone has been using up to the present, will all become invalid at the close of business March 2.
>
> Everyone asks, why must the government adopt such an extreme and in a sense reckless policy? In a word, it is an unavoidable way of curbing inflation, a truly harmful state of affairs for the people, disease which seriously affects our lives.

Shibusawa stated in this speech that the austerity measures were for the protection of the population as a whole—"the entire population. The rich must live in the same austerity." The freezing of funds and the conversion to the new yen, as well as levies of property taxes based on surveys made at the time, indeed had a profound impact on people's lives. One conspicuous effect was the financial ruin of the old upper-class families, and a resulting equalization of income distribution. This experience has long remained in people's memories. Even now, whenever the subject of redenominating the currency comes up, those days are brought to mind.

On March 3, the day the conversion to the new yen was concluded, the Price Control Ordinance was implemented in connection with the decision to seek price restraints by means of an official system of fixed prices (symbolized by a Ⓜ, *marukō*). These measures, however, did no more than temporarily suppress inflation, and from 1946 to 1947 the trend was toward a renewed burst of inflationary pressures. The stamping out of inflation had to await implementation of the 1949 Economic Stabilization Plan.

Production declined and then rapidly recovered, and at the same time severe inflation occurred. What accounted for these phenomena? What were the interrelationships among them—for example, between the revival of production and soaring prices? The following sections examine these questions.

Economic Recovery Issues and Options

Initial Conditions

The pattern for the postwar recovery was set in part by the inherited conditions to which the economy was subject at the outset. Here, let us examine the postwar economy's initial conditions with regard to the three points, national wealth, the labor force, and external economic relations.

Material losses due to the Pacific War were enormous. Eighty percent of the ships went down at sea or were burned, and one-third of the nation's urban residences were reduced to ashes. According to an Economic Stabilization Board report, direct and indirect damage amounted to one-quarter of the national wealth (Table 2–3). From 1935 to 1945 the national wealth should have increased by 35% as a result of forced savings during wartime, but the war wiped out the laborious efforts of those ten years.

The foregoing facts are important, but they convey no more than half the reality. If national wealth in 1945 had been at the same level as it was in 1935, it would be seen as extremely comfortable relative to the scale of the gross national product, which had fallen to one-half the 1935 level. Not only that, but a look at a breakdown of the remaining capital stock shows that the damages were greatest to plant and equipment in the consumer-goods-producing industries, which had been dismantled or converted to military production during the war, while the chemical and heavy industries sustained a surprisingly low level of damage. Generally speaking, plant and equipment in the chemical and heavy industries was considerably greater than before the outbreak of war (Table 2–4).

Falling heir to this legacy of the wartime economy, the Japanese economy entered the postwar period under conditions that made possible a rapid revival of production without large-scale capital accumulation.[3] Marginal capital coefficients stood at a low level.

Even so, the extent of accumulation of individuals' financial assets,

[3] This point has been recognized in the government Economic White Papers and other works, but Marxian economists stress the point that inflation was a means of capital accumulation.

Table 2–3. Damage to the National Wealth Due to the Pacific War

(¥ millions, in prices at time of defeat)

	Amount of Damage	National Wealth Prior to Damage	Proportion Damaged (%)	National Wealth Remaining at End of War	National Wealth in 1935	Rate of Increase over 1935 (%)
Structures	22,220	90,435	24.5	68,215	76,275	−10.6
Machinery & Tools for Industrial Use	7,994	23,346	34.2	15,352	8,501	80.6
Ships	7,359	9,125	80.6	1,796	3,111	−42.3
Electric & Gas Facilities	1,618	14,933	10.8	13,313	8,987	48.1
Railroads, All Vehicles	1,523	15,415	9.8	13,892	13,364	4.0
Telegraph, Telephone & Water	659	4,156	15.8	3,497	3,229	8.2
Capital Goods	7,864	32,953	23.8	25,089	23,541	6.6
Furniture & Household Goods	9,558	46,427	20.5	36,869	39,354	−6.6
Other	5,483	16,340	33.5	10,857	10,389	4.5
Totals	64,278	253,130	25.3	188,852	186,751	1.1

Sources: Economic Stabilization Board, *Taiheiyo senso ni yoru waga kuni higai sōgō hōkokusho* [Comprehensive Report of Damage to the Nation Due to the Pacific War], and Nakayama Ichiro, ed., *Nihon no kokufu kōzo* [The Structure of Japan's National Wealth].

Note: Direct damage was that which resulted from air raids, naval bombardments, etc., and indirect damage, that resulting from reduction to scrap, evacuations, inadequate maintenance, etc.

Table 2–4.   Productive Capacity at the Time of the Defeat

(¥ millions, in prices at time of defeat)

	Pre-1944 Peak	Capacity as of 8/15/45	% Remaining	1941, Year-end	Rate of Increase over 1941 (%)
Hydroelectric Power (1000 kw)	6,074	6,233	102.6	5,368	116.1
Ordinary Steel & Steel Products (1000 tons)	7,998	8,040	102.6	7,506	107.1
Aluminium (tons per month)	11,100	8,350	75.2	7,240	115.3
Machine Tools (tons)	190	120	63.1	110	109.1
Oil Refining (1000 kl)	3,739	1,443	38.5	2,359	61.2
Soap (1000 tons)	278	99	35.9	278	54.5
Cotton Staple Yarn (millions of spindles)	13.8	2.8	20.2	13.8	20.2
Cotton Textiles (1000 bolts)	393	123	31.4	393	31.4
Bicycles (1000)	3,600	720	20.0	2,880	25.0

—which at the same time were government liabilities—was noteworthy. Suzuki Takeo estimates that national bonds, wartime indemnity obligations, other government liabilities, cash, banknotes, and other monetary assets came to about ¥500 billion, of which about ¥200 billion consisted of fluid capital such as national debt, public bonds, corporate bonds, stocks, and so on (Suzuki, 1952). Suzuki compares these figures with the national income at that time of ¥146 billion. This ¥200 billion was the amount the Japanese government could under no circumstances avoid paying out, no matter how many times it went bankrupt. If these monetary assets should exceed the small quantity of wealth and property, a renewed outbreak of inflation would be inevitable.

Notwithstanding war casualties, the population increased from 73 million in 1944 to 78 million in 1947, primarily as a result of demobilization of troops and repatriation from abroad (Table 2–5). The employed population increased by 1,500,000 people, but it declined on a large scale in the industrial sector, while agriculture absorbed a labor force exceeding four million. Non-labor force increases were also large: according to a different estimate there were 1,979,000 people seeking em-

Table 2-5.   Population and the Number Employed, by Industry
(1000 persons)

	1930	1944	1947
Total Population of Home Islands	64,450	73,064	78,098
Number of Employed Persons	29,619	31,796	33,329
of which: Agriculture & Forestry	*14,131*	*12,814*	*17,102*
Industry	*5,875*	*10,016*	*7,233*
Commerce	*4,905*	*2,391*	*2,430*
Number of Unemployed	34,831	41,268	44,769

Source: National Census and Interim National Census. Cited in Mitsubishi Institute for Economic Research, *Nihon sangyō keizai sōran* [Conspectus of the Japanese Industrial Economy].

ployment in the cities alone (535,000 registered unemployed; 500,000 hidden unemployed; 604,000 demobilized military personnel; 203,000 repatriates; 137,000 natural working-age population increase). In sum, the postwar reconstruction had to be achieved under the heavy pressure of excess population.

Both capital and a labor force were available. One might have thought that if some degree of inflation could be tolerated, the reconstruction of the Japanese economy could be readily accomplished. However, an additional important condition must be pointed out: the Japanese economy remained under a blockade which was carried over from wartime. What originally caused the collapse of the Japanese economy during the Pacific War was the severance of marine transport by submarines, making raw materials impossible to obtain long before bombing raids on the main islands were conducted in real earnest (U.S. Strategic Bombing Survey, 1946).

National income statistics show that after the war the most severe observable decline was in imports and exports, as the blockade con-

Table 2-6.   Trends in Imports of Key Products

	1935	1945	1946	1947	1948
Rice (1000 tons)	39	0	16	3	42
Wheat (1000 tons)	445	—	340	694	695
Sugar (1000 tons)	141	0	0	50	602
Cotton (1000 tons)	737	9	159	108	109
Coal (1000 tons)	4,049	500	—	17	914
Iron Ore (1000 tons)	3,404	78	—	—	502
Crude Oil (1000 kl)	4,289	46	392	1,090	1,335

Source: Japan Statistical Research Institute, "Nihon keizai tōkei shū" [Collected Statistics on the Japanese Economy].

tinued to strangle the Japanese economy (Table 2–6). It can also be said, however, that the reverse is true: if imports and exports could be reopened, the Japanese economy had the potential to revive fairly rapidly. Because of the continuation of the blockade, the postwar Japanese economy fundamentally differed from defeated Germany in 1918, which had been able to return at once to international markets. This point needs to be particularly stressed, all the more so because numerous diagnoses of postwar Japanese inflation have been based on comparison with the German inflation experience following the First World War.

With its inherited capital stock and its surplus population employed in agriculture, the Japanese economy had taken a different shape from its former, prewar self, and an escape from this new impasse was ultimately sought in industrialization. Because, under the economic blockade, obtaining foreign raw materials was prohibited, the sole possibility for reviving production lay for the time being in goods which the Japanese people substituted, as it were barehandedly, for foreign raw materials. Domestically mined coal is a tangible example. This is what priority production (*keisha seisan*) was all about.

Priority Production
The concept of priority production was born of the forecast of a March 1947 crisis. For about one year, beginning in August 1945, mining and manufacturing production increased, although there was some slack, primarily in consumer goods. Factories which had made airplanes, warships, and shells converted to the production of pots and pans. However, there was a limit to production increases for producers' goods due to the difficulty in obtaining raw materials, and once the military raw materials inventories were exhausted, the production of consumer goods would also become impossible. After the summer of 1946 the fact that mining and manufacturing production overall began to stagnate was considered an ominous sign of impending collapse (Table 2–7). The National Economic Research Society's *Inventory Survey* estimated that military raw materials stocks on hand would be exhausted by about March 1947.

The only way to avoid this March crisis, absent a lifting of the blockade, was to strive to increase the domestic output of producers' goods. Coal comes to mind first in this regard, but the coal industry was afflicted by a shortage of workers and labor-management chaos; in addition, shortages of rolled steel were holding back production increases in the mines. Meanwhile, constrained by the coal shortage, steel production sagged in turn. The priority production system chan-

Table 2-7. The Stagnation of Production during the Latter Half of 1946
(1934–36 = 100)

		Mining & Manufac- turing	Metals	Machinery	Chemicals	Textiles	Food- stuffs
Jan.	1946	18.3	7.0	27.5	15.3	5.9	35.0
Apr.		28.7	14.1	50.3	24.2	8.5	36.8
Aug.		35.6	18.0	*61.3	31.9	13.7	*41.4
Sept.		*35.7	*19.1	60.2	31.3	16.1	40.7
Oct.		34.9	18.7	55.4	*32.2	16.9	40.8
Nov.		34.8	18.1	55.4	28.7	18.1	37.6
Dec.		33.1	17.3	49.3	27.9	*18.2	39.0

Source: Economic Advisory Board indexes of industrial activity revised
to the base years 1934–36. Cited in *Nihon Kōgyō Ginkō 50-nen
shi* [Fifty-year History of the Industrial Bank of Japan].
Note: * indicates peak for the year.

nelled such coal as was produced into the steel industry, and the resulting rolled steel output was in turn put back into coal; the attempt
to expand production from these two sectors in a reciprocal cycle was
first suggested by University of Tokyo Professor Arisawa Hiromi
(Arisawa, 1948:53–69).

From the beginning of 1947, priority allocations of materials, capital,
and manpower to coal and steel were stepped up. Producing 30 million
tons of coal was treated as a major goal for 1947. Six *gō* of rice were
rationed to coal miners and 3 *gō* to members of their families; as what
is still called the "Golden Hour" on Thursday evenings at 8:00, NHK
Radio (the national broadcasting corporation) broadcast a special
"Evening Program for the Mining Community." Public noticeboards
on street corners proclaimed the rate of progress in rice deliveries to
the government and in coal output the way the number of traffic fa-
talities and injuries is displayed today. The first Economic White Paper
stated that, if the production of coal increased by 20%, mining and
manufacturing production could be increased by 40%; and the Socialist
Katayama Cabinet's Trade and Industry Minister, Mizutani Chōzaburō,
donned a loincloth like a regular miner, put on a headlamp, and made
an inspection of the coal mines. The Occupation dispatched a special
commission of inquiry and encouraged production; and every region
had its own campaign to save the country by increasing coal production. In this way, with coal output at 29,340,000 tons and rolled steel
production at 740,000 tons in 1947, the priority production plan (*keisha
seisan hōshiki*), which should rightly be called Japan's autonomous
reconstruction plan, just barely achieved its goals.

During this period, due to water shortages and transport problems, materials were not allotted entirely in accordance with priority production expectations. Nevertheless, the Occupation authorities, once they recognized the economy's crisis situation, were instrumental in getting the revival of coal and steel production on track during this period; the Occupation did an about-face on its policies concerning importing and releasing such basic materials as crude oil, coking coal, and iron ore. In this sense, the importance priority production plan perhaps should not be overestimated. However, priority production brought home anew the realization that the Japanese economy, embracing as it did a capital stock inherited from the wartime economy and an overflowing surplus population, had no road to survival other than in the direction of industrialization.

Reconstruction Bank Finance and Price-Differential Subsidies

This period of priority production overlapped the period in which inflation, which had been damped down by the previously mentioned Emergency Financial Measures, became resurgent.

The recurrence of inflation was occasioned by the expansionist fiscal policies of the first Yoshida Shigeru Cabinet and Finance Minister Ishibashi Tanzan. In a fiscal policy speech of July 1946, citing Keynes's *General Theory*, Minister Ishibashi made a forthright and earnest appeal to the people for support for his views and convictions. As fiscal policy speeches go—consisting, as they usually do, of explanations in bureaucratese of budget figures from start to finish—Ishibashi's was totally unconventional:

> The goal of national finance, particularly in situations like that of our country today, is first, more than anything else, to give people jobs, to revive industry, to aim for full employment, and so to propel the national economy forward.
>
> If one were to ask, has our country been under conditions of full employment since the war, one could not say that anything of the kind has been the case. . . .
>
> Monetary expansion and soaring prices under such conditions can be remedied with deflationary policies, but the type of inflation we are experiencing is not inflation in the usual sense. . . .
>
> Starvation prices can only be cured by the production and flow of goods onto the market. . . .
>
> In order to achieve the goal of resuming production, there is no harm if, for example, government deficits occur, or if, as a result, an increased issue of currency is induced.

Taking as it did the opposite tack from the line of thinking behind the Emergency Financial Measures, which gave priority to rooting out runaway inflation, this speech was strongly criticized as an irresponsible advocacy of inflation. Nevertheless, it is true that tolerating a certain level of inflation for the sake of reviving production was not necessarily a mistaken policy at the time. One may well add that the policy authorities only expected the Emergency Financial Measures to serve the purpose of gaining them time pending a U.S. policy change or development of a long-term policy. Sticking to the Emergency Financial Measures line may have been seen as another option, but there was considerable potential for social unrest at that time. Even though Finance Minister Ishibashi was purged by the Occupation and the Yoshida Cabinet, defeated in the election, stepped down, the Japanese economy ultimately made its comeback by taking the endure-inflation route.

Considered analytically, both the capital stock and the labor force clearly were underemployed. The problem was simply that bottleneck factors, such as lack of raw materials from overseas, stood in the way. Finance Minister Ishibashi himself, in the above-quoted speech, spoke of the need to increase coal production, and the priority production system was partly responsible for solving the problem.

The measures that became the means of providing fiscal and financial support for the postwar recovery were Reconstruction Bank financing and price-differential subsidies. Both of these policies were promoted and extended under the Yoshida Cabinet. The bill for the Reconstruction Bank was sponsored and presented in the Diet by Finance Minister Ishibashi, and the subsidies expanded drastically under Ishibashi's fiscal policies. However, the full efflorescence of both occurred after Ishibashi's ouster, during the stage in which the priority production system came into its own.

Conceived of as a remedy for firms' funds shortages resulting from the cancellation of wartime indemnities after the freeze on deposits, the Reconstruction Bank was established in January 1947 with the object of "supplying needed funds to financial institutions having difficulty receiving a funds supply from other financial institutions, in order to promote the recovery of the Japanese economy." From that time until the end of March 1949, about two years later, the balance of funds outstanding grew swiftly, reaching ¥131.9 billion; as a single financial corporation, the Bank accounted for one-third of the loans outstanding in all commercial banks nationwide. Its top priority was the coal industry, which had an outstanding balance of ¥47.5 billion, or 30% of Reconstruction Bank financing. From the coal industry's point of view, 70% of its borrowings were from the Reconstruction Bank. The

Table 2–8.   Postwar Activities of the Reconstruction Finance Bank

(¥ millions)

Disbursement of Funds			
	End of FY 1946	End of 1947	End of 1948
Coal	1,036	19,874	47,519
Fertilizer	561	3,751	6,030
Electric Power	302	1,166	22,400
Iron	291	1,858	3,526
Machinery	835	2,806	6,521
Public Corporations*	—	18,199	18,181
Totals	5,986	59,463	131,965
Plant & Equipment	2,808	26,039	94,341
Working Capital	3,179	33,423	37,623

Bond Issues and Acceptances			
	FY 1946	FY 1947	FY 1948
Issues (A)	3,000	55,900	109,100
Bank of Japan Acceptances (B)	2,824	42,463	70,305
B/A	94	76	64

Source: Reconstruction Finance Bank, *Fukkin yūshi no kaiko* [Reconstruction Finance in Retrospect].

Note: * The Reconstruction Finance Bank made loans to 11 public corporations, which were set up for the sake of price and quantity control. They included the Public Coal Distribution Corporation, the Oil Rationing Corporation, the Price Adjustment Corporation, and the Fertilizer Rationing Corporation.

percentages in other industries such as electric power and fertilizers were considerable. One can understand from this perspective that the Reconstruction Bank worked to provide priority finance as backing for priority production (Table 2–8).

Price-differential subsidies were set up such that, when producers' costs exceeded the officially fixed (consumers') prices, the amount of the difference would be disbursed out of the general account in an attempt to make price stability compatible as a public finance obligation with stimulating the desire to produce (Table 2–9). The amounts disbursed came to ¥12.1 billion in 1946 (11% of the general account), ¥45 billion in 1947 (21%), and ¥114.1 billion in 1948 (24%) (Table 2–10). The largest recipient of subsidies was the steel industry: aside from the ¥21.3 billion directly received in 1948, subsidy support was indirectly channeled through the coal subsidies to specified industries. A look at the figures for June 1948 on the approximate proportion of

Table 2–9. Changes in the System of Controlled Prices

Prices		The 3.3 System (Mar. 1946)	The 7.5 System (July 1947)	Revised System (June 1948)
Overall Prices		8 times prewar levels	65 times prewar levels	110 times prewar levels
Wages		¥500/mo.	¥1,800/mo. (28 times prewar levels)	¥3,200/mo. (57 times prewar levels)
Rice (per *koku**)	Producers	¥300	Parity	Parity
	Consumers	¥286.65	Formula	Formula
Coal (per ton)	Producers	¥250	¥956	¥2,388.52
	Consumers	¥150	¥600 (48 times prewar levels)	¥1,000
		(Assessed)		
Pig Iron (per ton)	Producers	¥2,200	¥6,370	¥14,070
	Consumers	¥1,300	¥3,050	¥3,600

Sources: Data for the 3.3 system and the 7.5 system are from *Kakaku chōsei kōdan shiryō* [Documents of the Price Adjustment Corporation]. Those for the revised system are from Mitsubishi Institute for Economic Research, *Nihon sangyō keizai sōran* [Conspectus of the Japanese Industrial Economy].
Note: * 1 *koku* = 5.12 American bushels.

Table 2–10. The Status of Price-Differential Subsidies

(¥ millions)

		1946	1947	1948	1949
Expenditures on General Account	A	111,087	214,256	473,146	741,047
Price Adjustment Expenditures	B	10,318	23,853	62,500	179,200
Other Subsidies	C	1,713	21,225	51,628	19,556
B/A			8.7	11.1	13.2	24.2
(B+C)/A			11.0	21.0	24.1	26.8
Stabilizing Band Subsidies		—	10,199	53,764	95,765
of which, Iron & Steel		—	*3,545*	*21,372*	*40,428*
Coal for Designated Industries		—	*3,792*	*18,119*	*14,464*

Source: Miyashita Buhei, *Kokka shikin* [National Funds]. Final budget figures for each fiscal year.

producers' prices plus distribution costs consisting of subsidies indicates that these proportions were as high as 71% for pig iron, 46% for rolled steel, and 79% for coal directed to specific industries. Moreover, the Reconstruction Bank was in charge of financing for the public corporations which had been established because of price controls. It also financed firms' deficits pending revisions of officially fixed prices, thus serving as a backup for the price control system. In sum, Reconstruction Bank financing was concentrated in coal, price-differential subsidies were concentrated in steel, and priority production in these sectors was thereby supported.

Reconstruction Bank financing and price-differential subsidies were part of the priority production effort, and these two programs are viewed as having played a role in the revival of production. However, they also became factors in the acceleration of inflation. The initial policy decision that the Reconstruction Bank would be entirely financed by the government was not adhered to, and the balance at the end of 1948 showed that ¥109.1 billion in Reconstruction Bank bonds had been issued, 60% of which had been Bank of Japan acceptances (Table 2–8). This was a public bond issue concealed as a loophole in the New Public Finance Law (Shin Zaisei Hō), which extolled equilibrium in revenue and expenditures and the public offering of public bonds; hence, adverse criticism of "Reconstruction Bank inflation" began to mount. Furthermore, even if one considers price-differential subsidies to have been useful in bringing down individual consumer prices, from the macro point of view they expanded the scale of fiscal spending and were also linked to the increased issue of public bonds, which was hidden from view by the pressure to increase fiscal spending. In that sense they can also be said to have been a primary inflationary factor. The Dodge mission, which later set itself the task of ending Japan's inflation, criticized the price-differential subsidies as supporting the Japanese economy on a single stilt. This criticism also applies to the Reconstruction Bank's large-scale bond issue.

One further point regarding both the Reconstruction Bank and the subsidies is that chaos took over in government accounting operations. From 1948 on, when the revival of production became pronounced, subsidies were paid on the basis of old costs even though costs had declined as a result of climbing rates of operation, and suspicions were voiced that firms had taken excess profits. With regard to the Reconstruction Bank, it suffices to recall that not only did the Shōwa Denkō scandal prove fatal for that company, it also caused the collapse of the Ashida Cabinet.[4]

The Reconstruction Bank had no autonomy as a financial institution, and in addition to the fact that lines of responsibility were not clearly

---

[4] The Shōwa Denkō company bribed Cabinet officials in order to obtain special treatment from the Reconstruction Bank.

drawn among the authorities, there was also interference from the Occupation authorities. (It is in order to prevent recurrences of this type of situation that the autonomy of present-day financial institutions is guaranteed under the law.) Even so, the kind of glue-like sticking together done by politicians, bureaucrats, and businessmen during the postwar reconstruction, although quite open, may be quite worthy of being called state monopoly capitalism.

Analysis and Criticism
In the foregoing the postwar recovery and inflation have been described, but some of the points made there should be further discussed analytically. Due to the starvation-level consumption demand immediately following the defeat, output of producers' goods stagnated, and the degree of circuitousness of production was thought to have been reduced. This is indisputably a Hayek-like Ricardo effect. However, common sense tells us that, if the demand for consumer goods increases, a derivative demand for producers' goods should also develop. Why did this not occur? In the debate at the time, such things as the sabotage of capitalists and the antagonism of the workers were held up as the causes of production's stagnation in the basic industries, and criticism of this analysis met bitter retorts. Even if we take this to be the problem and assume that the question concerns only the contraction of production for such reasons, however, the prices of producers' goods should be expected to have soared if they were in short supply. But in postwar Japan's inflationary process, consumer goods prices, not producers', led the way in price increases (Table 2–11). This is indisputably the opposite of the German inflation following the First World War, but it would be difficult to explain such relative price relations using the above reason alone. Perhaps inflation's advance increased uncertainty about the future and made people scurry about acting short-sightedly. Linked to the view that stresses the contradiction between the recovery and inflation, this is an attractive hypothesis. By itself, however, it still leaves unanswered the question of how the recovery was hastened by inflation.

Table 2–11. Price Changes, 1946–49

				(1934–36 = 1)
	1946	1947	1948	1949
Wholesale Prices	16.3	48.2	127.9	208.8
Capital Goods	16.3	44.8	115.0	171.4
Consumption Goods	15.4	50.2	144.0	248.0
Consumer Prices	50.6	109.1	189.0	236.9

There is a theory that inflation reduces the real wages of workers and forces capital accumulation, and the theory has been applied to postwar Japan by more than one, economist. In reality, however, during the period of postwar reconstruction and inflation labor's share of national income was high, and even in the midst of continuing inflation real wages actually made a striking recovery. If inflation is so profitable for monopoly capital, it should have been unable to pay subsidies, however outrageously cozy the business-government relationship might have been. In fact, according to national income distribution statistics, those who benefitted from inflation were individual entrepreneurs. Even if we grant that inflation accelerated capital accumulation, not a great deal of capital accumulation was necessary during the postwar period of inflation since, as we have seen, the capital stock inherited from the wartime and postwar days was fairly large. Moreover, not a great deal was in fact accumulated. In the coal and steel industries, what was deemed necessary was maintenance and repairs. At the Reconstruction Bank as well, deficit finance —aside from equipment funds and working capital loans—played a major role in the economic recovery process. If the priority production system is viewed as an effort to increase production within the constraints of the economic blockade, this line of action is justifiable as well.

The Lost Revolution

The loss of the war delivered a heavy blow to the existing political and social order. For one thing, inflation proceeded apace while dire poverty among the populace continued. With the spread of the labor movement, the Socialist Party, like the Communist Party, was liberated. Thus, it is not strange that a tumultuous atmosphere, like that on the eve of a revolution, was brewing. Both the Paris Commune and the Russian Revolution were the results of the shock of defeat in war. In postwar Japan, the upsurge in revolutionary feeling manifested itself in the May Day observances of 1946, the strikes that flourished at about this time, and the wave of feeling that lasted from the labor offensive of October 1946 to the eve of the general strike which was planned for February 1, 1947. As it turned out, this February 1 strike was stopped by order of the Occupation. In the general elections which immediately followed, the Socialist Party became the leading party, and with the Democratic Party and the Cooperative Party it formed a coalition Cabinet. Unable to resolve conflicts within and outside the party, however, this Cabinet was forced to resign. Opportunity was already slipping away.

The stop order for the February 1 strike was a volte-face—a betrayal of Occupation policy—and is sometimes criticized as having twisted the development of postwar democracy. The opportunity for revolution that was consequently lost is looked back upon nostalgically from time to time. However, it is not clear how many general strikes it would have taken for Japan to achieve a democratic or socialist utopia if only this unjust intervention had not taken place. The stop order was typical of the way in which much of Japan's democratization was carried out—not voluntarily, but in accordance with the orders of the Occupation: it was a deplorable departure from the principle of autonomy. It is also debatable whether Japan would actually have prospered if the general strike had been conducted at that point and an ensuing revolution had succeeded. It is difficult to answer a hypothetical question, but one may well imagine that, with social fragmentation in the country further intensified, a dictatorship of state power might have become the only way to gain control over the situation. Furthermore, to stretch the point, Japan might have become entangled in a dangerous vortex of international conflict. Since there was as yet no leisure in which to experience such things as political and ideological freedom and the fruits of economic prosperity, there was no small danger that absolutism and austerity would revive under the name of democracy. In this sense, it was an extremely good thing that Japanese society in later years enjoyed, at one stage, bourgeois freedom and a bourgeois life, no matter what the system may become in the future. The fact that the Japanese people did not succumb to radicalism in the chaotic period following the war, but instead fought their way out to prosperity, may suggest the soundness of their instinct for survival in political crises.

While Japan was militarily occupied, economically blockaded, and subjected to displays of America's high standard of living, the people were scratching out their lives in abysmal penury. Here was an abundance of disillusionment, envy, dissatisfaction, and antagonism—the psychological materials for revolution. However, no socialist or communist revolution took place. From today's perspective we can see that a different revolution was in the making. The people were concentrating all their efforts on rushing full tilt into industrialization and raising living standards as much as possible.

It is strange that the Japanese people seem to have maintained a remarkable hold on their self-confidence in the midst of this chaos. There was a baby boom during the two or three years immediately after the war, in spite of severe commodity shortages. Were parents in those days of semi-starvation thinking about how they would raise these children or what kinds of jobs they would get? Was it confidence in the future, or irresponsibility? It is almost as though they had a premonition of the coming of rapid growth. At any rate, the roots of the Japanese economy's "growth revolution" (an odd juxtaposition of words) certainly can be traced to the psychological shock immediately following the defeat.

3

The Dodge Plan and the Korean War

A Shift in Policy Toward Japan

On January 6, 1948, U.S. Secretary of the Army Kenneth C. Royall gave a major speech on Japan policy at San Francisco's Commonwealth Club. After indulging in some self-congratulatory remarks to the effect that the demilitarization and democratization of Japan's economy had progressed rapidly under the American Occupation, the Secretary mentioned the hardships ahead, such as population increase and the tangled situation in Asia. "For political stability to continue and for free government to succeed in future," he stated, a "sound and self-supporting economy" in Japan was essential. Moreover, he added, the United States "cannot continue forever to pour hundreds of millions of dollars annually into relief funds for occupied areas." It was inevitable, he said, that some points of conflict should have arisen between the original concept of broad demilitarization and the new purpose of building a self-supporting nation. The Secretary went on to say:

> It is clear that Japan cannot support itself as a nation of shop-keepers and craftsmen and small artisans any more than it can exist as a purely agricultural nation. We can expect continuing economic deficits in Japan unless there is at least some degree of mass industrial production.
>
> We are building in Japan a self-sufficient democracy, strong enough and stable enough to support itself and at the same time to serve as a deterrent against any other totalitarian war threats which might hereafter arise in the Far East. (*New York Times*, Jan. 7, 1948)

The demilitarization and democratization policies of the Occupation's initial period were coming to an end, and Japan's revival as an industrial nation and its return to world markets were becoming the major points of America's Japan policy. This policy shift went through a number of vicissitudes, finally crystallizing in the National Security Council's recommendation concerning Allied Policy for Japan (NSC 13/2 and 13/3) of October 9 of that year:

> Second only to U.S. security interests, economic recovery should be made the primary objective of United States policy in Japan for the coming period. It should be sought through a combination of United States aid program envisaging shipments and/or credits on a declining scale over a number of years, and by a vigorous and concerted effort by all interested agencies and departments of the United States Government to cut away existing obstacles to the revival of Japanese foreign trade, with provision for Japanese merchant shipping, and to facilitate restoration and development of Japan's exports. In developing Japan's internal and external trade and industry, private enterprise should be encouraged. (Paragraph 15).

The difference between this and the U.S. Initial Post-Surrender Policy for Japan (September 23, 1945), as quoted in Chapter 1 (p. 18), is quite striking. What, then, were the main factors that produced this policy shift? The foregoing speech by Secretary Royall suggests two explanations for what became known in Japan as the "reverse course."[1]

One was the need to reduce the financial burden borne by the American people—the "taxpayer theory." The other was the "Cold War theory," positing that the aim was to induce Japan to serve as the Asian bulwark against infiltrations of Communist power. Loud insistence upon the plight of the taxpayer is an extremely American phenomenon, but in the American moral climate of the day the taxpayer and Cold War theories were complementary rather than contradictory; at least they were not clearly differentiated from each other. Reduction of the taxpayer's burden became a pressing bipartisan domestic political issue due to the gains made by the Republican Party in the 1947 off-year elections, but anti-communism, with its more partisan coloring, was much stronger in the Republican Party. The Cold War developed at an exceedingly rapid pace from 1947

---

[1] For some of the terminology in the succeeding paragraphs, I am indebted to Hata Ikuhiko's discussion in Volume 3 of his *Shōwa zaisei shi* [Financial History of Modern Japan] (Hata, 1976).

onward. In March of that year the United States decided to aid Greece and Turkey (the Truman Doctrine), and in June it announced a European recovery assistance plan (the Marshall Plan). In October the Cominform was organized by the Soviet Union and the nations of Eastern Europe. November's London Four-Power Conference of Foreign Ministers broke up over the Austro-German peace settlement. Since the summer of that year the civil war between Mainland China's Guomindang and the Communist Party had been gradually intensifying. As 1948 began, the Korean Democratic People's Republic was formed (February), and the Communist Party of Czechoslovakia seized political power in Czechoslovakia. In June a currency reform was implemented in the Western-occupied areas of Germany, in retaliation for which the Soviet Union imposed a total blockade on Berlin. The United States countered with a large-scale airlift operation, and the East-West confrontation took on a critical, explosive cast.

West Germany's currency reform at this time achieved unanticipated success and paved the way for the German economic miracle. The plan for this reform dates back to one originally put together in 1946 by Joseph Dodge, who headed the Fiscal Department of the U.S. military government in occupied Germany. At the end of 1948, amid news of the Chinese Communist Army's probable conquest of the Chinese mainland (its bloodless entry into Peking took place in December of that year), the U.S. government, which was trying to hasten the economic recovery of Japan, reappointed Dodge to work in occupied territory. His return to his position as manager of a Detroit bank was deferred, and he was instead placed in charge of directing the Japanese economy. This personnel decision was made primarily on the basis of the recommendation of Under Secretary of the Army William H. Draper; but Dodge was a member of the strongly Republican financial establishment, and domestic political considerations were also at work. His appointment was a maneuver aimed at pre-empting the party out of power (the Republicans) which was emphasizing the taxpayer theory. (John Foster Dulles played a similar role in later years in concluding the peace with Japan.)

Thus, the Dodge stabilization policy—popularly known as the Dodge Plan—was initiated in 1949. Its basic contents, however, had already been clearly stated in the recommendation concerning Allied Policy for Japan (NSC 13/2):

> The success of the recovery program will in large part depend on Japanese efforts to raise production and to maintain high export levels through hard work, a minimum of work-stoppages, internal

austerity measures and the stern combatting of inflationary trends including efforts to achieve a balanced internal budget as rapidly as possible. (Paragraph 15)

The Dodge Plan

Single-Stroke versus Stopgap Stabilization

By 1948 mining and manufacturing production had partially recovered, commodities were beginning to circulate again, and the rate of price increase had also begun to slacken somewhat (Table 3–1). Against this background, schemes for the reconstruction of the economy and for stamping out inflation were debated at home in Japan as well as among the Americans.

One such dispute was the "Arisawa-Kimura Debate," which grew out of Kimura Kihachirō's criticism of Arisawa Hiromi's contention that the government should wait until production had recovered to a certain prewar level and then stamp out inflation. Kimura held that the recovery of production was predicated on eliminating inflation. This was the confrontation between the at-one-stroke stabilization theory advocated by Kimura, Suzuki Takeo, and others, and Arisawa's conditional-at-one-stroke theory; however, both adhered to Marxism in a broad sense, i.e., were in the left-wing camp. Here, stabilization means stabilization of the price of the currency, and what many people had in mind in this connection was something like the stabilization of the mark after the First World War (the Rentenmark miracle).

In contrast, the stopgap stabilization theory was conceived by government authorities. The following excerpt is from a document of March 1948 drawn up by the Economic Stabilization Board (the forerunner of the Economic Planning Agency):

Table 3–1. The Revival of Production and the Blunting of Inflation

(% relative to previous year)

	Industrial Production	Agricultural Production	Effective Prices	Consumer Prices	Bank of Japan Notes in Circulation
1947	17.9	2.4	57.4	115.6	134.6
48	33.8	15.0	−7.3	73.2	62.1
49	24.1	1.2	−16.4	25.3	0.0

Source: "Kihon Nihon keizai tōkei" [Basic Statistics of the Japanese Economy], and "Nihon keizai tōkei shū" [Collected Statistics of the Japanese Economy].

The aim of stopgap stabilization is, in a word, to take hold of and use to good advantage a time when, in view of the international situation, the potential for foreign capital assistance and food supplies to our country is greatest; to rely on the implementation of a general policy which embraces each of the economy's three aspects, goods, capital, and labor; to sharply brake inflation's advance; to make possible both our nation's economic reconstruction and its participation in the international economy; and to establish the conditions for moving toward a future full-fledged stabilization.

Stopgap stabilization does not require the policy reversal implicit in a deflation which disregards the degree of sacrifice entailed by bringing inflation to an absolute halt and thereby engendering a depression. It will suffice if a continued "feeling of stability" is achieved, rather than an abrupt slowdown in inflation.

The specific timetable and goals for this stopgap stabilization program were envisaged as follows:

1. *A preparatory period* lasting until October 1948: waiting for full-scale assistance and improvements in the food situation.
2. *First period*, from November 1948 to October 1949: increasing rations, breaking the vicious wage-price spiral, putting mass production into operation, securing a substantially balanced budget.
3. *Second period*, ending March 1950 at the latest: establishing a single exchange rate, bringing in private foreign capital, promoting exports.

Table 3–2. Economic Recovery Plan, First Draft

	1952 (A)	1930–34 (B)	(A) as % of (B)
Mining & Mfg. Output			
Coal	44 million tons	31.17 million tons	141
Ordinary Steel & Steel Products	23 million tons	21.95 million tons	105
Spindles (for cotton yarn)	5.83 million	8 million	73
Calories	2111 calories	2242 calories	
Rice	67.92 million *koku*	61.02 million *koku*	111
Exports	$16.47 million	—	—
Imports	$16.57 million	—	—

Source: Hayashi Yūjirō, ed., *Nihon no keizai keikaku* [Japan's Economic Plans], p. 43.

In addition, the government prepared an economic plan for the time-span beyond this period of stopgap stabilization. The Economic Recovery Planning Commission, with Prime Minister Ashida Hitoshi as Chairman and Chief of the Economic Stabilization Board Kurusu Takeo as Vice-Chairman, held its first meeting on May 17, 1948, at which time it announced the first draft of its economic recovery plan. The principal goal of this plan was to restore by 1952 the standard of living to its average level for 1930–34 (Table 3–2). The promotion of exports and the increased self-sufficiency which alone could provide the imports necessary to support this standard of living, along with the suppression of inflation, were taken up as priority items. Even these objectives, modest from today's perspective, were considered no easy matter in those days when Japan's population had increased to 25% over the prewar figure.

Both the stopgap stabilization plan and the reconstruction plan were expressions of a policy effort which attempted to anticipate the state of affairs under difficult circumstances. Unlike the Marxists, who at that time possessed overwhelming intellectual influence and who took as a model Germany's experience after the First World War with bringing inflation under control, the advocates of stopgap stabilization, setting out from a position of realism, sought to avoid the increases in unemployment and bankruptcy which accompany the abrupt elimination of inflation.[2]

However, when America's global policy began to demand stabilization of the Japanese economy at one stroke, the stopgap stabilization plan had to be tossed out, no matter how much weight it carried at home in Japan. Since the stopgap policy was itself conceived with the aim of extricating the economy from the blockade carried over from wartime (see Chapter 2) and in hopes of economic assistance and capital imports from the U.S., its demise when contradictions with American policy arose was inevitable. The recovery plan, even more than the stopgap stabilization plan with its emphasis on increasing self-sufficiency, was in serious contradictions with the stated goals of American Occupation policy. In an effort to cope with the sudden change that implementing the Dodge Plan represented, the Economic Recovery Planning Commission made some adjustments in the language of the plan, such as substituting "implementing disinflation and normalizing the economy" for "conquering inflation," but this was hardly ade-

---

[2] It is thought that post-World War I France implemented what is here referred to as stopgap stabilization. Among Marxian economists of the time the French formula was less highly esteemed than the German stabilization, however.

quate for the job of achieving a logical transition to the new policy.

By the time the Economic Recovery Planning Commission had finally settled on a plan, on May 30, 1949, the Ashida Cabinet had been replaced by the Yoshida Cabinet, and the new administration shelved the Commission's plan. It was reported that Prime Minister Yoshida Shigeru had criticized the plan as "autarchic in conception and lacking in international feeling." Economic Stabilization Board Chief Aoki Takayoshi, who found himself caught between the Scylla and Charybdis of the Commission and the Prime Minister, made a personal visit to Yoshida's villa in Oiso to gain confirmation of the Prime Minister's intentions, but his report to the Commission upon his return merely referred to "the Prime Minister's obstinacy in old age" and apparently explained nothing in detail. In September of that year the matter ended with a decision to officially withdraw the recovery plan.

The Super-Balanced Budget and Disinflation Policy

On December 18, 1948, General Headquarters of the Occupation (GHQ), "in line with the efforts the United States is making to contribute to worldwide economic recovery and which are being carried out in other countries as well," issued a nine-point directive on economic stabilization. The nine points of this program included anti-inflationary provisions which became the nucleus of the Dodge Plan, such as (1) balancing the general budget, (2) tightening up on tax collection, (3) restricting credit, and (4) stabilizing wages; but they were also deeply tinged with considerations of control, as seen in (5) the strengthening and expansion of price controls, (6) the improvement and reinforcement of trade and foreign exchange controls, (7) the upgrading of the materials rationing system, (8) increased domestic production of raw materials and manufactured goods, and (9) the improvement of food cargo collection. It is thought that the former were policies coming straight out of Washington, while the latter were conceived of by the Occupation officials in Tokyo.

In the event, implementation of the stabilization plan was driven forward by Joseph Dodge, who was sent to Japan with the rank of Minister after the matter was entirely entrusted to him by President Truman. Since Dodge was a classical liberal, the clampdown doctrine, as stated in the latter half of the program's nine points, was quietly discarded, and stress was laid on the revival of sound public finance and on the price structure. The nine points came to be equated with a balanced budget. Dodge's proclamation of April 15, 1949, expressed his beliefs:

There seems to be astonishingly little comprehension among the Japanese people of the real situation of their country. Nothing should have been expected as the result of the war but a long term of hardship and self-denial. The nation continuously has been living beyond its means. . . . Wealth must be created before it can be divided.

The Japanese people should demand a balanced budget and should then direct their attention to the elimination of excessive expenditures, wastefulness, subsidies, over-employment and the general dependence on government instead of individual or group accomplishment.

. . . This practice of the general use of subsidies is abnormal and undesirable. It creates fictious and unnatural price relationships. Also it is more costly than the mere figures indicate. The amount collected in taxes for subsidies is first reduced by the cost of tax collection and then progressively reduced by the other administrative costs of the government and the operating costs of every Kodan or government department handling the transaction until the remainder is actually applied to a consumer price of food, material or product. Thus the consumer taxpayer inevitably receives back only part of what he pays out for this purpose. But the taxes are paid by all of the people and except for subsidies granted to hold down the price of basic foods consumed by all the people, the tax proceeds going into subsidies are distributed for the benefit and protection of special groups of people.

Something can be said in favor of certain price increases perhaps costing the consumer less than some taxes are now costing him. Too much of the price of too many materials and products is collected by the Tax Bureau of the government instead of in the market.

Dodge's strong convictions and high moral sense are, in all honesty, deserving of respect. At the same time, why did the Americans—MacArthur was the same way—like to highhandedly sermonize like this? What is more, like a puppy that wags its tail when scolded by its master, most of Japan's political parties of the day advocated immediate implementation of the nine points.

In 1949 Dodge attempted to achieve a genuine balance in the general budget. The 1947 Public Finance Law prohibited the issuing of national bonds, and a formal balance was even achieved in the general account; but "hidden public bond issues" passing through special accounts and government institutions (such as the one for Reconstruction

Table 3-3. The Dodge Super-Balanced Budget (FY 1949)

(¥ 100 millions)

(a) General Account

	1948	1949			
		Government Draft	SCAP Draft	Initial Budget	Notes
Price Adjustment Expenditures	625	700	1,987	2,022	Large increase due to hidden subsidy appropriations
Settlement of Matters Pertaining to End of the War	1,071	1,100	1,250	1,252	Outlays for the Occupation
Public Works Projects	495	750	500	615	Curtailed
Unemployment Relief	10	150	0	30	Curtailed
Totals, Incl. Other Items	4,737	5,787	7,030	7,047	

(b) Overall Receipts & Disbursements

		1946	1947	1948	1949
Aggregate	Annual Expenditure	3,899	6,942	16,707	45,240
	Annual Revenue	3,876	6,954	16,701	44,957
Net Budget	Annual Expenditure	1,253	3,699	9,273	25,362
	Annual Revenue	2,148	4,203	10,161	23,795
Difference		−897	−509	−887	1,567

Source: Shōwa zaisei shi [Shōwa Financial History], Vol. 3, Tables 4–15 and 4–16.

Bank bonds) reached a colossal sum, which was directly linked with the creation of inflationary money (Chapter 2). "Hidden subsidies" were being paid through special accounts for foreign trade administration by selling imported raw materials below the government's cost of acquisition abroad. Dodge published all such factors in tables and assembled a "super"-balanced budget with a net general surplus of $157.6 billion, which was used for such things as the amortization of Reconstruction Bank bonds (Table 3–3). Under the Dodge Plan, postal rates and fares on the National Railways were increased on a major scale, the Reconstruction Bank's new lending to enterprises was brought to a halt, and the proceeds from the sale of American aid commodities were set aside as a Counterpart Fund equivalent to U.S. aid to Japan. On April 23, 1949, the US$1: ¥360 exchange rate—

which was to remain in force until 1971—was established.

As the first Economic White Paper aptly stated in June of 1947, the Japanese economy following the defeat was in such a state that "the nation, the principal firms, and household budgets are all running deficits." As efforts were made to cover these deficits, inflation advanced, while overseas the deficits were taken care of by U.S. aid to Japan.

In order to reduce American assistance, Dodge put Japan's public finances in the black by tightening up on tax collections and holding down expenditures. He encouraged the self-reliance of business firms by cutting price subsidies (which meant a shakeout for those firms which could not be self-sustaining) and compelled households to make tax payments while at the same time exhorting them to save. The individualistic or microeconomic way of thinking, which had been influential in the era of commodity and price controls, gave way to the simple macro theory of the classical balance between savings and investment. In this process, in order to "clarify where government responsibility lies," Dodge had compiled in tables the main factors causing inflation which lay obscurely buried in other accounts. To put the matter in the current idion, this was an attempt to cope both comprehensively and clearly with public welfare and its defrayment, with benefits and costs, but without mistaken intentions or decisions. This point of view may well be judged the starting point for any reform of a public finance system. Dodge in fact made clear distinctions among the government proper, government enterprises, and private economic activity, and each made its contribution to restoring the balance between revenue and expenditure.

How did the Japanese government under the Occupation handle the Dodge stabilization policy? Succeeding Ashida's coalition of Democrats and Socialists, which was brought down as a result of the Shōwa Denkō scandal, Yoshida Shigeru's Democratic Liberal Party (Minshū Jiyūtō, the forerunner of todays Liberal Democratic Party) won a sweeping victory in the general elections of January 1949, laying the foundation for its long-term, stable, and conservative hold on political power. Prime Minister Yoshida straightforwardly accepted the Dodge Plan as a requirement imposed by the Occupation. Subjectively, Finance Minister Ikeda Hayato may not necessarily have been a member of the deflation faction, but he made strenuous efforts to implement the super-balanced budget. These qualities of straightforwardness and decisiveness seem to have won the Yoshida Cabinet all the more public support.

At the same time, however, there was another side of the coin. Under the Dodge Plan the excess of withdrawals over payments in the public-

Table 3–4. Progress under the Dodge Plan

	Labor Pro-ductivity (Prewar = 100)	Volume of Exports (1953 = 100)	Government Receipts (Fiscal years; – indicates budget sur-plus; ¥100 millions)	Bank of Japan Lending (¥100 millions)	Incidence of Bad Checks (No. per 10,000)
1947	24.9	—	59.2	– 181	0.3
48	32.4	19.8	40.1	196	1.0
49	42.2	40.9	– 84.3	367	4.7

Sources: Economic Planning Agency, "Kihon Nihon keizai tōkei" [Basic Statistics of the Japanese Economy]; "Gendai Nihon keizai no tenkai" [Development of the Contemporary Japanese Economy (Data Section)]; *Pore kara Daresu e—Senryō seisaku no keizaiteki kiketsu* [From Pauley to Dulles—Economic Consequences of the Occupation Policy].

to-government balance was completely reversed as government funds began to exceed private funds; the Reconstruction Bank's financing activities were halted, and the Counterpart Fund was in many instances applied to debt amortization instead of being used as a new supply of funds. In response to such financial stringency, the government and the Bank of Japan put into effect a "policy for alleviating the monetary stringency," consisting of such measures as a relaxation of operations and an easing of the policy of keeping interest rates artificially high, and active use of Trust Fund Bureau funds. Bank of Japan lending increased sharply during this period, which also saw the emergence of the over-loan phenomenon, a practice which continued from that time until the 1960s (Table 3–4). An attempt to ameliorate from the financial side the deflationary effects of the Dodge fiscal policies, the overloan was typical of a surplus budget with an easy money policy. This testifies to the Japa-nese government's ambivalence, submitting to Dodge's policies on the one hand and resisting them on the other; and somehow it also seemed to have the understanding and support of the Occupation authorities in Japan, who were not necessarily always of the same mind as U.S. Government officialdom in Washington.

If one seeks the ideological basis for this opposition, one can see the shadows of the stopgap stabilization concept and the recovery plan which, once defeated, were supposed to have been buried. It might be noted parenthetically that the technique of supplementing the fiscal balance from the monetary side also became a special feature of the Ikeda public finance policies in the first half of the 1950s and left a trail as the subsequent practice of "flexible use" of Treasury loans and investments.

The Domestic Consequences of the Dodge Plan

As a result of the implementation of the Dodge Plan, the volume of Bank of Japan notes contracted; black market prices fell steeply; the abolition of commodity and price controls progressed (in the single year beginning April 1949 the number of controlled commodities was reduced from 290 to 63, and the number of price-controlled items dropped by three-quarters, from 2,128 to 531); and trends in the rationalization of firms and in efficiency increases were remarkable. Was it because the economic structure was simple that the effects were felt so extremely rapidly?

Mining and manufacturing production, however, after increasing until the middle of 1949, only fluctuated thereafter. Exports at the fixed ¥360 rate expanded on a large scale during the first half of 1949 and virtually doubled during that year, but with the devaluation of the pound in October of that year some misgivings were raised about the future. As a result of the crackdown on tax collections, the financial stringency, and the sluggishness of demand, inventories increased. An example is coal inventories, which were directly affected by the Dodge Plan, and which exceeded 4 million tons at the end of March 1950.

The third Economic White Paper warned that the possibility of harm due to inflation had become remote, but that the Japanese economy had entered a critical stage of "devastation due to deflation" (this expression carries an undertone of the stopgap stabilization theory proponents' opposition to the Dodge Plan). The possibility of a stabilization crisis began to be talked about.

The Dodge austerity policy also delivered a direct blow to the labor movement. In a long letter of July 22, 1948, in which he quoted former President Franklin D. Roosevelt, General MacArthur had given instructions for an amendment to the National Public Service Law prohibiting strikes by public employees. On this basis, Government Order No. 201, making such strikes illegal, was issued. It was at about this time that walkout tactics were adopted, and labor-related incidents occurred in rapid succession. On December 11, 1948, GHQ announced that it would not approve wage increases which produced price increases, thus seeking to support the balanced budget policy in this area as well.

In June of 1949, while the Dodge Plan was in effect, amendments to the labor laws were enacted. The Japan National Railways (JNR) and the Japan Tobacco and Salt Corporation were launched as independent public corporations (*kōsha*), and strikes by public servants· were prohibited. An administrative retrenching in which 260,000 people would lose their jobs was proposed, in a more direct connection with the Dodge Plan. In May a law providing for a fixed number of public employees was passed. At JNR, where the number of employees had swelled to 620,000 by the absorption of repatriates following the war, the personnel reduction became a focal point for the government-labor confrontation. Amid turbulent public feeling, as "liberated peoples' commuter trains" were operated by radical trade unionists and rumors of a November revolution circulated, JNR sent out dismissal notices on July 1. There followed in rapid succession some of the most dramatic incidents in postwar history, including the disappearance and death of JNR President Shimoyama Sadanori on July 5 and two instances in which sabotaged trains derailed, killing nine people.

As a reaction against the political character of labor organization activities up to that time the Mindō (Minshuka Dōmei) tightened its hold on labor leadership, as is seen in National Railways Labor Union Directive No. O, which confirmed Mindō's position. The situation led to the formation of two other umbrella labor federations, Shinsanbetsu in December of 1949 and Sōhyō in March of 1950.

In another quarter, the Cold War entered a new stage with the Soviet Union's development of the atom bomb in September of 1949 and the formation of the People's Republic of China in October of the same year. On January 8, 1950, the Cominform criticized the Japanese Communist Party and drove it toward a reckless advocation of extreme leftist armed struggle. On the fifth of June the Occupation authorities ordered a purge of the Communist Party cadres.

Currency reform in Germany became the impetus for the Berlin blockade. This shows all too well how deeply interrelated are a nation's currency and its domestic and foreign politics. The Dodge Plan revived a free economy, but, operating as it did in the adverse international environment of the East-West Cold War, it left behind a lasting scar.

The Impact of the Korean War

On June 25, 1950, the North Korean army crossed the 38th parallel and attacked South Korea, occupied Seoul in short order, and, putting the South Korean army to rout, advanced to the south. The United States came to the assistance of South Korea, sending in first its navy and air forces and then army troops; the United Nations, too, decided on sanctions against North Korea. The Korean War had begun.

As we have seen, prior to this the Japanese economy had faced a deflationary crisis as a result of the implementation of the Dodge Plan.

Table 3–5. Influence of the Dodge Plan and the Korean War
(%, as proportion of figure for same month of previous year)

	Dodge Plan (Mar. 1950)	Korean War (Mar. 1951)
Mining & Mfg. Output*	5.8	46.0
Export Volume*	56.2	40.3
Wholesale Prices	15.3	46.9
Consumer Prices	8.7	14.7
Bank of Japan Notes	−0.4	27.3

Source: "Gendai Nihon keizai no tenkai" [Development of the Contemporary Japanese Economy], Table 1–15.
Note: * January.-March as compared with the same period for the previous year.

The outbreak of the Korean War produced a sudden change in the situation. Japan became a supply base. As orders were concentrated in special procurements and munitions, exports grew rapidly along with the worldwide military expansion. Markets boomed, inventory backlogs were sold out, and mining and manufacturing production also grew at a fast tempo from early autumn of that year, for an increase of about 50% in the year after the war began. The balance of payments improved, capital became plentiful, and profits rose as well. It appeared that perhaps the Dodge Plan would simply be forgotten (Table 3–5).

As indicated in the speech by Army Secretary Royall quoted at the beginning of this chapter, the shift in America's policy toward Japan was in one respect governed by the "taxpayers theory" and in another by the "Cold War theory." It is for this reason that the international political background was included in the foregoing discussion of the Dodge Plan. However, the Dodge Plan itself is considered to have represented a period when the taxpayers theory and the Cold War theory were as yet undifferentiated. Prior to the Korean War, America's rather passive Asia policy consisted of pinning hopes on a future Sino-Soviet confrontation, promoting Japan's economic stability, and considering how best to establish a line of defense (the possible abandonment of South Korea and Taiwan). The Korean War stepped up U.S. involvement in Asia and resolved the debate on taxpayers versus Cold War theory in favor of the latter. On his third visit to Japan, which followed the Korean War, Dodge pointed out that Japan's accumulation of foreign exchange as a result of the Korean War "is an exceptional and temporary phenomenon, one which, moreover, has limits." He stressed that "there is no greater folly than to submit to the wave of inflation which is on the rise everywhere in the world." However, even these words of warning did not prevent hopes from rising in Japan for Japanese-American economic cooperation and an early peace.

While for Japanese the adversities of war in a neighboring country were a boon, a "wind of the gods" (*kamikaze*), the situation also showed the fragility of the Japanese economy's peaceful base at the time and revealed the self-centeredness and vanity of the Japanese people. Compared to the hardships on the road to long-term development, the prosperity due to the Korean War was no more than a temporary phenomenon.

Significance and Lessons

The Dodge Plan produced (1) an end to the postwar inflation, (2) a return to world markets, and (3) the revival of a free economy. In that sense it was a great watershed in postwar economic history. It is often said that the Germans, more than the Japanese, will always remember the ordeals of inflation; but Japan will not soon forget inflation. The commitment to a blanced budget established under the Dodge Plan continued for about 15 years, until the 1965 special public bond issue. The exchange rate set at US$1 = ¥360 under the Dodge Plan lasted until 1971, about twenty years. The tax system (the Shoup Report), the system of public corporations (three public corporations and five government enterprises), the money supply system (overloans), and the leadership of the labor union organizations (the Sōhyō [General Council of Trade Unions of Japan] system), had their origins in this period, as did a number of other institutions which also survived for a long time afterwards.

The Dodge Plan brought to a close the upheavals of the 1940s. In the wake of another round of upheavals in the 1970s, it has now become possible to see more clearly the meaning of the policy choices in the Dodge Plan. Stabilization or recovery? Stabilization at a single stroke or stopgap stabilization? How to cope with the increased unemployment accompanying a drop in inflation? To what extent is controlled intervention necessary, and to what extent effective? These were questions that once again in the 1970s demanded answers.

At the time when the Dodge Plan was being implemented, the Japanese economy could not have failed to become disoriented when confronted with sudden changes in the international situation, particularly changes in America's global policy. From today's vantage point one can see that throughout 1948 the United States government was steadily setting up the initial strategic moves toward single-stroke stabilization for the Japanese economy. The Japanese, however, did not notice the shift in American policy until virtually the end, and a sluggish, stopgap stabilization policy flourished in the meantime. The Dodge proclamation came like a bolt from the blue. This apparent obtuseness has a particular meaning: it testifies all too well to what Prime Minister Yoshida Shigeru very aptly termed "lack of international feeling" when he was commenting on the recovery plan.

However, the problems of thirty years ago are not to be laughed at. In the Japan of 1971 it was impossible to keep up with all the reading about hopes for a gradual contraction in Japan's balance of payments surplus, while the United States was urgently demanding a revaluation of the yen. If we substitute the earlier dictum, "Set a single exchange rate at an early date," for "Revalue the yen immediately," do not the frame of mind and behavior of Japanese government officials and economists just prior to Dodge's arrival resemble their frame of mind and behavior just before the announcement of Nixon's New Economic Plan—which came as the same kind of shock? Moreover, the same exercise was repeated both in 1973 (the adoption of a floating exchange rate system) and in 1977 (the uproar over the strong yen). Watching the same pattern occur again and again, one has the sense of some kind of fated confrontation, something which can only be called the incompatibility of Japanese and American culture.

Under the Dodge Plan, Japan returned to world markets and revived its free-economy system. However, it found itself in an Asia fragmented by the Korean War, while itself enfeebled by the defeat and inflation. Dealing with these realities became the task of the Japanese economy at the beginning of the 1950s.

4

The Special Procurement Boom:
Economic Outcome of the Korean War

The San Francisco Treaty

On September 8, 1951, at the San Francisco Opera House, the treaty of peace with Japan was signed. It came into force on April 28 of the following year, 1952, and the defeated Japan of World War II thereby regained its independence.

According to U.S. Special Envoy John Foster Dulles (then Advisor to the Secretary of State), who undertook the drafting of and final arrangements for the treaty, it was an "amicable and generous peace." According to the leftist faction of the Japan Socialist Party, labor unions, and the sophisticated progressives of the Peace Discussion Societiy,[1] this treaty was not a full-fledged peace settlement but a one-sided peace which excluded China and the Soviet Union. Together with the U.S.-Japan Security Treaty, which was concluded at the same time, in the leftist view it placed Japan in a "Manchuria-like position" vis-à-vis the United States. Public opinion was divided,

Under the San Francisco Treaty Japan's international position steadily improved. The U.S.-Japan Security Treaty did not obstruct the restoration of diplomatic relations between Japan and the Soviet Union and China. At the time, the one-sided peace and the restoration of independence were to Japan's advantage, and appeared to be natural choices. This view, however, is from the perspective of the present, in the light of subsequent history. At the beginning of the 1950s Japan was in an extremely unstable position. Above all else it was intimidated by the ominous shadow of the Korean War. The United States, for its

---

[1] *Heiwa Mondai Danwa Kai.* The "Peace Problems Discussion Society's January 1950 Proclamation Concerning the Peace" contained the following points: (1) Economic independence will not be achieved by a one-sided peace. (2) A peace on all fronts is desirable. (3) As a neutral and inviolable nation, we rest our hopes on participation in the United Nations. (4) We oppose offers to establish military bases here. Refer to contemporaneous issues of the magazine *Sekai* ["World"].

part, planned for a peace that was "amicable and generous" compared with the Treaty of Versailles imposed on Germany after World War I, because it feared that, in the strained atmosphere of the Korean War, Japan would go Communist. The peace-on-all-fronts doctrine captured a segment of public opinion because it appealed to Japan's wish to avoid becoming involved in a shooting war like that in Korea. The leftist Socialist Party led by Chairman Suzuki Mosaburō rapidly expanded the vote in its favor by appealing, "Young men: do not take up arms!" Within the conservative parties, which constituted over two-thirds of the National Diet, there was a powerful faction which advocated rearmament and the independent adoption of a constitution.

The San Francisco Treaty is significant for having determined that Japan would restrict rearmament to a minimum and devote all its energy to economic recovery. This policy, which was advocated by Prime Minister Yoshida, was criticized at home for making a mockery of the idealism of the pacificist constitution by creating an army "without fighting capacity" and entering a military alliance with the United States. Abroad it was criticized as a contrivance to feed parasitically on a neighboring country's wartime devastation while scheming to selfishly expand the home economy. Such elements were admittedly present. However, considering Japan's actual circumstances internationally and the state of people's lives at that time, this policy choice was undeniably realistic and rational. After the end of the Korean War, when both Stalinism and McCarthyism went into decline, when East-West tensions were eased and there was movement toward international multipolarization such as that which occurred in the Sino-Soviet confrontation, the realism of this choice became still more evident. In the so-called "reactionary policy" phase, the health of pacifism and democracy was at any rate preserved in the name of economic recovery. This shows that the lessons of the Pacific War had been learned well.

The Special Procurement Boom

Price and the Balance of Payments
In conjunction with the outbreak of the Korean War, prosperity came to call on the Japanese economy as economic activity suddenly expanded. Not surprisingly, in an economy that had been suffering from depressed business conditions, the Korean War was hailed as a "wind of the gods" (*kamikaze*). However, particularly because this boom was created by the war and the American military forces's orders for supplies that the war generated, even in the midst of prosperity all manner

of distortions and instabilities combined to produce striking results. The first was a revival of inflation. One year after the beginning of the Korean War, wholesale prices showed a steep rise of 47% and consumer prices were up 15%. Even in comparison with the rest of the inflation-ridden world, these were extraordinary price increases (Table 4–1).

The inflation immediately following the war had occurred under the economic blockade, and consumer prices soared above producers' goods prices. By contrast, however, the inflation of the 1950s was led in by the steep price advances produced by the Korean War, and this time producers' prices overtook consumers'. This was inflation in its classic form, while the immediate postwar inflation was outside the usual mold. In the period of inflation directly after the defeat, the government gave price-differential subsidies for basic commodities, supplementing producers' prices. The inflation of the Korean War period, in contrast, made possible the smooth abolition of price-differential subsidies for basic materials, as determined in the Dodge Plan.

The soaring international prices arising out of the Korean War were, however, a temporary phenomenon. As a result of the hawkish General MacArthur's dismissal in April of 1951 and Soviet U.N. representative Malik's June peace proposal, the mood of worldwide military expansion ebbed and market conditions sagged dramatically, dealing a severe blow to speculators. There were business failures at trading companies in the Kansai area. And at just about that time, the inflation which had begun with exports spread to wages and domestic raw materials. Thus, just as Japanese industry was shorn of the last of its subsidies, with its unmoderated high costs (low productivity) exposed in the open market, it came face to face with competition in the shrinking markets overseas. It is said that the US$1 = ¥360 exchange rate undervalued the yen somewhat when it was established, but inflation seems to have rectified the situation all too well.

The second distortion was the instability of the international pay-

Table 4–1. Price Increases during the Korean War (1949 as base year)

Year	Wholesale Prices	Consumer Prices	Nominal Wages	U.S. Wholesale Prices	U.K. Wholesale Prices
1949	100.0	100.0	100.0	100.0	100.0
50	118.2	93.2	126.5	104.5	102.4
51	164.1	108.5	139.1	116.1	111.2
52	167.3	113.9	160.5	112.9	111.2
53	168.4	121.4	182.1	111.6	114.7

Source: From various indexes.

Table 4–2.   Fluctuation in the Balance of Payments

($ millions)

	Exports	Imports	Trade Balance	Aid	Special Procurements
1946	67	303	−236	192	—
47	184	449	−266	404	—
48	265	547	−282	461	—
49	536	728	−198	534	—
50	924	886	38	361	149
51	1,358	1,645	−287	157	592
52	1,295	1,701	−407	5	824
53	1,261	2,050	−790	—	809
54	1,614	2,041	−426	—	596
55	2,001	2,060	−53	—	557

Sources: "Gendai Nihon keizai no tenkai," etc. Exports and imports follow the IMF formula. Accurate statistics on assistance for 1949 and earlier are lacking.

ments balance. For a number of years after the Second World War it was American assistance that supported Japan's balance of payments. During the Korean War this was replaced by the U.S. military's orders for labor and working materials (collectively known as tokuju, an abbreviation for tokushu juyō, special demand). Special procurements from 1950 to 1952 reached a cumulative total of $1.56 billion, cancelling out the $0.65 billion deficit in the foreign balance for the same period (Table 4–2). This means that Japan's basic imports (food, raw materials) were covered by special procurements, which were considered to be temporary, unstable income. Moreover, since special procurement orders were placed in Japan because of its close proximity to the theater of war, it was geographic conditions that turned a nation lacking normal international competitiveness into a supply depot for the U.S. military forces. As a result of the multiplier effects produced by the special procurements, domestic income levels rose. Without them, the costs of industrial goods could not have been maintained at such high levels as to weaken the export drive. Thus, the special procurements insulated the Japanese economy from normal international competition. The economic leaders of the day alternated between euphoria and despair over trends in special procurement orders.

Japan-U.S. economic cooperation was much publicized at that time, but in reality it was not all that extensive. It was thought that, in place of the assistance that would disappear with the end of the Occupation, the United States would attempt to make use of Japan's industrial strength in its plans for military expansion. On the American side, an influential group headed by William F. Marguat, Chief of SCAP's Economic and Scientific Section, was attempting to hasten the rearming of Japan, while on the Japan side considerable maneuvering was devoted to securing some kind of aid or other from the United States. In the Ikeda-Robertson talks of October 1953 the Japanese would not concede to a gradual increase in Self-Defense Forces personnel, and economic assistance was limited to an agreement on $50 million worth of surplus agricultural commodities (Hata, 1976, Vol. 3: 500–511, 533–540).

This means that the Japanese economy at that time had not established a normal export base. After reviving in 1950 to 32% of the prewar level, the index of export volume had risen no higher than 36% in 1952. During this period mining and manufacturing production increased 50%, and import volume also increased one and a half times. Rolled steel exports expanded unexpectedly in 1952 owing to the steel strikes in the U.S., but cotton textiles peaked and flattened out. Sluggishly expanding fibers and unstable steel made up 30% of exports (Table 4–3). Among doctrinaire leftists of the day, the view that stressed Japanese capitalism's dependency on America and Japan's militarization and colonization carried most weight.[2] As objective analysis of the situation at the time, this view was mistaken. However, the importance of special procurements to the economy gave this mistaken view some measure of apparent reality. In actuality, the idolization of America that began with the Occupation was at last beginning to pall; the rise of an anti-American mood led to such incidents as the

Table 4–3. Principal Export Items

	1936	1951	1952
Steel Products (1000 tons)	501 (2.1)	975 (15.1)	1,607 (20.5)
Cotton Textiles (million yards)	2,701 (13.5)	1,600 (23.4)	762 (11.4)
Raw Silk (1000 pounds)	66,585 (11.0)	9,430 (3.1)	9,573 (2.1)
Marine Products (1000 tons)	131 (2.2)	70 (2.6)	100 (3.6)
Sewing Machines (1000)	— (—)	826 (1.6)	881 (1.5)
Ships (No. of vessels)	221 (0.2)	243 (1.2)	414 (0.9)

Source: Customs statistics. Figures in parentheses indicate proportion of total export monetary value the items represent.

[2] As a result of the self-criticism that followed the denunciation of Stalin in the Soviet Union, there are few Marxists today who agree with these ideas.

bloody clash between police and anti-Security Treaty demonstrators at the 1952 May Day celebrations.

Still, as long as the special procurement orders continued to pour in, it was natural for the economy to seek an equilibrium in response to them. Nothing is accomplished by viewing this equilibrium as unsound just because it was based on the special procurements. The point was, how could the revenue obtained best be put to use in the next phase of development? Viewed from today's vantage point, the Japanese economy succeeded in traversing an extremely hazardous bridge during the Korean War.

Production and Consumption

About one year after the Korean War began, an essay entitled "The Special Qualities of the Japanese Economy" by Hitotsubashi University Professor Nakayama Ichirō was published (in Nakayama, 1954). In this essay Professor Nakayama noted that, although mining and manufacturing production had increased by 50% in the year during which the Korean War had been in progress, thus recovering to prewar rates, the level of consumption had increased no more than 5% and was still sagging 20% below prewar levels. According to Nakayama, the phenomenon of production and consumption levels moving counter to each other in this way has in fact been characteristic of the Japanese economy for a long time. It is a fact that when in the past the Japanese economy has advanced in such remarkable leaps and bounds that it has attracted worldwide attention, such as during the First World War or in the period following Japan's departure from the gold standard early in the Depression, always hovering in the shadows have been low levels of consumption by the population. In the atmosphere of the Korean War, this unfortunate feature of the Japanese economy was doggedly trying to reappear. Professor Nakayama gloomily sounded a warning against perpetuating this pattern.

However, as 1952, the third year of the Korean conflict, began, peoples' lives had improved remarkably; in particular, they were better dressed. A 14% improvement in one leap returned consumption levels to approximately prewar levels (Table 4-4). As production and exports levelled off with the abatement of the war boom, consumer purchasing power sustained prosperity. Textiles were a typical case: while production operations were being curtailed because of stagnating external demand, the volume of textile purchases by urban households took a 60% leap. The Economic White Paper at the time termed this a "consumption boom," but it was actually an explosion of consumer demand which had been suppressed since the war—the final phase of the Korean

Table 4-4. Changes in Economic Indexes, 1946–53

(1934–36 = 100)

	1946	1950	1951	1952	1953
Real Gross National Product	61.6	64.7	99.0	110.6	119.1
Mining & Mfg. Output	27.9	73.3	100.0	108.1	131.4
Agriculture, Forestry, & Fisheries Output	77.9	99.8	108.2	117.3	105.9
Export Volume	* 7.4	32.0	35.8	35.8	37.7
Import Volume	*20.8	37.1	55.3	56.0	77.4
Level of Consumption	—	—	83.7	95.3	106.0
Real Wages	**30.2	85.5	92.2	100.0	107.5

Source: "Gendai Nihon keizai no tenkai," appended table.
Note: * 1948 data. ** 1947 data.

War boom whose first stage had been exports. The journey there was a treacherous process of transforming export inflation into domestic inflation.

Were Nakayama's apprehensions wide of the mark? The answer probably is yes, and then no. Household budgets were still scanty, but the other side of the consumption boom coin was expanding income differentials, etc. The Engel coefficient for urban worker households in 1952 was still 49%, far higher than either the prewar (40%) or 1975 (32.4%) levels. The savings rate of people who had just barely risen above the level of selling their belongings for food (deficit budgets) just after the war was no more than 4.6% (1975: 22%). Even if people were better dressed, personal effects were still beyond their reach (35 pairs of shoes per thousand people per year were sold, compared with today's figure of about 500 pairs).

On the other hand, a *nouveaux riches* class emerged from the procurement boom, textile boom, and stock price increases, and their lavishness fed the public imagination and appetite for consumption.[3] In a best-selling novel of 1952 called Ōban (General Manager) by Shishi Bunroku, the hero Akabane Gyūnosuke ("Gyū-chan") buys a used Datsun before the Korean War and a Ford in 1951, begins to build onto the family retreat that was used in the days of the titled nobility, and takes up golf. In 1952 he buys a new, eight-cylinder, 180-horsepower black Lincoln for ¥4.5 million, and drives it around the Outer Garden of the Meiji Shrine, shouting, "Light as a feather! Light as a feather! It's absolutely like flying above the clouds!" As though giving substance to this story, from 1951 to 1953 passenger car imports

[3] Masuda Yoneji's *The Ruin of the Postwar Nouveaux-Riches* (*Sengo Narikin no botsuraku*) (1965) describes the atmosphere during this period.

approximately quadrupled, imports of gold equipment increased by about sevenfold, and watch imports went up about eightfold.

Seen in this way, the consumption boom of the early 1950s, like that during the First World War, included the worst features of untamed capitalism. However, at the same time the signs pointed to the advent of a full-fledged mass consumption society. While income differentials continued to expand, in 1952 the incomes of the employed increased by 22 % and agricultural incomes grew by 18 %. This can be viewed against the background of postwar political democratization, as exemplified by the labor union movement, the success of the land reform, and so on. The consumption boom was, in one respect, supported by such increases in mass purchasing power. In the first half of the 1950s radios, sewing machines, and motor scooters became the most prized consumer items after clothing; they were the forerunners of the 1960s' "three sacred treasures"[4] (television set, washing machine, refrigerator) and the "three C's" of the 1970s (car, color television, air conditioner). As private radio broadcasts began in September 1951 and NHK (the national broadcasting corporation) began television broadcasts in February 1953, the footfalls of the consumer revolution gradually grew louder. Matsushita Electrical Appliances had already inaugurated its divisional corporate structure and was making preparations for a chain of retail stores. In the sewing machine industry, new-entrant firms were former weapons makers. They pioneered in such innovations as the interchangeability of parts, and it was not long before they were preparing to launch into the export market.

Certainly the consumption boom had a one-sided character while the special-procurement prosperity lasted, and there was also something immoderate about it. However, there is no denying the desire of the people themselves to improve their lives.

The Reappearance of the Dual Structure

Wide wage differentials between employees of large firms and those of smaller firms—much wider than those in other advanced nations—had been a feature of the Japanese economy since the 1920s; they were said to be a manifestation of a "dual structure"—a modernized and a traditional sector coexisting in the same economic structure.

Wage differentials very nearly disappeared in the abysmal poverty of the immediate postwar years, which was a common disaster suffered by all workers. For example, during the period when deposits were frozen, each person could receive only 500 new yen per month in salary. In

[4] A double entendre on the Three Sacred Treasures of the Imperial House: the Sacred Mirror, the Heavenly Sword of the Clouds, and the Crescent Jades.

Table 4–5. Wage Differentials in Manufacturing Industries, by Scale of Operation

	500 persons or over	100–499 persons	30–99 persons	20–29 persons	10–19 persons	9 or fewer persons
1950	100.0	84.2	67.3	56.7	52.5	48.9
51	100.0	79.6	61.8	53.9	49.4	46.7
52	100.0	79.1	58.8	54.9	51.0	49.2
53	100.0	79.3	60.0	55.1	52.9	50.2

Source: Iida et al., 1976, Vol. 1: 175.

the course of the democratization movement, property taxes were levied, distinctions in treatment between laborers and white-collar employees were diminished, and incomes were further equalized.

During the Korean War years, however, the "dual structure" reappeared. Even in the midst of the economic boom the large companies did not increase their hiring to any significant extent, and the surplus labor force became temporary workers seeking employment in small enterprises and individually managed firms. Thus, if we devise a scale on which the wage level in manufacturing firms employing 500 people or more is 100, the value for firms employing 30 to 99 persons dropped from 80 prior to the Korean War to 60 in 1953 (Table 4–5), with a particularly notable increase in the wage differential for medium-sized firms (chūken kigyō).

This reappearance suggested that the Japanese economy was fated to be hounded by the dual-structure problem.[5]

The End of the Special Procurement Boom

When Japan recovered its political independence with the San Francisco Treaty, there was a hue and cry that economic independence must be achieved along with it. The dilemma was that there was no way to maintain a balance in international payments without the special procurement orders. Beginning in about 1952, adopting an interventionist stance and setting its sights on achieving economic independence, the government embarked upon a policy of fiscal investments. In private industry a plan for thoroughgoing rationalization was undertaken. In 1953, on the heels of the consumption boom of 1952, an investment boom occurred.

The special procurement boom itself had peaked in 1951 and was already ebbing, and it might have died a "natural death" (the diagnosis

[5] On the genesis of the dual structure, see Nakamura, 1983.

of the Economic White Paper at the time) at the end of 1952 had it
not been for the government's investment policy. The investment boom
of 1953 was also linked to the special procurement boom in the sense
that it was based on expectations of accumulated special procurement
income from the Korean War and after. But, influenced partly by the
poor harvest of 1953, the balance of international payments rapidly
deteriorated; a policy of monetary stringency (the one trillion yen
budget) was implemented in response to the worsening situation, and at
length the special procurement boom gave up the ghost.

When Stalin died in February of 1953, the Tokyo stock market
declined dramatically, revealing the perceptions of the peacetime vulner-
ability of the Japanese economy, dependent as it was on the special procurement orders. In the autumn of that year, Itō Masutomi's Society
for the Preservation of the Economy, which had collected the savings of
ordinary people and, in the expectation of inflationary price increases,
put them into stock investments in an amount said to total ¥4.5 billion,
was forced into collapse. There is a well-known story that Itō boasted
of the financial backers whose support he sought, "If they let my ship
go down, there'll be a riot." The ensuing recession and the extinction of
inflationary expectations turned 1954 into a year of ruin for the postwar
parvenus.

In 1955, with the Korean War at an end, with the Geneva talks on
peace in Indochina under way, and with tension over the Straits of
Taiwan reduced, the Japanese economy enjoyed its best year of the
postwar period in quantitative terms, based on rapid export growth
and an abundant harvest. During this year an international payments
balance was finally achieved without the special procurement income.
For the Japanese economy this was the year that proved there was a
way to live by peace and not by war. The decade of postwar recovery
had ended, and the curtain was about to rise on the decade of rapid
growth.

In order to reach that point, however, we must take a look at the
planning that was being done for a gradual process of modernization
while the special procurements were still being relied on. This will be
the topic of the next chapter.

5

The Bases for Economic Growth

Trade versus Development

As outlined in the preceding chapters, the Japanese economy achieved rapid expansion with the help of special procurement orders during the Korean War; but at about the time of its return to independence, worldwide business conditions were already showing signs of a downturn, and distortions in prices, costs, international payments, income distribution, and so on were becoming pronounced. The Japanese economy had come face to face with the danger that, if neglected, this situation could become an obstacle to the economic recovery that was taking shape.[1]

Breaking out of this locked-in situation and achieving economic independence was the task of the day. Here, economic independence was considered to require the balancing of international accounts without reliance on aid or special procurement orders, and the management of domestic enterprises without reliance upon subsidies. These two conditions were also aims of the Dodge Plan. The fact that policymakers were attempting to achieve these goals while raising the standard of living as much as possible provided a reason for not relying on a simple deflationary policy.

Debates such as those on "international tradism" versus "developmentalism," or on "liberalism" versus "statism," were waged over the means of achieving economic independence. Nakayama Ichirō, who adhered to international tradism, contended that a small country like Japan with a surplus population and inadequate raw materials should seek a way out of the dilemma via international trade, industrialization, and capital accumulation, a course that would be faithful to the lessons

---

[1] This chapter draws heavily on "Chōki shinyō ginkō seido tanjō no haikei" [Background to the Birth of the Long-Term Credit Bank System], in *Nippon chōki shinyō ginkō 10-nen shi* [Ten-year History of the Long-Term Credit Bank of Japan].

of economic theory and history. Arguing from the standpoint of developmentalism, Arisawa Hiromi and Tsuru Shigetō held that great things could not be expected from international trade, given the existing division of world markets, and that the nation should therefore promote the planned development of domestic raw materials. The former is essentially liberalism, while the latter advocates the use of central planning (Nakayama, 1954; Arisawa, 1953). On repeated occasions, this debate addressed fundamental questions of the Japanese economy's optimal degree of international dependence and the optimal level of government interference.

In connection with the points made by the development theorists, it is worth recalling just how unstable the international economic situation was at that time. Tensions between the United States and the Soviet Union were at their height. Japan and mainland China—its traditional market—had just been forced into mutual isolation by the Korean War. The free convertibility of international currencies had not yet been restored, and Japan, caught between the two stools of the pound zone (Southeast Asia) and the dollar zone, suffered as a result. The Bretton Woods system, which had made its debut after the war amid so many lavish hopes, was also effectively "on ice" because of the dollar shortage (Gardner, 1980, 278 ff.). From the perspective of subsequent events, it can be said that the decision to opt for international tradism in the midst of all this was sagacious; but in fact there probably was no other real choice for the Japanese economy.

The Effort to Establish an Independent Economy

Rationalization Plans

The greatest obstacle to the adoption of international tradism was the high materials costs of Japanese industries, especially the high cost of iron and coal. During the Korean War, Japan's steel bars sold for $100, equivalent to the peak price overseas, which showed that Japan was in the position of a marginal exporter. By the time the Korean War boom had run its course, Japanese coking coal sold for $20 while the same item imported from the U.S. cost $17 to $18, and it was said that the quality of the import was also superior (Japan Iron and Steel Federation, 1959). In the priority production system for 1947–48, the quantitative expansion of these two industries, steel and coal, had been taken as the supreme mandate, but now their qualitative improvement became an issue. The continuation or revival of subsidies was repeatedly proposed and debated. Such devices as applying the export link system

Table 5-1. Results of Plant and Equipment Investment under the First Iron and Steel Rationalization Plan

(¥ millions)

	1951	1952	1953	1954	1955	Totals
Pig-iron Manufacture	2,549	3,970	2,895	1,124	1,528	12,066
of which: Blast						
furnace construction						
& improvements	*1,955*	*2,598*	*835*	*524*	*876*	*6,788*
and: Pre-processing						
of raw materials	*20*	*412*	*1,249*	*196*	*133*	*2,010*
Steel Production	3,181	3,093	3,261	2,006	1,299	12,840
of which: Steel						
production plant &						
equipment	*2,192*	*2,255*	*1,116*	*1,242*	*1,067*	*7,872*
and: Oxygen-producing						
equipment	*511*	*514*	*519*	*421*	*102*	*2,067*
Rolling mills	8,199	16,510	18,185	9,178	6,397	59,069
of which: Rolled						
ingots	*1,436*	*3,518*	*4,522*	*2,302*	*447*	*12,226*
and: Sheets	*3,367*	*8,068*	*7,748*	*3,507*	*2,831*	*25,221*
and: Hoop steel	*3,471*	*2,168*	*1,729*	*599*	*74*	*7,041*
Totals, including						
other items	22,689	32,563	33,596	18,289	13,239	120,386

Source: Ministry of International Trade & Industry, "Sangyō gōrika hakusho" [Industrial Rationalization White Paper].

to rolled steel destined for the shipbuilding industry were also implemented.[2] However, the major aim was reduction of costs through planned investment—the "rationalization" of target industries.

The First Iron and Steel Rationalization Plan (three years, beginning in 1951; planned scale of investment, ¥63 billion; actual investment, ¥120 billion) gave tangible form to these objectives in the iron and steel industry (see Table 5-1). The primary goal was replacing the old-style pullover/hand sheet mills with spanking new imported strip mill facilities in a rationalization of the rolling mill sector.

This change amounted to a fundamental reform in the production process—the adoption of a mass production system. It was reported that, with the switch from pullover/hand sheet mills to strip mills, the per-ton cost of steel plate was cut by ¥4,700, even if only lower

[2] From 1953 to 1955 MITI forced raw sugar importers to subsidize ship exports at the rate of 5% of their (very considerable) profits by requiring them to present proof that they had allied themselves with and subsidized a shipbuilder. Without such proof, MITI would not issue the license necessary to import sugar (Johnson 1982:232).

operating costs and more efficient use of raw materials are calculated. The effect of the switch to the strip mill method was to further expand the secondary processing sector. Moreover, it was reported that producers trying out the continuous process electrolytic tin plating method realized cost savings of 39% on their tin-plated sheets compared to those produced by the old soaking method.

This type of rationalization of the large producers in the rolling mill sector induced a trend in the open-hearth furnace sector toward either building in-house blast furnaces and becoming integrated producers, or being absorbed into one of the groups of leading firms (*keiretsu*). When blast furnace operators expanded into the rolling mill sector, the supply of pig iron—the cornerstone on which open-hearth furnace operations were built—would shrivel, at a time when scrap iron imports were beginning to run short. The blast furnace users who had strengthened the rolling mill sector abandoned importing coking coal and iron ore from mainland China, a trade which had gone on continuously until the eve of the Korean War; instead they became dependent upon more distant sources in North America and Southeast Asia. This meant an increase in transport costs, and there was no alternative to still greater emphasis on quality control and selection of raw materials. The result was the quality products that were to give Japan's iron and steel manufacturers such a good reputation worldwide; they shipped in high-quality raw materials at stable prices from all over the world and used them efficiently by building integrated pig iron manufacturing plants near harbors to facilitate transport. The success of the First Iron and Steel Rationalization Plan was symbolized above all by the construction of Kawasaki Steel's Chiba plant. This iron and steel rationalization also set out to serve as a means of coping with the launching of the European Coal and Steel Community. As a result of its success in the steel industry, Japan was able to establish a base for developing the heavy and chemical industries.

In contrast to the success of steel, the rationalization of coal mining ultimately failed. A bit more than a year after the beginning of the Korean War, the coal mining industry was enjoying such a boom that there were coal shortages everywhere, but this meant that coal had gotten a late start on rationalization planning (Ohki, 1960). A program loudly touted as a drastic rationalization in the form of hinged bar mining, mine shaft development, and so on, languished, and there was no real progress until the industry found itself confronting the protracted 70-day strike in the fall of 1952. The coal industry was old, and in the end it was unable to free itself from the fetters of its excessively antiquated patterns of labor-management relations. The instability of

Table 5-2. Plant and Equipment Investment by the 18 Major Firms in the Coal Mining Industry

(¥ millions)

	Mine Shaft Construction	Development Projects	Facilities Improvement Projects	Electric Power Projects	Maintenance Works	Totals
1950	747	2,560	2,700	492	2,613	9,112
51	1,062	3,640	3,830	700	3,706	12,438
52	1,400	4,822	5,079	421	4,915	17,137
53	1,900	3,125	3,188	824	5,647	14,684
54	2,000	2,953	3,303	224	2,627	11,107
55	1,665	2,077	1,534	253	2,760	*9,061

Source: Ministry of International Trade & Industry, "Sangyō gōrika hakusho" [Industrial Rationalization White Paper].
Note: *Includes ¥7.72 million for projects using coal.

the coal supply due to the coal shortages of 1950–51 and the miners' strike in 1952 caused demand to shift to electric power and oil as sources of energy (Table 5–2).

In the unusual drought of autumn 1951, when electric power shortages became evident, the construction of large-scale hydro-electric plants was expedited in order to increase the capacity to make peak hour adjustments (see Table 5–3). It was at this time that development of the Tadami River and construction of the Sakuma Dam and the

Table 5-3. The Electric Power Development Plan

	The 9 Public Electric Utilities	Electric Power Development Co.	Local Government	Independent, In-house Generation	Totals
Generating Power					
Hydro power (1000 kw)	1,612	2,675	469	270	5,026
Steam power (1000 kw)	843	—	—	238	1,081
Totals (1000 kw)	2,455	2,675	469	508	6,107
Funds (¥ 100 millions)	3,106	2,741	682	362	6,891

Source: Ministry of International Trade & Industry, Public Utilities Bureau, "Saihensei go no denryoku hakusho" [Post-reorganization Electric Power White Paper].
Note: This was the plan (1951–60) at the time that the Law for the Promotion of Electric Power Development was adopted (1951).

Mihoro Dam were undertaken. The concept of generating hydro-electric power and then combining it with limestone, a domestic raw material, to foster the domestic production of synthetic vinylon fiber was a dream of the developmentalists. In the midst of this rising tide favoring hydro-electric power over steam-powered plants, imports of steam-powered model plants (the Karita, Mie, and Kanagawa plants), and experiments using crude oil instead of coal were promoted. Just as in the coal industry, an 86–day strike was conducted in 1952 by the Electric Power Industry Workers' Union (Densan rōso), which had hoisted its banners in favor of wage demands in accordance with the market-basket formula (20,000 yen a month, up 56%), and the strike turned into a serious confrontation with a post-reorganization electric power company. This walk-out was probably the decisive labor-management battle of the post-independence period. Defeated in the end, Densan was forced to disband, and was replaced by the more moderate Federation of Electric Workers' Unions (Denrōren). Labor-management relations in the electric power industry took a turn toward stability.

It was also about this time that an expansion of the fleet of ocean-going ships was charted, in response to the longer sea routes that resulted from the switch from mainland China to the United States as point of origin for raw materials imports. In addition, many industries were about to stake their futures on rationalization in the first half of

Table 5–4. Effects of Rationalization Investments

Industry	Percentage Cost Reduction	Improvements
Pig-iron Manufacture	4	Pre-processing of raw materials
Steel Production	10	Oxygen-process steel production & mass-production-sized open-hearth furnaces
Sheets	27	Continuous process rolling mills compared to old-style facilities
Steel Pipe	30	Flettsmunn process compared to old seamless pipe facilities
Oil Refining	15	Newly-built refineries compared to old-fashioned ones
Rayon Fibers	25	Continuous process compared to prior method
Ammonium Sulfate	21	Simultaneous production of urea

Sources: *Sengo tekkō shi* [Postwar History of Steel], and "Sangyō gōrika hakusho" [Industrial Rationalization White Paper].

the 1950s, when the Korean War prosperity had run its course. Their efforts included: (1) the ammonium sulfate industry's conversion from the electrolytic process to the gas process; (2) the automobile industry's preparations for producing small trucks for the domestic market; and (3) the nurturing of the synthetic fiber industry, which was seeking to reduce the burden of raw material imports. These efforts laid the foundation for the rapid growth of later years.

The startling thing about investment in rationalization in this period is the extremely large effects it produced. Postwar investment was limited in size because of unused capacity inherited from the wartime expansion. A look at the cost reductions effected by means of rationalization investments shows that they amounted to 20% to 30% in not a few industries (see Table 5–4). These cost reduction effects were all the more remarkable in view of the fact that Japanese industry was importing a great deal of brand-new machinery from abroad because access to foreign technology had been interrupted during the war, making much existing machinery and equipment obsolete. For example, it is said that, of those items approved for special depreciation as rationalization machinery in the rolling mill sector, which was the heart of the rationalization program in steel, 70.3% were in fact imported machinery items. The technological gap between Japan and the rest of the world was great, a fact which still further expanded the investment frontier.

On the other side of the coin, however, were conditions that gave cause for second thoughts about rationalization investment in such a backward economy. (1) It was thought that markets were limited and there was no hope of increasing operating rates for the brand-new equipment. (2) It was thought that the workers displaced by the new facilities would form a second-class labor force and, uniting around their low wages as an issue, would pit themselves against the new plant and equipment. (3) The more rationalization investments increased machinery imports, the less domestic markets would expand (Nurkse, 1953). In the economic press, strong apprehensions were expressed to the effect that rationalization investment would produce surplus plant and equipment as a result of excess competition.

Rationalization investment at that time was, moreover, "piecemeal" rationalization, in contrast to the comprehensive "investment-calls-forth-more-investment" modernization such as occurred during the rapid growth period. For this reason, however, the entrepreneurial spirit of the firms that undertook this investment should be all the more highly appreciated.

Changes and Competition in the Enterprise System
Those who bore the lion's share of the burden of the above-mentioned rationalization plan were firms which, after the break-up of the zaibatsu, the elimination of excess concentration, and the dismantling of economic controls, were free and on an equal footing, but at the same time were in a weakened condition. The greater the extent to which a firm had undergone this levelling and been weakened thereby, the more it tried to outdo its competitor firms by rationalization investment. Thus, rationalization planning turns out to have moved forward in tandem with intense competition among firms.

Let us listen in on President Miki Takashi's speech at the ceremonies commemorating the founding of the Yawata Steel Company:

> If anyone thinks Yawata is all right because it is big, it must be said that to do so is a serious anachronism since those who think like that are pursuing the dream of the government-managed monopolies era. The facilities capacity of the Yawata Iron and Steel Foundry as a percentage of nationwide capacity was 72% of iron foundry facilities at the time of the Japan Steel Corporation's formation in 1934, but at present it is half that, 33%. Moreover, steel-making facilities and rolling mills, then 36% of the national total, have dropped to a mere 18% and to 26%, respectively. This is indicative of the fact that during these past sixteen years other companies have expanded capacity more than we have, and at the same time it also means that the plant and equipment of other companies are brand-new. Thus, if we do not take seriously competition with these new factories, it will not be an easy matter for us to keep our heads above water (*Fifty-year History of the Yawata Steel Works*).

In contrast, the Fuji Steel Company was attempting to restore some balance through rationalization: Fuji had inherited many facilities for supplying semi-finished products and pig iron for external sale:

> Relative to plant and equipment in the rolled steel division, facilities in the pig iron division were in excess supply, and the variety of rolled steel products was also extremely limited. Thus, this company, seen as a single independent private enterprise, was unable to implement rational integrated steel operations without modification to its character as an independent private enterprise. We have taken as our fundamental policy, first, that the most important thing for us is to increase the production of rolled steel,

our final product, and to diversify our product line; and for that purpose we have sought to renovate and build up rolling facilities while at the same time and in support of these aims we have worked harder at maintenance of both the pig iron and steel production divisions and at quickly establishing a rational and economic production and sales system. Overcoming numerous difficulties, this entire company has striven with all its might to achieve these goals (*Kamaishi Seitetsujo 70-nen shi* [Seventy-year History of the Kamaishi Iron and Steel Works])

However, as described above, the end result of this policy was that several open-hearth producers, who were dependent upon purchases of pig iron, turned to constructing their own blast furnaces. Under the decisive leadership of President Nishiyama Yatarō, the Kawasaki Steel Corporation expanded with the construction of a factory in Chiba; elsewhere Sumitomo Metals, in search of a foothold for an advance into blast furnaces, merged with Kokura Steel. In the background of the First Iron and Steel Rationalization Plan were ripples such as these, set in motion by the casting of the stone known as the policy for the elimination of excess concentration.

An industry in similar circumstances was paper manufacturing. When the giant Ōji Paper Company was divided into three parts, GHQ sternly forbade the Tomakomai works in Hokkaido, with the most up-to-date facilities of all, to form linkages with other factories. At the Tomakomai factory, the peculiarities of the site and of the product mix were excessive, and in order to compensate for them, the Tomakomai Paper Company (which later re-adopted the name Ōji Paper) undertook construction of a brand-new factory at Kasugai in Aichi Prefecture, and this project became the spark touching off rationalization investment by other companies in the paper industry.

Reorganization of the electric power industry, as proposed by the government, triggered heated debate and opposition; and in the end the Diet failed to pass the measure. The government was finally forced to issue an Emergency Ordinance dissolving the Japan Electric Power Generation and Transmission Company and creating nine regional power companies (Tokyo Electric Power, Kansai Electric Power, etc.) in its place. At first, however, imbalances in supply and demand among the regions were striking. In particular, the three central companies (in Tokyo, Chūbu, and Kansai) which were cut off from the hydroelectric power belt created for themselves a base from which to advance into large-scale steam-powered electricity generation in later years. In this way, the changes in the postwar enterprise system were closely intertwined with the development of industry-wide rationalization plans.

The Development of the Industrial Finance System

The development of rationalization as described above was in addition conditional upon (1) the introduction of foreign technology, (2) the protection and control of industry by the government, and (3) a reorganization of the financial system.

Importing foreign technology was a way for Japan to catch up with the rest of the industrialized world in areas in which it had fallen behind during the war. There were many examples of technology imports with capital tie-ups before the war, but during this period after the war technology was commercialized and offered to many firms. This fact made technology imports one means of competition among domestic firms. On the basis of the Law Concerning Foreign Investment (Gaishi Hō) of May 1950, foreign technology imported during this period inspired tie-ups such as those between Toshiba and G.E., Mitsubishi Electric Machinery and Westinghouse, Matsushita and Phillips, Nissan and Austin, Isuzu and Hillman, Hino and Renault. In addition, many firms were provided with technology such as that of RCA in television manufacturing (obtained by, e.g., NEC [Nihon Denki]); high-level German diesel engine construction know-how (Mitsubishi Shipbuilding); Westinghouse's technology for making transistors (Sony); Cluett-Peabody's Sanforizing technology (Kanebō); and so on. Technology imports proceeded all the more vigorously during the decade of rapid growth (1955–64), and the success of these technology imports in the first half of the 1950s led the way.

The Temporary Commodities Demand and Supply Adjustment Law was abolished in April of 1952, and the government officially recognized the free enterprise system. However, the government still possessed the means to exercise powerful economic control: foreign exchange controls (80% of raw-materials imports were items receiving foreign exchange allocations), restrictions on foreign capital investment, and others. For example, with the intention of building up capacity by means of a system of foreign exchange allocations for plant and equipment, the government was able to stimulate export promotion by means of the export link system (an example of which, in the sugar import industry, was described in footnote 2). Moreover, the government's intervention in industry was deepening, as could be seen, for example, in the passage of the Export-Import Transactions Law and the implementation of an advisory 20% curtailment of production in cotton spinning in February 1952. Not only that, but March 1952 saw the enactment of the Enterprise Rationalization Promotion Law, which was aimed at economic independence through the modernization of plant and equipment in key industries. The core of this program was the special depreciation system for heavy machinery (50 % in the first year), which, when combined with tax exemptions and reductions on key products, played a large role in promoting rationalization. The Electric Power Development Promotion Law was also passed in July of that year, and the Electric Power Development Company was launched. Thus, the government was constructing a new relationship with industry, one which included both the aspect of control and that of protection and nurture.

Finally, let us touch on the reorganization of the financial system which took place during this period. Under the Dodge Plan the activities of the Reconstruction Bank were suspended, along with the financing activities of the U.S. counterpart funds, and in their place the city banks came to occupy the pre-eminent position in finance. At the same time, however, under the tight fiscal and monetary policies called for by the Dodge Plan, the government's fiscal budget showed a surplus, and the volume of Bank of Japan lending to city banks in a condition of "overloan"—in which the ratio of their loans to deposits exceeds 100 %—became commonplace. This was thought to mean that restrictions should be placed on the activities of the city banks, and all kinds of policies for counteracting the banks' tendency toward illiquidity were proposed, by Ishibashi Tanzan, Kiuchi Nobutane, Ikeda Hayato, and others. On the basis of these proposals, (1) government financial institutions such as the Export-Import Bank of Japan (1950), the Japan Development Bank (1951), and the Small Business Finance Corporation (1954) were established; (2) the Investment Trust was launched (1951); (3) the Loan Trust (Kashitsuke Shintaku) was authorized; and (4) the Long-Term Credit Bank Law was enacted (1952).

It was expected that these measures, by providing alternative sources of funds for businesses, would relieve some of the pressures on banks that resulted in overloan conditions, and they were steps that at last came to grips with the burgeoning burden of rationalization investment. As firms' equity/capital ratios dropped significantly due to inflation, they made a start at dealing with the problem by using various reserve fund systems, revaluing their assets, and so on; but since the results of these measures were not adequate, the establishment of a long-term finance organization was expedited. Thus, diversification of the industrial capital supply came about in an environment in which priority was given to indirect finance (Table 5–5).

These measures were at the same time part and parcel of a reevalua-

Table 5-5. Industrial Capital Supply Conditions

(¥100 million)

	1951	1952	1953	1954	1955
Private Lending	6,402	7,965	7,358	4,051	5,552
of which:					
City Banks	} 3,793	} 3,984	} 3,534	879	1,029
Long-term					
Credit Banks				509	502
Trust Accounts	*201*	*411*	*265*	*403*	*865*
Government Lending	721	973	931	1,175	982
Industrial Debentures	360	370	413	184	245
Stocks	695	1,224	1,658	1,421	975
Totals	8,593	10,227	11,065	10,648	6,792

Source: "Honpō keizai tōkei" [Economic Statistics for the Nation].

tion of the system implemented when Japan regained independence with the termination of the Occupation, and were, as well, a departure from Dodge's fiscal austerity, the first steps toward positive fiscal and monetary policies such as the decision under Finance Minister Ikeda's leadership to issue government savings bonds.

The rationalization efforts of the first half of the 1950s were promoted by firms, banks, and the government in the manner described above. This was the starting point for the new government-industrial complex which took the place of the controls and subsidies of the wartime and postwar periods. A major shipbuilding scandal in 1954 involving pay-offs to conservative politicians proviced a scathing critique of this government-industrial complex and ultimately brought to an end the Yoshida regime's long-standing grip on power. However, this does not in any sense mean that Japan's industrial finance system was perfected at that time and remained unchanged thereafter. During the following decade of rapid growth Japan's industrial finance system in fact exhibited a flexibillty befitting a growing economy. Rather than reflecting this situation, however, the "Japan, Inc." theory, generalized from impressions of this period that had become fixed, instead appears to result in many anachronisms when applied without modification to today's Japanese economy.

Consolidation of the Conditions for Rapid Growth

The Japanese economy found itself in a period of transition from reconstruction toward development at the time when its independence was restored. The economic conditions of the reconstruction period may be summarized as follows:

(1) The postwar reconstruction had to start from extremely low levels of production and consumption.

(2) Thus, the pressure of consumption demand was strong, the propensity to consume was high, and the rate of saving was even negative at times, depending on the year.

(3) Difficulties in the procurement of raw materials restricted supply. Since a large capital stock remained as a legacy of the wartime economy, plant and equipment investment went no further than maintenance and repair outlays. In other words, the marginal capital coefficient was remarkably low.

(4) With raw-material imports covered by American aid and revenues from the special procurement orders, an expansion in the volume of domestically manufactured producers' goods was sought while at the same time a cushion was provided against the deterioration of business conditions by subsidies and Treasury loans and investments.

Table 5–6. Conditions for Capital Accumulation

	Over-loan Ratio (%)	Equity Capital Ratio (%)	Rate of Dependence on Gov't. Funds (%)	Tax-exempt Income (¥100 million)	Increases in Reserves (¥100 million)	Difference after Revaluation of Assets (¥100 million)
1950	15.3	28.3	11.4	10	37	6,277
51	19.3	36.7	8.6	36	118	981
52	13.3	36.0	17.1	73	741	
53	14.8	36.7	7.2	115	1,010	
54	11.2	39.8	15.9	178	1,106	6,035
55	1.2	38.1	7.6	335	1,043	

Notes: (1) Overloan Ratio: City banks' borrowings from Bank of Japan ÷ deposits ("Honpō keizai tōkei" [Economic Statistics for the Nation]).

(2) Equity Capital Ratio: Statistics Division of the Economic Planning Agency ("Kihon Nihon keizai tōkei" [Basic Statistics on the Japanese Economy]). Second half of each year.

(3) Rate of Dependence on Government Funds: Data on government funds as a proportion of total industrial capital are from Nakamura (1981). The rate for 1947 was 25.0% and for 1960 it was 4.3%.

(4) Tax-exempt Income and Increases in Reserves : Data from a survey by the Tax Bureau, Ministry of Finance (as shown in *Nippon Kaihatsu Ginkō 10-nen shi* [Ten-year History of the Japan Development Bank]).

(5) Differences after revaluation of assets are for the period 1950, 1951–52, and 1953–55, collectively.

Table 5-7. The Pattern of Growth in the Postwar Reconstruction Period

(%)

	1946–51	51–55	65–70 (For Reference)
Economic Growth Rate (Real)	9.5	8.6	12.1
Percentage Personal Consumption per GNP (Nominal)	64.8	63.6	53.6
Percentage Plant & Equipment Investment per GNP (Nominal)	8.3	10.8	18.0
Personal Saving Rate (Nominal)	4.7	10.7	18.5
Labor's Share (Nominal)	89.5	84.9	80.6

Source: "Kokumin shotoku tōkei" [National Income Statistics].

In 1952, however, when independence was restored, such conditions were disappearing. Production and consumption levels had recovered for a time, but the aid and special procurements which had supported the recovery were about to come to an end. In addition, the expansion of exports was obstructed by the ruinous cost structure of raw materials. In order to work around the high prices of coal and iron, huge amounts of plant and equipment investment would be necessary. It was impossible for the capital coefficient to remain at a low level forever (Table 5–6).

As national income statistics show, the low levels of the marginal capital coefficient, the rate of investment, and the savings rate, which had become characteristic of the recovery period, were considerably modified during the period from 1951 to 1953 (Table 5–7). The rate of private investment in plant and equipment and the household saving rate both exceeded 10%. Even if this is considered a rather far cry from the rapid-growth period in which both investment and savings rates approached 20%, it did permit the Japanese economy to follow a path into a take-off period toward growth in Rostow's sense. Inflationary expectations, dependence on special procurements, and the dual structure seemed to be as strong as ever. However, mass consumption caused expansion of markets; and firms, intent on catching up with the technological level of the advanced countries, embarked upon rationalization plans. In the midst of this expansion, new relationships arose among firms, banks, and the government in place of the previous mode of control, and these relationships themselves were about to change further. It was during this period that Japan's efforts to make "death-defying leaps" toward chemical and heavy industrialization achieved success. The First Iron and Steel Rationalization Plan and the construction of Kawasaki Steel's Chiba plant were symbolic of this.

Part

II

Growth

6

The Beginning of Rapid Growth

From the Cold War to Peaceful Coexistence

In July 1955 talks were held by the leaders of the United States, the Soviet Union, Great Britain, and France at the Palais des Nations, Geneva, "to find a basis for agreement on how to make life safer and happier." The Geneva summit meetings became symbolic of a shift away from the Cold War toward detente and peaceful coexistence.

The Korean War, which began in 1950, ended in July 1953. Dien-bienphu fell in May 1954, and the French withdrawal from Indochina was negotiated at the Geneva Conference on the Far East, held from April through July. In April 1955, the Afro-Asian Conference was held in Bandung, where ten principles were enunciated, including anti-colo-nialism, national sovereignty, and peaceful coexistence. Austria, which had been partitioned and occupied by the United States, the Soviet Union, Great Britain, and France, regained its unity and independence as a permanently neutral state by a treaty signed in May 1955.

Soviet Premier Stalin died in March 1953, but in his last years he said that for capitalism, munitions were like the straws that a drowning man grasps for. Lenin's thesis of 1916, "The more rotten capitalism gets, the more rapidly it develops," was not valid in the postwar era, according to Stalin. However, following the 1953 recession which took place simultaneously with a slowdown in military expansion, the American economy made a swift recovery in a comparatively short period of time. From 1954 to 1955 a full-fledged boom hit the free industrialized nations. Echoing the riots in Poland and Hungary and the Hundred Flowers campaign in China, the de-Stalinization speech at the 20th Congress of the Soviet Communist Party in February 1956 was indicative of the "thaw" in the socialist nations and, at the same time, of its attendant difficulties.

At home, in the meantime, politics achieved a kind of stability with the formation of a two-party system consisting of the Liberal Democrats (LDP) and the Japan Socialist Party (JSP): the Liberals (Jiyūtō) merged with the Democrats (Minshūtō) to form the LDP, while in the opposite camp the Right and Left Socialist factions reunited to form a single Japan Socialist Party in 1955. Meanwhile, one-third of the Diet seats were held by the reform faction, making Constitutional amendment impossible. In 1956 Prime Minister Hatoyama Ichirō visited the Soviet Union; the Soviet-Japanese Joint Declaration issued on the occasion of his visit made possible Japan's entry into the United Nations, which had been obstructed by the Soviet veto until then. In the labor world, the leadership of the General Council of Japanese Trade Unions (Sōhyō) passed out of the hands of politically-oriented Secretary Takano Minoru and into those of labor union-oriented Chairman Ohta Kaoru and Secretary-General Iwai Akira.

The world had been vastly changed by World War II, and a return to prewar normalcy was unthinkable. However, the Cold War, which dominated the immediate postwar decade and which brought with it the Korean War, should be called a postwar aberration—one which, moreover, cannot have continued. Although it was advancing by taking two steps forward and one step back, the world was at a turning point around 1955, as it was about to enter a new stage of peaceful coexistence and multipolarity. The rapid growth of the Japanese economy began precisely during this transition. During the decade 1945–1954, although Japan's postwar pacifism and democracy sparkled like a brightly lit display of fireworks, its economy depended on special military procurement orders and foreign aid and was supported by the dual economic structure domestically—all of which left a dark chasm yawning between the ideal and the reality. If the decade 1955–1964 seems brighter than the one that preceded it, this most likely results from the remarkable improvement in people's standard of living and the first reduction in this gap between the real and the ideal.

The Beginnings and Development of Rapid Growth

The Postwar Economy's Best Year

As the government's Economic White Paper stated the following year, 1955 was the postwar economy's finest year. Not only did the rate of economic growth that year exceed 10% in real terms, but prices stabilized (the consumption deflator increased by 1.1% while the private inventories deflator rose by 0.8%) and the balance of payments showed a $300 million surplus ($500 million according to the foreign exchange statistics in use at the time). Inflation, which had tormented Japan's postwar economy, had been conquered, and the goal of economic independence, achieving a balance of payments equilibrium without special procurement income, was finally attained. The economic situation that year is referred to as the "*sūryō* boom" (literally, quantitative prosperity, a translation from the German *Mengenkonjuktur*): a high real growth rate in the midst of stable prices (Table 6–1).

What produced the ideal economic expansion that year? After the Korean War, Japanese industry was preparing for its take-off into economic growth by filling the technical gaps that developed between Japan and other advanced industrial countries during and after the war. From the fall of 1953, the economy was deflating owing to the adoption of very tight fiscal and monetary policies such as the trillion-yen budget, a contraction of treasury loans and investments, and stricter application of high central bank penalty interest rates. On top of this, the above-mentioned boom occurred among the nations of the Free World. Differences in the pressures of internal and external demand and their time-lag effects produced export increases and price stability. The distinctive feature of this rapid growth process was the joint operation of two factors, investment in industrial rationalization (an infla-

Table 6–1.   Changes in Gross National Expenditure

Year	Nominal Component Ratio (¥ trillions)	Real Rate of Growth (%)					
		1955	1956	1957	1958	1959	1960
Personal Consumption Expenditure	61.5	8.9	6.6	6.7	7.2	8.9	9.0
Government Current Expenditures	10.2	−1.2	−0.4	−0.2	5.8	5.1	4.4
Private Housing	2.9	7.7	12.9	12.5	8.8	18.9	19.9
Private Plant & Equipment	10.8	8.6	**38.7**	18.3	**−4.5**	27.0	**38.8**
Government Fixed Capital Formation	6.3	−0.1	0.9	**22.6**	17.3	15.7	13.8
Private Inventory Investment	3.7	10-fold	30.4	12.5	**−48.1**	**75.0**	32.0
Exports	11.7	17.2	15.9	13.0	3.9	15.2	14.1
Imports	10.6	10.9	**38.8**	11.1	**−10.2**	**29.6**	21.9
Gross National Product	8.86	10.8	6.2	7.8	6.0	11.2	12.5

Source: "Kokumin shotoku tōkei" [National Income Statistics].
Note: Figures in boldface indicate particularly noteworthy changes.

tionary factor) and stringent financial policies (a deflationary factor). Quantitative prosperity was characteristic of low-pressure economies (Japan, West Germany) surrounded by a global high-pressure economy (cf. Hansen, 1957).

Typical of export growth was the case of the shipbuilding industry. The volume of steel ship construction increased rapidly from 410,000 tons in 1954 to 730,000 tons in 1955, 1,740,000 in 1956, and 2,290,000 in 1957. Particularly striking was the tanker boom, a result of the thriving demand for supertankers arising from the worldwide switch to oil as an energy source, the completion of large oil refineries in western Europe with Marshall Plan aid, and so on. Shrewd Greek shipowners placed large numbers of orders with the Japanese shipyards, where lead times were short and prices were low. For the shipbuilding industry as well, rationalization was proceeding apace, with the use of welding instead of riveting as in prewar days, the development of block construction methods, and so on; and this ultimately bore fruit in the form of exports.

Another factor sustaining the quantitative boom was the bountiful harvest of 1955. The poor harvest of 1953 had made increased food imports necessary and became a factor in the balance of payments deficit. In 1955, however, rice production reached 12,380,000 tons, a 30% increase over the previous year, and this made it possible for Japan to become self-sufficient in rice. This may also be viewed as evidence that the success of the land reform had extended into agricultural production itself. The impact of the abolition of the landlord system as a result of the land reform was greatest in the Tōhoku region, and increases in productivity in this region were remarkable.

To offset the large excess disbursements from the Special Treasury Accounts for foreign exchange and for foodstuff control that resulted from the balance of payments surplus and the large harvest, the Bank of Japan hastily curtailed its lending. Along with price stability and balance of payments equilibrium, slack monetary conditions are characteristic of quantitative booms. "Financial normalization" proceeded against a background of monetary ease: (1) The Bank of Japan revised its financial control system; instead of focusing heavily on high penalty rates for banks borrowing excessively at the discount window, it returned to financial administration based on the discount rate. (2) The bond markets revived while, against a background of falling interest rates, the conditions for issuing private debentures were revised. (3) The view that government financial institutions such as the Export-Import Bank and the Japan Development Bank should be curtailed or done away with gained currency.

The quantitative boom, however, did not last long. In the transition from the export boom to the investment boom, beginning in mid-1956 constraints on the supply of funds surfaced; a bottleneck and price increases developed, and a large balance of payments deficit soon followed. The sharp increase in prosperity from 1956 to 1957 made that year the year of the Jimmu boom.[1] Thus, the quantitative boom was shortlived. However, as has been pointed out on more than one occasion, it is of no small significance that rapid growth began with a quantitative boom. While rapid growth is a tumultuous ride on the high seas of fortune, it was at the same time the path to normalization.

Boom and Bust after Jimmu

The prosperity that began as an export boom spread to domestic consumption and investment.

The state of household budgets in the mid-1950s was such that the Engel coefficient for urban households was 45% (nearly half of disposable income was spent on food), and the rate of saving had moved from the negative side of the ledger (immediately following the war, when people were eking out a living by selling their personal effects) to a level of 10%. The spring labor offensives began around this time: unions in all sectors of the economy negotiated with managements once a year, in March and April. Wage increases won in the mid-1950s averaged around 5%. According to monthly labor statistics, average monthly income was less than 20,000 yen. The standard of living was still low. However, the diffusion and establishment of new consumption patterns was a stimulus to consumption.

In 1953 television broadcasting was begun, and 300,000 black-and white television sets were produced in 1956, 1 million in 1958; the output of washing machines also reached the 1 million level in 1958. The production of transistor radios began in 1955, about the same time as in the United States; and as many as 35.7% of urban households owned cameras in 1957. It was also at about this time that such new materials as synthetic fabrics and polyvinyl chloride plastics entered the household. The expansion of consumption is characteristically linked with such things as mass production and new products.

Toyopet Crown, which upgraded the reputation of domestically produced cars, began production in 1955, but it was scooters and light three-wheeled vehicles that reigned supreme in the streets at the time.

---

[1] The boom of 1956–57 was dubbed by journalists the "Jimmu boom," after the legendary Emperor Jimmu, whose reign, according to tradition, began in 660 B.C. The implication was that this was the biggest thing since Jimmu's time.—Trans.

Moreover, there was a nationwide boom in the construction of department stores and movie theaters, and fashions such as the A-line and the V-line became popular. The appearance of the Generation of the Rising Sun—named after a group appearing in Ishihara Shintarō's novel *The Season of the Sun*, signified the advent of the consumption ethic, a marked departure from the declining aristocracy and black marketeers of the decade 1945–1954.

However, the essence of the Jimmu boom was a rapid expansion of investment in plant and equipment. Private plant and equipment investment in 1956 increased 57.6% in nominal terms and 48.2% in real terms over the previous year's levels—a record which has not been surpassed to this day. Orders for machinery increased 80%, and such was the desire to obtain rolled steel or machinery that, contrary to previous practice, payment in advance became more popular than the usual method of payment on account. In conjunction with the investment boom, enterprise profit showed an increase of 37.5% in 1956 and 51% in 1957. No wonder the business upturn of those years was regarded as the biggest boom since the prehistoric reign of Emperor Jimmu. Such a sudden flourishing of plant and equipment investment would be startling if it had occurred in a vacuum. Underlying this plant and equipment investment, however, was a technological revolution, which will be explored in a later chapter.

The sudden increase in plant and equipment investment during 1956 and the first half of 1957 produced a complete change in the Japanese economy, which had been tranquilly enjoying quantitative prosperity (Table 6–2). In the monetary area, bank lending expanded sharply in contrast with the considerable monetary slack of the previous year; conditions of supply and demand for funds became stringent, and central bank lending to city banks increased. Steel and machinery were in short supply because expansion was going on at such an intense pace, and transport bottlenecks developed, with backlogged goods piled up in the vicinity of railway stations. The situation was exacerbated by a drought in 1956 that caused a shortage of electric power which, in turn, constrained the production of chemical products. Investments were steeped up in order to break this bottleneck, but they became a factor further contributing to the existing supply and demand constraints. The overheating of the economy produced a rapid increase in imports in response to domestic price increases and a balance of payments deficit.

When it was forecast that in 1957 foreign exchange reserves would approach the minimum required level of $500 million, the government and the Bank of Japan turned to a tight money policy. This stringency

Table 6–2.   Changes in Economic Indicators

	1955	1956	1957	1958	1959	1960
Mining & Mfg.						
Output (%)	7.3	22.7	17.3	−1.6	20.3	24.9
Wholesale						
Prices (%)	−1.8	4.4	3.0	−6.5	0.9	1.1
Consumer						
Prices (%)	−1.1	0.3	3.0	−0.4	0.9	3.6
Money Wages (%)	2.5	9.8	5.0	−0.4	8.4	8.8
Foreign Exchange						
Reserves						
($100 millions)	7.38	9.41	5.24	8.61	13.22	18.24
Bank of Japan						
Lending						
(¥100 millions)	319	1,399	5,519	3,793	3,379	5,002
Call Rate (%)	5.84–	4.75–	7.67–	19.95–	7.67–	8.40
	8.03	8.76	20.81	8.03	8.76	

Source: Economic Planning Agency, "Gendai Nihon keizai no tenkai" [Development of the Contemporary Japanese Economy], appended statistical tables.

put great pressure on business firms in the midst of expanding their investments; the banks, too, driven by the need to obtain funds, temporarily raised the call rate above 20%. The Suez crisis of October 1956 also had considerable imapct on soaring domestic and foreign prices and increasing speculative imports.

What is particularly noteworthy about the fiscal and monetary policies of this period are the ¥100 billion tax cut and the ¥100 billion fiscal spending policy. In the three years since the retrenchment policy of 1954, the general account budget had been maintained at a level of ¥1 trillion. With "full employment" as his slogan, however, Prime Minister Ishibashi Tanzan, who was elected President of the Liberal Democratic Party by a majority with a thin margin of seven votes, pointed the way toward the positive budget policies which he pursued beginning in 1957. Ishibashi, who as Yoshida's Finance Minister in 1947 had been rejected as an irresponsible inflationist, attempted to put his views as a pure Keynesian before the nation for a second time. As Ishibashi was reported to have said at the time: "There are people who say that inflation is written all over Ishibashi's face. But this does not mean that I am going to put an end to positive fiscal policies. If my intention of increasing jobs until unemployment is eliminated and tripling production is thwarted, then I will resign. I became Prime Minister because I wanted to do things my way" (*Nihon Keizai shimbun*, Dec. 15, 1956).

The result was a ¥100 billion tax reduction and the implementation of policies calling for expenditures of ¥100 billion. With the national budget on the scale of ¥1 trillion at that time, this was the equivalent of tax reduction and fiscal spending involving ¥10 trillion today. The focus of policy implementation was to direct resources toward fully developing social capital, such as roads and housing, and, in particular, to break the transport bottleneck. Furthermore, the 100 billion yen tax reduction consisted almost entirely of a reduction in income taxes. The intent of the tax reduction and the increased fiscal spending was to launch a cyclical process whereby the fruits of rapid growth would on the one hand revive the private sector and on the other remove obstacles to growth and, in so doing, stimulate further growth. This way of thinking set the pattern for public finance policy during the period of rapid growth.

In the short term, however, these policies threw fat on the fire of the overheated economy and, instead of producing the desired effects, wound up cutting the boom short. Such lags between the initiation of a policy and the materialization of its economic effects were encountered on subsequent occasions amid the economy's ups and downs. In June of 1957 it was decided that a number of long anticipated public works projects would have to be postponed. Prior to that, Prime Minister Ishibashi had already fallen ill, and he resigned with the parting words, "I followed my political conscience." His bold vision of a society advancing from full employment into social welfare and peaceful diplomacy came to an end in mid-stride without being fulfilled.

The Iwato Boom
The Jimmu boom's growth curve showed a steep angle, which made its collapse all the more dramatic. Prices and production immediately showed the effects of the monetary stringency imposed in the spring of 1957; and with the rapid decline in imports, the balance of payments quickly approached equilibrium at the end of that year. As 1958 began, manufacturing showed signs of a sharp recovery.

However, although production levels had been increasing rapidly, business firms regarded the period up to autumn 1958 as a depression since they were holding large inventories while prices hovered at low levels and since the revival of business earnings was not at all rapid. This sort of gap between the micro and macro levels—time lags in the effects produced by booms—was repeatedly experienced in later booms and recoveries (Fig. 6–1).

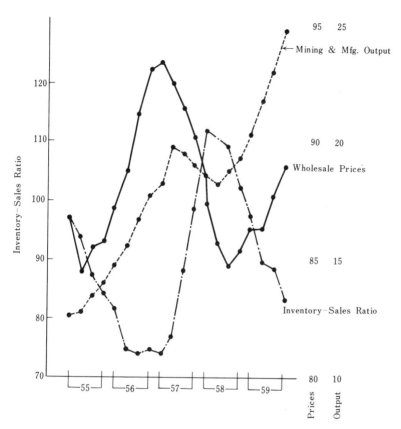

Figure 6–1. Prices, Output, and Inventory-Sales Ratios
  Source: Economic Planning Agency, "Keizai hendō kansoku shiryō nenpō" [Annual Bulletin of Survey Materials on Economic Fluctuations].

By 1959 Japan was hailing a period of prosperity called the Iwato boom,[2] a boom in the sense that the economic upturn had permeated the entire economy and surpassed the Jimmu boom. The difference between the Jimmu boom and the Iwato boom is that while the former

---

[2] This time the nickname referred to an era even more ancient than the time of Jimmu, when, in the mists of prehistory (so the legend goes), the Sun Goddess Amaterasu-Ōmikami was lured out of her sullen seclusion in a cave (*iwato*) by a conclave of deities.—Trans.

had a feverish and abrupt character, the latter was durable. If one views quantitative prosperity as the thesis and the Jimmu boom as its antithesis, the Iwato boom was the synthesis of the other two. In contrast to the 31 months of upswing, including the quantitative boom, which are generally considered to constitute the Jimmu boom, the upswing of the Iwato boom lasted 42 months. This record was exceeded by the protracted period of prosperity that lasted 57 months in the latter half of the 1960s, but the two together were in all likelihood historically rare phenomena as periods of long-term prosperity.

If one considers the historical significance of the Jimmu boom to be that it set the Japanese economy on a high-growth track, then that of the Iwato boom is that the effect of rapid growth penetrated every nook and cranny of the economy and ultimately brought about full employment. However, rather than further comparing the Iwato with the Jimmu boom, let us examine the conditions which made for the durability of the Iwato boom.

Fundamentally, the Japanese economy, riding the wave of the technological revolution, had reached an important milestone: the growth of demand was more balanced than during the early 1950s, supply capacity increased in an orderly fashion, and it was difficult to upset the supply and demand equilibrium. Unlike the Jimmu boom, which was led by demand effects of plant and equipment investment that production capacity could not match, consumption and export demand during the Iwato boom diversified in response to emerging production capacity and absorbed supply. The name "Iwato" is reminiscent of the ancient gathering of countless gods at Takamagahara, and to the extent that this boom calls to mind the diversification of demand, the name is well suited to the event since the gods represented diverse forces which might conceivably have included such things as exports and consumption. In particular, the price-stabilizing effects of the supply and demand equilibrium for basic materials made it possible to evade the problem raised by speculative inventory investment.

Yet another factor was the prudent administration of monetary policy. Taking a lesson from the overheating of the Jimmu boom, the Bank of Japan inaugurated a reserve deposit system in September of 1959 and raised the discount rate at the end of that year. This preventive stringency was in response both to reconstruction demand upsurge triggered by the Ise Bay typhoon and to fears of price increases. To initiate this type of tight monetary policy before a disequilibrium in the balance of payments developed was exceptional during the period of rapid growth. For this reason, contrary to what one might expect, by about the summer of 1960, when the economy had entered an interim period of adjustment, this policy contributed to the prolongation of the prosperity.

Supply and demand equilibrium and prudent monetary management were also in evidence during the long-term prosperity of the latter half of the 1960s. However, one should not conclude that, on the basis of those two factors alone, prosperity should have continued indefinitely. Although there was, in fact, a supply and demand equilibrium during the Iwato boom, the heart of the boom was investment; and in any event, once the investment rate had exceeded a reasonable level as defined by the ratio between the growth rate and the capital coefficient, the economy could not help but enter a leveling-off period. In reality, the twilight of the Iwato boom, like that of the Jimmu boom, turned out to be a hurried sunset. In 1960 the Ikeda Cabinet, which came to power in the wake of political unrest triggered by revision of the U.S.-Japan Security Treaty, set forth in rapid succession its programs for income doubling, the liberalization of trade, and a low interest rate revolution. It contributed still further to prosperity in the private sector with unprecedentedly brisk activity on the securities exchange; but at the same time the international balance of payments took a downhill slide toward deficit. In the summer of 1961 fiscal and monetary stringency was once again imposed.

An Evaluation of Growth and Cycles

Postwar No More
Ten years after Japan's defeat in the Pacific War, its economy had made a remarkable recovery, but the outlook for the Japanese economy in the mid-1950s was still viewed as extremely poor. In the opening paragraph of its report entitled "The Problem of Japan's Industrial Structure" (1955), the Ministry of International Trade and Industry's Research Task Force on Industrial Structure made the following statements:

> Even today, ten years after the end of the war, the political and economic situation surrounding our national economy bears as perilous an aspect and weighs down upon us as much as ever. . . . Ten years after the end of the war, after having passed from devastation to recovery, when, today, we confront the problems of the Japanese economy, it is inevitable that we should discover that the conditions which in a former day facilitated the solving of our

problems have vanished and that, moreover, new difficulties have arisen.[3]

The famous paragraph from the 1956 Economic White Paper that announced the end of the postwar recovery was also lacking in optimism to a degree perhaps mystifying to people of later periods:

> It is no longer the "postwar" period. We are now on the verge of confronting a different situation. Growth through recovery has ended. Growth henceforth will be sustained by modernization.

This, in fact, is the correct view that growth would come by means of modernization. At the same time, however, there was also a concealed but profound fear that a slackening of the growth rate would accompany the end of postwar reconstruction.

The foregoing is not related here for the sake of a good laugh at the lack of foresight of the people of that day. In fact, it is always difficult to foresee the future. The transitions from the quantitative boom and the Jimmu boom to the Iwato boom in the latter half of the 1950s forced repeated surprises and hard lessons on the country. Only in the aftermath of this process did the significance of these transitions from boom to boom gradually became clear. Let us undertake an evaluation of this sequence of events from two points of view.

The Revival of the Business Cycle
During the war and in the immediate postwar period autonomous business cycles were not observed due to controls, the war, and inflation. And although the business cycle mechanism was not yet fully autonomous during the dramatic shift in economic circumstances between 1955 and 1960, this shift taught the lesson that this cyclical mechanism was an undercurrent of economic life. Since it is thought that no fully autonomous business cycle had previously existed, it was not at all strange to call the economic fluctuations of this period the business cycle. Gained from experience during this time, the know-how for diagnosing conditions such as the lead and lag relationships among the indices of business activity has been handed down to this day. The progression from overheating of the economy → balance of payments deficit → tight money → sharp recovery came to be seen as the established pattern for economic fluctuations.

---

[3] It should, incidentally, be noted that, even in 1955, the Japanese language was still written in the classical *kambun* (Sinicized) style, and government documents took a sensational tone.

Table 6-3. Dating of Business Cycles

Trough	Peak	Trough	Duration of Upswing (months)	Duration of Downswing (months)
Nov. 1954	June 1957	June 1958	31	12
June 1958	Dec. 1961	Oct. 1962	42	10
Oct. 1962	Oct. 1964	Oct. 1965	24	12
Oct. 1965	July 1970	Dec. 1971	57	17

Source: Economic Planning Agency, "Nihon keizai shihyō" [Japanese Economic Indicators].

Swings in inventory investment were noted as the principal factor producing the cylical pattern of business activity. Contending that the increased level of imports of 1956–57 was due to inventory investment and would therefore reverse itself autonomously, Shimomura Osamu criticized the monetary stringency as unnecessary, engaging in a debate with Gōtō Yonosuke and others. It would be difficult to judge whether or not the monetary stringency was necessary, but the fact that the tight money policy was linked to an immediate drop in prices and a sharp falling off of imports created the impression that Shimomura's theory was correct. There is no mistaking the fact that this "inventory debate" went a long way toward promoting understanding of the business cycle mechanism.

An additional point, also related to inventory fluctuations, is the fact that the amplitude of the business cycles during this period was marked by virtually unmodulated extremes (Table 6–3). A number of factors are cited as reasons: the fierceness of inter-firm competition, inter-bank competition and business dependence on borrowed funds, the complexity of the distribution system, and a trend toward excess demand. The fact that basic materials had been placed under an import quota system also brought increased requests to authorities to bend the quotas. Basically, however, the investment activity of private firms became brisk while rapid growth prevailed, and the importance of this investment activity lay in its impact on the business cycle.

Investment-Centered Rapid Growth
From 1955 onward the Japanese economy achieved an unusually high level of rapid growth, by any historical standards. The reasons for it can be explained along various dimensions and in various terms. The technological revolution and the process of catching up with the advanced nations, which are considered to be the heart of the story, will be taken up in another chapter. With regard to the beginning of rapid

growth, however, let us here review the background in which plant and equipment investment showed such extraordinarily rapid increases.

As we have seen, at the time of the defeat the Japanese economy was suffering from a low level of output due to the interruption of raw materials supplies from abroad, but the capital stock inherited from wartime was quite considerable. The postwar recovery was achieved by putting this capital stock to work, obtaining raw materials from abroad with foreign aid and special military procurement income and by obtaining domestically manufactured producers' goods through the priority production system and rationalization. Since high growth was not expected to continue beyond the recovery period, it was not generally thought that plant and equipment investment was being undertaken in earnest on an all-out scale.

If growth were to continue beyond the recovery period, the capital stock would have to be expanded with longer-term objectives in mind. Since only minimal investment had been carried out prior to 1955, increases in plant and equipment investment aimed at expanding the capital stock rose dramatically. This suggests that even the rapid increases in plant and equipment investment in 1956–57 were not keeping pace with the expansion of the capital stock (Table 6–4). The rapid growth rate of plant and equipment investment can best be explained as a function of capital stock adjustments (the acceleration principle).

At the same time, there was a great deal of room for modernization of the plant and equipment which, as a legacy of the war, was old and very much out of date. Firms that had begun to be confident that

Table 6–4.   Capital Stock and Plant & Equipment Investment

(%)

Year	Economic Growth Rate	Growth Rate of Plant & Equipment Investment	Growth Rate of Capital Stock	Plant & Equipment Investment as a Proportion of GNE (Nominal)	Plant & Equipment Investment as a Proportion of Capital Stock
1955	10.8	8.6	—	10.8	7.9
56	6.2	38.7	6.2	15.5	9.2
57	7.8	18.3	7.3	16.6	10.0
58	6.0	− 4.5	6.3	14.7	9.0
59	11.2	27.0	7.7	16.3	10.6
60	12.5	38.8	11.2	19.6	13.3

Source: "Kokumin shotoku tōkei" [National Income Statistics], etc.
Note: GNE = Gross National Expenditure.

growth would continue set about as though with one accord to renovate their plant and equipment. Such was the process of plant and equipment investment: the material realization of the technological revolution. In that sense as well, this investment in technical progress can be said to have constituted the nucleus of economic growth.

7

The Technological Revolution and Its Impact

The Mechanism of Rapid Growth

From the mid-1950s onward the Japanese economy was running flat-out on the path of rapid growth. Booms such as the "Jimmu" (1956–57) and the "Iwato" (1959–61) arose in the course of that process. The rapid growth process was the Japanese economy's "historical period of ascendancy" (in the words of Shimomura Osamu); it was a mechanism whereby "investment called forth more investment," and it was made manifest in industry's technological revolution, the consumer revolution, wholesale population shifts, the achievement of full employment, and so on. The aim of this chapter is to convey, even if only in small measure, some of the flavor of that multifaceted development. There is no way to narrate these dramatic and exciting pages of history but by means of an overwhelming accumulation of example after impressive example.

However, when one broadens the perspective to take a macro view of rapid growth, one notices only the most ordinary economic activity taking place. From the mid-1950s onward, plant and equipment investment expanded rapidly and rose as a proportion of the gross national product as well. In a single bound it jumped from its earlier level of 10% to nearly 20%. One can appreciate what a remarkable expansion this was from the fact that investment's share of GNP doubled at a time when the economy as a whole was expanding swiftly. It is precisely this fact which may be considered the link between individual episodes in the technological revolution and the macroeconomic rapid growth mechanism. However, it should be kept in mind that, while plant and equipment investment expanded on a large scale, increases in the capital stock were not all that great. That is, the nature of plant and equipment investment in the decade from 1955 to 1964 suggests that it could be adequately explained by the acceleration principle, even without any particular technological revolution or

Table 7–1.   Capital Formation in the Rapid-Growth Period

(¥ trillions, %)

	1955	1960	Annual rate of increase
Real Gross National Product (a)	17.2	26.2	8.8
Real Private Plant & Equipment Investment (b)	1.3	3.7	22.9
Investment Rate (b)/(a)	7.7	14.0	
(Nominal Values)	(10.8)	(19.6)	—
Real Gross Private Capital Stock (c)	18.9	27.5	7.8
Average Capital Coefficient (c)/(a)	1.1	1.0	—

Sources: "Kokumin shotoku tōkei" [National Income Statistics], etc.

the like (Table 7–1). Repeated reference has already been made to the fact that great productive capacity was inherited from the wartime and the prewar period, so the country got by in the early postwar years with very modest increases in plant and equipment investment. When production rose as a result of recovery and new plant and equipment began to be considered necessary, the degree of expansion in capital investment inevitably had to be high in reaction to the low levels of investment prior to that time. An additional point is that, if viewed only in accordance with the usual methods of growth accounting, the contributions of increases in the capital stock to economic growth were not all that large.[1]

This sort of skeptical macro view undeniably contains an element of truth. However, where and how is it linked to the actual drama of rapid growth? It is precisely such linkages that may in fact be the core of economic history: the points at which universally applicable economic theory and historical events cross swords, as it were. At any rate, in order to fill in some of the gap between the two views of rapid growth, attention is drawn to two important points.

The first is that, roughly speaking, capital stock was expanding in proportion to the gross national product; but examining the figures in somewhat greater detail shows that around 1955, the capital stock was rather large relative to the gross national product. The point of departure for rapid growth was a high average capital coefficient. The fact that an investment boom occurred while the average capital coefficient was high, and that as a result the capital coefficient began declining, suggests that the capital stock was antiquated and that there was ample room for modernization. One would not err greatly in identifying enterprises'

---

[1] This point is discussed in greater detail in Kosai and Ogino, 1980.

desire to invest as the prime mover, in the sense that firms boldly seized their opportunities to modernize.

Secondly, even though from a macro point of view the expansion of investment was a natural occurrence, its achievement required an economy-wide effort at adaptation that may be termed extraordinary. To sustain a 20% expansion in plant and equipment investment, a large-scale production increase in capital goods and producers' goods had to be contrived, and in order to do that, a large labor force of inexperienced workers had to be attracted and put to work in these new industries. Even from one this single example one can comprehend how great was the strain produced by rapid growth. Furthermore, in order to prevent inflation and a balance of payments rupture from occurring as investment rapidly expanded, households had to be encouraged to save assiduously without explicit orders from anyone. Without such a "fortuitous" accumulation of countless events of this kind, the gears of rapid growth would not have turned.[2]

As promised earlier, let us now turn to the substance of the technological revolution of the 1950s.

The Unfolding of the Technological Revolution

The Second Rationalization Plan for Steel

In order to see how the plant and equipment investment of the latter half of the 1950s differed from prior stages both quantitatively and qualitatively, let us compare the Second Rationalization Plan for Steel with the First. Implemented during the first half of the 1950s, the First Steel Rationalization Plan played a pivotal role in the economic take-off, as we saw in Chapter 5.

In the harsh foreign and domestic environment following the Korean War armistice, the First Rationalization Plan was undertaken with the sense of urgency of a nation with its back to the wall: firms were fighting for their very existence, and from the national point of view the goal was to lower the steel prices that held the key to economic independence. In contrast to this, the Second Rationalization Plan was sustained by the successes achieved by the First. Looking back on the years 1955–56, *Nippon Kōkan 50-nen shi* [Fifty Years of Nippon Kokan

---

[2] There is a view that the provision of adequate housing and social security was delayed, the high rate of saving was a contrived phenomenon, and that at work therein are the intentions of the ruling capitalist class. This author, however, considers rapid growth to have come, not from someone who wrote and directed the process, but from a more grass-roots level.

K.K.] bears witness: "Each steel company, from past experience, had confidence in the Japanese economy's capacity for growth in the future" (p. 299). As we saw in the previous chapter, it was the continued prosperity of the industrialized nations under a relaxation of international tensions that produced this self-confidence.

If an industrial boom arises out of private demand rather than the expansion of military demand, a broadening of the uses of such products as consumer durables must be contrived. If the boom is worldwide and long-term, reliance on scrap iron is impossible and an iron supply must be secured. Thus, the major foci of the Second Rationalization Plan became the construction of strip mills to produce thin plates for consumer durables; the spread of oxygen converters, which used little scrap iron as a raw material and, as far as product is concerned, were well suited for the manufacture of tin plates; and the construction of integrated coastal steel mills for pig iron production. (Steel mills at that time were producing on a scale of 2 million tons per year, a figure that reached 5 to 6 million tons per year as the 1960s began.) In contrast to the ¥120 billion invested under the First Rationalization Plan, investment exceeded ¥500 billion under the Second (Table 7–2). In this way Japan's volume of steel output overtook that of France and of England (and afterwards surpassed that of West Germany as well); in number of hot strip mills (seven at that time) it took second place behind the United States; and in oxygen converter capacity, coke ratio, and ratio of pig iron output, Japan reached the leading position in the world. Quality improvements and new product developments such as high-quality steel sheets, light gauge steel, seamless electrical pipe, and high tensile strength steel became the material foundation that supported the technological revolution in the demand industries.

Since history is continuous, one cannot simply draw an arbitrary line, but there is no mistaking the fact that, in comparison with Japan's first rationalization, its second became endogenous in the sense defined by Rostow (1971). Demand for steel now came from consumer durables industries, not from public works. From the standpoint of funds as well, the Second Rationalization Plan was carried out with almost no direct reliance on government funds. Thus one must not think of the industrial finance system during the period of the First Rationalization Plan as having been too rigid. In contrast to its piecemeal character during the rationalization of the early 1950s, from the middle of the decade on, the financial system gained breadth and at the same time a deepening of its structure.

Table 7–2. Plant and Equipment Investment under the Second Iron and Steel Rationalization Plan

(¥ millions)

	1954	1955	1956	1957	1958	1959	1960	1961	1962	Totals	%
Pig-iron Manufacture	—	85	4,577	14,938	12,998	24,167	29,177	7,031	1,367	94,340	17.7
New Blast Furnace Installations	—	53	1,790	7,448	7,178	11,218	13,406	2,661	375	44,126	
Steel Production	991	562	2,149	4,126	5,631	17,695	12,785	5,447	1,418	50,774	9.5
Converters	—	—	697	2,016	2,226	9,938	8,081	3,651	716	27,368	
Rolling Mills	514	924	22,635	46,267	55,099	54,479	49,429	23,022	7,796	260,165	48.8
Hot Strip	—	—	9,895	16,541	18,060	9,447	4,646	2,187	781	61,321	
Rail Steel	—	—	1,339	1,705	2,172	3,731	6,379	7,622	3,483	26,429	
Maintenance & Repairs	—	—	4,506	5,936	7,312	8,954	14,600	—	—	41,308	7.7
Other	—	60	2,319	5,807	12,017	24,343	42,000	—	—	86,546	14.3
Totals	1,475	1,631	36,187	77,074	93,057	129,638	147,992	35,500	10,580	533,133	100.0

Source: Ministry of International Trade & Industry, Heavy Industry Bureau, "Tekkōgyō no gōrika to sono seika" [The Rationalization of the Iron and Steel Industry and Its Results].

The Energy Revolution and the Resource Shift

In the first half of the 1950s a lowering of iron prices and coal prices was seen as the key to economic independence. In the end, however, the problem of the high price of coal was solved by substituting electric power and petroleum for coal during the rapid growth beginning in the latter half of the 1950s.

This development of electric power also gave a strong impetus to the switch from the primary use of hydro power and secondary use of steam power during the decade 1945–54 to primary use of steam power and secondary use of hydro. This switch received official sanction in the form of the 1953 World Bank loan for thermal plants, the Matsunaga Plan put forward in 1955, and the 1956 Five-year Plan for Electric Power Development. At the end of 1955, 7,400 kw were produced by means of hydro power and 4,100 kw by steam power; at the end of 1961, however, this order had been reversed, with 9,444 kw of hydro power and 9,750 kw of steam power. At the time of the World Bank loan for thermal generating plants, the Karita thermal plant at 75,000 kw was renowned as the latest and most powerful of its kind, but the development of high-capacity thermal electric generating plants proceeded at a rapid pace, and in the span of only a few years a 220,000 kw plant (in 1960) and a 375,000 kw plant (Owase, 1965) were built. Thus, the concept of steam-powered plant capacity changed drastically during these ten years (Figure 7–1).

The economic advantages resulting from a steam-powered, highly efficient, high-capacity operating base became all the more striking with the advent of exclusive burning of crude oil and a fall in the unit price of fuel, along with full use of all manner of automatic controls. As the development of the Middle Eastern oil fields progressed, the price of crude oil declined dramatically, and the cost of transporting it dropped markedly due to the acceleration of supertanker construction. Intense competition among foreign and domestic oil firms who foresaw the growth potential of the Japanese market was also a reason for the drop in the prices of petroleum products that occurred during this period. The situation was exactly the opposite of that during and after the oil crisis of 1973.

This energy revolution had a great influence on related industries. Under the foreign exchange allocation system whereby the first thermal electric generator was imported and the second was produced domestically, the heavy electric machinery industry developed. On the other hand, the electric steel furnace industry, which depended upon hydroelectric power, lost the very foundation for its operations. The carbide industry in 1960 led the world with production on the scale of 1,500,000

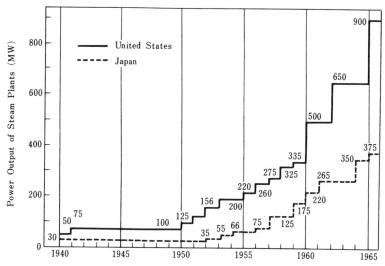

Figure 7-1.   The Scaling-Up of Steam-Powered Generators
    Source: Sakisaka Masao, ed., *Nihon sangyō zusetsu* [Japanese Industry
    in Charts].

tons, and was linked to the polyvinylchloride industry and the vinylon
and acetate industries. This industrial grouping, peculiar to Japan, was
the developmentalists' once-dreamed-of ideal of industrialization on
the basis of domestic resources; but, along with the raw materials shift
into petrochemicals, it was pushed onto the economy by the switch to
steam power as the primary source and hydro as secondary in the development of sources of electric power.

    The signal for the full-fledged commercialization of the petrochemical
industry was the adoption in July 1955 of the Policy for Nurturing the
Petrochemical Industry, a policy supported by the clearing of munitions factory sites, by Development Bank financing, and by the introduction of imported technology. In the case of petrochemicals, imports
were liberalized from the beginning; instead of damaging domestic
industry, increased imports of petrochemical-based synthetic resins
such as polyethylene expanded domestic markets and prepared the way
for the development of domestic production. In addition, once the
limits had been reached in chemical fertilizers, the capital invested in
chemicals was looking for a point of entry into the field of organic
chemistry. Hirschman (1958) states that, when there is a certain degree
of preparation domestically, imports do not impede the development

of domestic industry; rather, the development of markets by means of imports is a prerequisite for industrialization, and the petrochemical industry may be an example of this.

The raw material base for the petrochemicals industry was primarily naphtha. This differed considerably from the United States and Europe, which relied on natural gas or waste gas from well heads. However, at the beginning of the 1960s the composition of Japan's petroleum consumption was biased toward crude oil, which, based on the rate of acquisition, appears to have provided a plentiful supply of gasoline and stabilized the price of naphtha (Sato, 1961). There was also a plan to make full use of naphtha distillate. This situation is reflected in the fact that, in addition to chemical firms, industrial complexes which included electric power and petroleum refining were formed. These complexes underwent a transformation into mass-scale undertakings: from four centers operating on a scale of 20,000 tons of ethylene, primarily polyethylene, in the 1955–60 period, they expanded to five centers as the 1960s began. The first of these five centers produced at a level of 80,000 tons, the others at 40,000 tons, primarily propylene and acetoaldehyde.

The very development of synthetic fibers was a major raw materials switch, and, beginning in the early 1960s, a further shift in raw materials technology was taking place within the industry. Acetoaldehyde, the raw material for acetate, had been made from carbide and acetylene, but it was converted to a petrochemical formula. By switching the production procedure for the raw materials for nylon from the complicated process of benzol → carbolic acid → cyclohexanone → caprolactam to such methods as the benzene direct method, the Zimmer method, and the photosynthetic method, the process was shortened, and major decreases in raw materials costs were anticipated as a result. Such a raw materials shift in the organic chemicals industry also had an impact on industrial structure; for example, it elicited a degree of cooperation exceeding what had previously existed among enterprise groupings (*keiretsu*); large numbers of new entries were spawned; and so on.

The Development of Consumer Durables Industries

Paralleling the development of the energy and materials sectors, rapid growth and modernization proceeded in the manufacturing sector as well. Typical was the development of such consumer durables industries as automobiles and electric machinery and appliances. The development of the automobile industry has been characterized as a series of advances toward mass production. According to Maxcy and Silberston's classic study (1959), the optimal scale for the four principal processes of automobile production are: assembly, 60,000 to 100,000; forging, 100,000; machining, 500,000; and press, 1 million (per year in all cases). In contrast, Japan's top producer, Toyota, was in 1955 at last on the verge of completing its five-year plan for plant and equipment modernization, the goal of which was to produce a total of 3,000 per month of all its various makes. The poor performance of earlier passenger cars was explained in these terms by Toyota: "Since the cost goes up when you make only passenger cars, we had to make trucks and passenger cars from the same parts and had to try to increase the overall volume of production, even if only a little." When this method was abandoned and production undertaken of the Toyopet Crown (announced in January 1955), which was from the first designed to be purely a passenger car, the large, high-quality finished steel sheets used for the roof and the hood "could not be made at a profit by domestic steel companies because too few automobiles were produced"; they had to be imported from the United States, and this broke down the inter-industry linkage. From this perspective, the mechanism of the automobile industry's development is also clear.

The motorization that followed was swift. After the explosive expansion of domestic demand for motocycles had run its course, production for export began, while three-wheeled vehicles were replaced by small four-wheeled ones as demand rose. In the process, modern mass production plants for small passenger cars (initial monthly production, 10,000 units of one model only) such as the Toyota plant at Motomachi and the Nissan plant at Oppama were built. Toyota and Nissan in 1956 installed transfer machines that used cylinders, and in 1962 Nissan brought in fully automated presses which, along with new plant construction, signaled the modernization of the automobile industry (Kokumin Keizai Kenkyū Kyōkai, 1961).

These developments in the auto industry had a great impact on the economy. Thin sheet production in the steel industry was powerfully stimulated. Industries such as special steel and machine tools, which had long been in existence but had not developed due to the obstacles posed by limited markets, were invigorated and proceeded to develop further: the scale of production in the machine tool industry expanded sharply, from 5 billion yen in 1955 to 100 billion yen in 1962, and both the production lot size and the scale of the firm in Japan became the international standard. The rationalization of the small subcontracting firms was a third major effect.[3] Adopting the "supermarket" system

---

[3] As a policy, too, major importance was attached to the basic sector rationaliza-

(now often called the just-in-time system) in 1956, Toyota matched the speed of the parent plant's finished assembly-line conveyor belt to the production of subcontracting firms by synchronizing the production of the latter with their own assembly line. The mechanization and semi-automation of small firms was at first carried out with second-hand machinery inherited from the parent companies, but later on subcontracters took to installing new machinery at their own expense. This further expanded the market for the machine tool industry. While all this was going on, an independent, specialized type of producer not satisfied with merely being part of a group of subcontractors came into being. These independents typified the *chūken kigyō* (independent medium-size firms) identified by Nakamura Shūichirō, which were to become one of the pillars of economic growth.

Development of this kind was not confined to the automobile industry. In electric machinery and appliance manufacturing as well, mass production of washing machines and refrigerators became possible when the steel industry was able to introduce the automatic, continuous-process stamping machines which were at the heart of quality improvements in silicon steel sheets, and when transfer machines were introduced in the electric machinery and appliance industry. The development of radio and television parts manufacture (variable condensers, condensers, and so on) was remarkable, and this developed into an export industry as well. Also important is the fact that Japan's electrical machinery and appliance manufacturers pioneered civilian uses. Semiconductors, which had been developed for military use, were also mass-produced in Japan. They cannot be called consumer durables, but the development of computers also began about 1962; and in 1964 the HITAC 5020 was installed at the University of Tokyo as the nation's largest mainframe computer.

Until that time viewed as exogenous, the heavy and chemical industries were brought close to people's daily lives by the development of the consumer durables industries. The latter industries became the knot that joined the technological revolution and the consumer revolution. Three mechanisms seemed to be at work in this process: (1) As the degree of diffusion of consumer durables increased, costs and prices fell as a result of mass production effects, further hastening diffusion. (2) A strong demonstration effect was at work as, along with the diffusion of consumer durables, a middle-class consciousness was becoming

---

tion of the machinery industry. While this policy did bring profits to the large producers in the machinery industry, at the same time it shows that the view that funds, subsidies and so on were concentrated exclusively on monopoly capital is incorrect.

widespread. (3) The diffusion process typically mirrored the life cycles of products as they emerged on the market, peaked, and ultimately gave place to still more recent products (Figure 7–2).

The Repercussions of the Technological Revolution

Impact on the Organization of Industry and Finance

Rapid growth, whose nucleus was the technological revolution, had a major impact on the industrial sector and finance. New industry entrants and the firms producing new products flourished, and in short order growth firms joining the ranks of the major firms appeared. Interfirm competition became even more vigorous.

We have already seen how the zaibatsu were broken up as a result of the democratization, and this became the starting point for inter-firm competition after the war. During the procurement boom following the Korean War, the revival of the zaibatsu was a much-discussed possibility. In the event, however, what formed were *keiretsu* (financial groupings), with banks at their cores instead of the main companies (*honsha*) of the former zaibatsu. The "one-settism" discussed by Miyazaki Yoshikazu tried to describe a situation during the period of rapid growth in which fierce plant and equipment investment competition took place as each *keiretsu* cluster around a bank attempted to have a firm in every field of industry. However, it does not necessarily follow that the inter-firm competition of the rapid growth period was only and exclusively a path to the revival of the zaibatsu or to formation of the *keiretsu*. Rapid growth did not occur as a result of direct orders from the top executive offices of the *keiretsu* banks, which wanted to see enterprise groupings lined up in a row as "one set." Rather, rapid growth resulted from the fact that at every producing enterprise all over the country people were striving to catch up with the technologically advanced nations. Of the companies that became the stars of rapid growth, such as Toyota, Nissan, Hitachi, Matsushita, Honda, etc., no small number were headed by outsiders or newcomers with comparatively remote connections with the zaibatsu or the bank groups. Nor do Yamata, Fuji, and Kawasaki Steel necessarily fit into the framework of the bank *keiretsu*. The behavior of these firms cannot be termed one-settism. The rapid growth that followed the break-up of the zaibatsu, rather than a revival of finance capital, produced a new industrialism. It can be shown that throughout this period, the higher the growth rate of the firm, the lower was its rate of dependence on bank borrowings; neither were enterprise ties with banks fixed (Table 7–3).

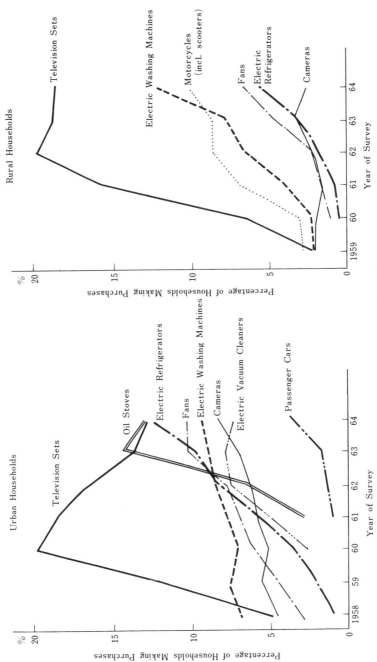

Figure 7-2.   Shifts in Purchasing of Key Consumer Durable Goods
Source: Economic Planning Agency, "Shōhisa dōkō yosoku chōsa" [Survey and Forecast of Consumer Trends].

All through the period of rapid growth the development of industry proceeded swiftly, and the expansion in scale of the large enterprises was striking. The rate of concentration in industry, however, even showed a downward trend, primarily in the high-growth areas, and the share of small and medium-sized firms changed hardly at all, although there was repeated replacement of firms. When we consider that the historical record shows that conspicuous accumulations of wealth have been usual in every instance of economic development, the relative moderation in this area in contemporary Japan may be regarded as astonishing. Surprise at the vitality of Japanese industry elicited a plethora of jouralistic interest in around 1960. The image of Japanese industry as backward and as showing an inverted, abnormal pattern of development that had dogged it for so long at last came to be perceived as a worn-out stereotype.

Changes in Industrial Geography
The industrial development which accompanied the technological revolution had a great impact on the geographic location of industry.

The energy liquefaction revolution dealt a severe blow to the regional economies of Kyushu and Hokkaido, which were based on coal. Development of coastal industrial zones proceeded apace as part of the process of converting this "weakness" of dependence on foreign raw materials into strength. As coastal steel plants, coastal oil refineries, and coastal electric power plants sprang up along the Pacific seaboard belt that links Tokyo to Yokohama and to Osaka, Kobe, and Kyushu, and as industrial complexes were built, the machine industry clustered around these high-consumption areas. Once again, as it had done more than once before in its history, Japan turned away from mainland China and opened itself toward the Pacific Ocean.

Between 1955 and 1960, the population increased by 4,140,000: 2,440,000 in the southern Kanto region; 600,000 in the Tokai region; 1,230,000 in the western Kinki region; and 270,000 in Hokkaido. In all other regions the population decreased. During this period, the population of the Tokyo metropolitan area grew from 6,970,000 to 8,310,000; that of the city of Osaka from 2,550,000 to 3,010,000; and that of the city of Nagoya from 1,340,000 to 1,590,000. The urban population increased by 9,050,000 while the rural population declined by 4,900,000. Industrialization was a process of urban population concentration as well (Table 7–4). During this time, many of the internal migrants who had concentrated in the cities congregated under communal roofs in search of old-style family ties: the average number of persons per urban household, surprisingly, grew from 4.73 in 1955 to 4.86 in

Table 7–3. Sales Growth Rates and Financing Patterns, 1955–63

		I 8-fold or more (21 Firms)	II 5–8– fold (34 Firms)	III 3–5– fold (55 Firms)	IV 2–3– fold (53 Firms)	V Less than 2-fold (40 Firms)
Funds Procurement						
(1955–1963)						
Borrowed Funds	%	32.5	36.6	41.0	41.8	47.0
Equity Capital	%	36.2	23.3	22.3	22.5	7.1
Financial Ratios						
(1963–1st half)						
Proportion Borrowed						
Funds	%	32.3	35.5	38.7	30.3	39.1
Proportion Equity						
Capital	%	38.7	28.7	28.0	1.6	29.4
Liquidity						
(1963–1st half)						
Deposits/Sales	%	32.0	27.1	22.8	20.4	18.0
Deposits/Borrowings	%	49.9	25.8	20.9	15.0	21.1
Rate of Increase						
(1955–1963)						
Borrowed Funds	%	9.57	8.27	6.59	4.31	2.74
Deposits	%	17.40	8.73	5.06	2.86	2.19
Percentage Interest Expense						
(1963–1st half)		7.88	8.30	8.34	8.50	8.54
Proportion of Financing						
by Main Banks						
(1955–1st half)	%	65.2	42.9	55.5	41.1	38.9
(1963–1st half)	%	44.5	35.1	51.6	40.4	41.9
Stability of City Banks'						
Ranking as Lenders		0.681	0.705	0.796	0.787	0.808

Notes: (1) Classified and aggregated in accordance with the financial
statements of 203 leading manufacturing firms.

(2) Funds procurement consists of the proportions of increases
in borrowed funds (including discounted bills) and in equity
capital divided by increases or decreases in gross assets +
discounted bills outstanding.

(3) Of the financial ratios, that for proportion of borrowed funds
is the percentage of borrowed funds including discounted bills
divided by gross assets + discounted bills outstanding; and that
for proportion of equity capital is the percentage of equity
capital divided by gross assets.

(4) Percentage interest expense (1963–1st half) is interest expense
divided by borrowed funds (including discounted bills) and

Table 7–4.   Population Increases, by Region, from 1955 to 1960

(10,000 persons)

Nationwide	414		
Southern Kanto	244	(Cities)	(905)
Western Kinki	123	City of Tokyo(23 wards)	124
Tokai	60	Osaka	46
Hokkaido	27	Nagoya	25
Tohoku	−1	Kobe	21
Eastern Kinki	−1	Yokohama	19
Kyushu	−3	Kawasaki	18
Chugoku	−5	Kyoto	10
Hokuriku Tosan	−8		
Northern Kanto	−9		
Shikoku	−12	(Rural Districts)	(−490)

Source: "Kokusei chōsa" [National Census].

1960. The next five years, in contrast, saw a swift decline in this figure (the move toward the nuclear family), to 3.9 persons per urban household in 1965.

During this period major shifts were occurring in the population. Where did this population come from? And where did it work? Under what sort of conditions? It is in connection with precisely these points that the impact of rapid growth, the nucleus of which was the technological revolution, is most typically revealed. The result is what is known as the break-up of the "dual structure."

total debentures. Average of percentages for each firm.

(5) Proportion of financing by main banks is that proportion of borrowed funds from the city banks provided by that city bank which is the largest supplier of financing.

(6) Stability of city banks' ranking as lenders is given by coefficients of concordance (average value of the rank order coefficients of correlation) for city bank short-term loans for the first half of 1955 and 1959–63.

(7) "Nenji keizai hōkoku" [Economic White Paper] (1964).

8

Income Doubling and Trade Liberalization

The Security Treaty and the Miike Strike

1960 was a year of political turmoil. It was the year of *Anpo*, the U.S.-Japan Security Treaty, which gave the United States the right to station troops and maintain military bases in Japan. The 1951 treaty, which had been controversial in Japan from the start, came up for renewal in 1960, and the government of Prime Minister Kishi Nobusuke entered into lengthy negotiations with the U.S. that resulted in some modifications and limitations on the American forces' freedom of action in Japan. However, the revisions did little to change the basic situation—U.S. troops stationed on Japanese soil; and renewed opposition centered on the fear that this would add to Japan's burden of responsibility for the Far Eastern conflicts involving American military forces. In the wake of the initialing of the treaty renewal in Washington in January 1960, opposition activity intensified; the Diet was besieged from morning till night with petitioning activity, and the streets leading to the parliament building appeared to be blocked with demonstrations that spread the width of the streets as the marchers linked arms. The entry of police into the Diet on the night of May 19–20 to enforce an extension of the Diet session and ratification of the Security Treaty threw fat on the fire of the opposition movement. A general strike was called on June 4; President Eisenhower's Press Secretary James Hagerty was forced to escape by helicopter from a mob of demonstrators at Haneda Airport on June 10; a college student died when the Zengakuren (National Federation of Student Self-Government Organizations) student demonstrators burst into the Diet on June 15; and a planned visit to Japan by President Eisenhower, who had come as far as Manila, was cancelled. Then, like the ebbing of a spent wave, a sudden calm reigned with the automatic renewal of the Security Treaty on June 19 and Prime Minister Kishi Nobusuke's announcement of his resignation on June 23.

1960 was also the year of the Miike strike, the postwar period's most dramatic labor–management confrontation. At the previous year's end, the Mitsui Mining Co., backed by a business community desirous of converting from coal to petroleum as a source of energy, proposed dismissing several thousand workers at its Miike coal mine in Kyushu. The company's union dug in its heels; and in a dramatic scene on January 5, 1960, a union-hired helicopter dropped back the dismissal notices for 1,278 workers over the company's Yamanoue Club. Management declared a lockout on January 25, and in response the union called for a full-scale strike against Mitsui. After the formation in March of a new union cooperative with the company, the two unions clashed repeatedly. There were incidents of harassment at company housing, bloody free-for-alls between strike-breaking work crews and picketers, sieges, stabbing attacks on strikers by gang members, struggles over the company's coal hoppers at Mikawa, sea fights offshore from Miike, and so on. The Ikeda Hayato Cabinet was formed on July 18, and on the afternoon of the 19th Labor Minister Ishida Hirohide exhorted labor and management to resolve the conflict. Ordering by virtue of his *ex officio* authority that the matter be submitted for compulsory arbitration to the Central Labor Relations Committee, Ishida narrowly averted a pre-dawn clash on the 20th between 10,000-some odd picketers and a 10,000-man police force over enforcement of a provisional injunction. The Central Labor Relations Committee's arbitration proposal (arbitrators: Fujibayashi Keizō, Nakayama Ichirō) called for an adjustment period of one month, after which the company was to cancel its dismissal designations; at the same time those who were to have been dismissed were to resign voluntarily. The matter in fact ended in defeat for the union.

What was the significance of the Security Treaty? of the Miike strike? The crisis over the Security Treaty may be termed a manifestation of nationalism, yet there was no particular upsurge of anti-American feeling initially. Pacifistic feeling also contributed to the opposition movement, but, ironically, today the Security Treaty is internationally viewed as a brake against militarization in Japan. The fact that the Ikeda Cabinet's "tolerance and patience" had an immediate tranquilizing effect on the Security Treaty disturbances leads one to conclude that the reason for this mass movement on such an unpredecented scale lay in the Diet's inept handling of procedural problems and, perhaps, in some trivial differences in political style. This, however, means that a new society, one in which symbolic differences of this kind are fraught with great meaning, was being born in Japan. What was being challenged was the Kishi Cabinet's rather secretive political style, the importance Prime Minister Kishi attached to the Cold War, and his predisposition to aspire to power. What challenged it was a new middle class that cherished a modest, unassuming peace and was reluctant to take part in the international power game. Kishi's departure also marked a permanent farewell to the prewar generation of political leaders: Kishi was the last postwar prime minister to have also served in a prewar Cabinet.

The significance of the Miike strike is that in the midst of the advancing energy revolution, the Mitsui Company's traditional methods of labor administration failed while at the same time the philosophy of "struggle at the workplace" and the tactical line calling for worker "control at the point of production" were proven bankrupt. These were the philosophy and tactics espoused by the Miike labor union, which combined the peculiar village consciousness of a coal-mining barracks community with the classical ideology of class struggle. This is not to say that there was no drama of human courage and suffering in this struggle; nevertheless the clashes between the company and the union, and between the union and the breakaway workers' group, became filled with malice and a kind of internecine hatred, the obverse of the mutually indulgent relationship that had prevailed until then. Self-centered cunning was prominent in the proceedings, and the protracted strife cast a wide pall of gloom. The Miike conflict revealed the antiquated character of both labor and management in the coal industry, which was already heading for trouble.

The Security Treaty and Miike were rites of passage into Japan's period of modernization in the 1960s; they were an exorcism for that purpose, a rite of purification. The society that emerged from the disturbances consisted of, on the one hand, a minority of fragmented radical factions that placed themselves outside society and, on the other, the new middle class majority, who were both the promoters of rapid growth and its beneficiaries. Indifference to the decline of statism and class ideology was the social consequence of the Japanese economy's approach to full employment and the breakdown of the dual structure during rapid growth. Internationally, too, prescribed ideologies were losing their luster and new theories of modernization were becoming popular. W. W. Rostow's *The Stages of Economic Growth* was translated; Edwin O. Reischauer, an advocate of the modernization view of Japanese history, was appointed U.S. Ambassador to Japan by newly elected President John F. Kennedy. The Hakone Conference in the autumn of 1960 was the beginning of a flourishing ascendancy for the theory of the modernization of Japan.

Income Doubling and Trade Liberalization

The Income Doubling Plan

1960 was also the year of income doubling. The long-term plan with the announced aim of doubling national income within ten years had already been submitted by the Kishi Cabinet the year before for deliberation by the Economic Council, but it was in the hands of the Ikeda Cabinet that the plan took on great significance. June 15, 1960, was the day that college student Kamba Michiko died in the fighting that followed radical students' invasion of the Diet. In the tense political situation while the dispatching of the Self-Defense Forces was under discussion, Minister of International Trade and Industry Ikeda Hayato, who was one of the candidates to succeed to the prime ministership after Kishi's widely expected resignation, was asked by his Secretary Itoh Masaya, "What will you do if you become Prime Minister?" Ikeda is said to have replied, "Isn't it all a matter of economic policy? I'll go for income doubling." According to Itoh's biography *Ikeda Hayato—Sono sei to shi* [Ikeda Hayato: His Life and Death], Ikeda was full of a sense of mission and confidence that no one could lead the nation better than he. The fact that the idea for income doubling was borrowed from Nakayama Ichirō's wage-doubling theory and Ikeda's dissatisfaction with the Economic Planning Agency's drafting of the Income

Table 8–1. The Income Doubling Plan and Results Achieved

	1970 Levels		Rate of Increase (%)	
	Goal	Actual	Goal	Actual
Total Population (10,000s)	10,222	10,372	0.9	1.0
Number Employed (10,000s)	4,689	5,094	1.2	1.5
Number of Employees (10,000s)	1,924	3,309	4.1	4.3
Gross National Product (¥ trillions)	26.0	40.6	8.8	11.6
Per Capita National Income (¥ 10,000s)	20.8	31.8	6.9	10.4
Mining & Mfg. Output	431.7	539.4	11.9	13.9
Energy Demand (coal, 100 millions of tons)	3.0	5.7	7.8	12.0
Exports ($100 millions)	80.8	202.5	10.0	16.8
Imports ($100 millions)	98.9	195.3	9.3	15.5

Source: Economic Planning Agency, "Gendai Nihon keizai no tenkai" [Development of the Contemporary Japanese Economy].

Notes: Gross national product and per capita income are in 1958 prices. For mining and manufacturing output, 1958 = 100. Rate of increase is relative to averages for 1956–58.

Doubling Plan do not negate the fact that income doubling was the pillar of Ikeda's policy (Table 8–1).

The charm of the National Income Doubling Plan as a government document lies in its magnanimity:

> The ultimate aim of this plan is to move ahead toward a conspicuous increase in the national standard of living and the achievement of full employment. To that end, the maximal stable growth of the economy must be contrived.
>
> If internal and external economic conditions should take a more favorable turn than assumed in this plan, it will be possible to achieve the goals set herein within the plan period. If such conditions are realized without destroying economic or social stability and, moreover, without harming future capacity for growth, this will be quite desirable for the Japanese economy, and it will not be necessary to restrain growth.

The theories of Shimomura Osamu cast a long shadow in this affirmation of growth. A fierce debate among economists like Okita Saburō, Tsuru Shigeto, Shinohara Miyohei, and Yoshino Toshihiko took place over Shimomura's bold derivation of a capital-output coefficient of 1 for plant and equipment investment, and a marginal propensity to import of 9%.[1] However, the heart of Shimomura's theory, which was confidence in the Japanese economy's capacity for growth, slowly and imperceptibly captured people's hearts.

The source of such growth capacity lay in the free activities of private firms:

> In this plan the private sector, which is the principal sector of the economy, seeks economic rationality through free business enterprises and the market mechanism, and there is respect for the position that they conduct autonomous activity in accordance with their originality and ingenuity. . . . Private firms should contribute to the growth and development of the economy by displaying to the utmost the latent energy they always contain. That is what in the end produces increases in national income and improvements in the lives of the people.
>
> In this plan the fields of economic activity have been divided into two. For the government and public sector, in which the government primarily possesses direct means for implementation,

---

[1] See *Ekonomisuto,* 1960; Kinyū Zaisei Jijō Kenkyūkai, 1959; Murakami, 1971.

it formulates a plan which as much as possible possesses the potential for implementation in concrete terms; and for the private sector, which fundamentally relies upon the originality and ingenuity of business firms for its activity, the plan restricts itself to something in the nature of forecasts, and weighs a policy of guidance in desired directions where necessary.

As can be deduced from the fact that it appears twice even in a brief quotation, the "originality and ingenuity (*sōi to kufū*) of the people" was a popular expression at that time. This may well be compared with the frequent use of the term "efficiency" (*kōritsuka*) in the Economic and Social Development Plan of later years. Income doubling itself is often seen as displaying the success of the Japanese industry–government combine, but it is also interesting that the National Income Doubling Plan itself, as is seen in the final paragraph of fhe above quotation, actually takes a rigid position of neoclassical synthesis. The plan itself, which focuses on the growth rate, indicates the diffusion of modern economic thought, and its modernist tone makes the document fresh and clear.

As might be expected from the assertions about originality and ingenuity, this plan made liberal use of new terms and translations of foreign terms such as "social overhead capital," "the Pacific coast belt region," "human resources," and so on. The policy proposal is also bold:

With regard to foreign exchange, we are actively pursuing liberalization. Direct rice controls should be abolished and indirect controls substituted for them.
    As for our nation's [contribution to] economic cooperation . . . in the target year it will reach the level of 2.9% of GNP.

Although the international goal of contributing 1% of national income to economic aid had previously been quite unattainable, in the Income Doubling Plan nearly three times that amount is assumed. The plan's drafters seemed emboldened when writing of matters ten years in the future. As for abolishing the direct controls on rice, it is no less than a miracle that such a bold proposal could get past the sharp-eyed, vigilant documentary examination of the relevant ministries. This point in fact later became an issue in the Diet, and it was said that government circles were thrown into great confusion over it. The propaganda function of economic plans was probably not well understood even by those in the government. Such easy-going buoyancy disappeared from subsequent plans; in contrast to the sweeping optimism of the Income Doubling Plan, later plans seemed arid and insipid.

Examples of ineptitude can also be found in the Plan, however – for instance the stated intention of mining 70 million tons of coal in 1970 irrespective of the fact that the coal industry was losing ground to oil already in 1960. Since this plan predated the introduction of an econometric model, it lacked consistency among the variables of primary importance such as GNP, mining and manufacturing production, plant and equipment investment, and so on. More fatal was the fact that price stability was taken for granted during the plan period since the plan assumed that the dual structure of the labor market could be relied on until 1967, when the labor supply would begin to decline. In reality, the dual structure declined swiftly in the midst of the income-doubling boom, and consumer price inflation began in short order.

Trade Liberalization

1960 was also the year of trade liberalization, which, like the Income Doubling Plan, was pioneered by the Kishi Cabinet.

It has been stated a number of times that the Japanese economy had been in a state of blockade since the middle of the Pacific War. Even after the reopening of private trade, imports were placed under a system of licenses and foreign exchange quotas in order to maintain balance of payments equilibrium and to protect domestic industry. In about April of 1960, those items which had been moved to an automatic approval system came to 40 % of all imports. In Western Europe, by contrast, liberalization within the region had been under way since 1949; there was a move toward trade liberalization against the dollar in 1954, and a still further acceleration of the tempo of liberalization was occasioned by the restoration of currency convertibility at the end of 1958.When the general meeting of GATT opened in Tokyo in 1959, plans for the liberalization of trade and foreign exchange landed on the agenda because Japan's dilatoriness was severely criticized by the other nations, primarily the United States.

At the end of 1959, the Proposals for Trade and Foreign Exchange Liberalization issued by the Research Institute for Economic Policy of Japan (Sōgō Seisaku Kenkyūkai) had considerable impact on public opinion in that they clearly specified the necessity for liberalization and set an explicit schedule for it.

In January of 1960 the government set up a Cabinet Council for the Promotion of Trade and Foreign Exchange Liberalization, which, on the 24th of June, during the final days of the Kishi Cabinet's tenure

Table 8-2. Time Schedules for the Liberalization Plan

Proposal by the Comprehensive Government Policy Research Society			Outline Plan for Trade & Foreign Exchange Liberalization
Liberalization by Sept. 1960	Scrap iron, pig iron, soybeans, raw cotton, raw wool, salt, iron & steel products, some machinery (bearings, bicycles, textile machines, sewing machines, optical instruments, radios, etc.), potassic salt, zinc & others.	Early Liberalization	Pig iron, ordinary steel & steel products, galvanized iron sheet,* zinc ore, optical instruments, textile machinery, construction equipment, farm equipment, electrical machinery & appliances for use by the public, ships, railroad cars, machine components, benzol, toluol, xylol, potassic salt, calcium cyanamide, pharmaceuticals (excluding vitamins, etc.), raw cotton, raw wool, silk & cotton products, bicycle tires & tubes, rubber hose, beer, miscellaneous grains, processed vegetables (excluding tomatoes),* processed fruits (excluding canned bananas & pineapple),* special crops (excluding black tea and rapesped),* silk cocoons, canned salmon & trout, wood products,* petroleum wastes.*
Liberalization by the end of 1961	Petroleum, pulp, copper, barley, feed, some machinery (prime movers, construction machinery, heavy electric machinery, etc.).		
Liberalization by the end of 1963	Coal, rice, sugar, remaining machinery (automobiles, machine tools, applied electronics devices, etc.)		
		Near-Term Liberalization (within 3 yrs.)	Petroleum, special steel, ferroalloys, aluminium, magnesium, machine tools (excluding items in process of technological development), carbolic acid, acetone, butanol, soda-ash, caustic soda, paint, natural nitric soda, vitamins, woolens, rayon staple products, synthetic fiber products, plate glass, bicycle tire tubes, sundry goods, processed lard, industrial oils & fats, edible oils.
		Long-Term Liberalization	Copper, lead, nickel, machinery in process of technological development, construction machinery, metal working equip-

Table 8–2. (cont.)		ment, tools, chemical apparatuses, passenger cars, heavy electrical equipment, electronic equipment for industrial use, ammonium sulfate, urea, hemp products, pulp, leather products, wine, whiskey, special forest products.
	Difficult to Liberalize	Sulfur, manganese ore, grain flour, bananas, canned pineapple, sugar, dairy products, wheat.

* Straddles two categories

in office, agreed on an Outline Plan for Trade and Foreign Exchange Liberalization (Table 8–2):

Thus far Japan's government has administered trade and foreign exchange because of difficulties involving the postwar recovery and the international balance of payments, but during the past few years, we have gradually relaxed these restrictions and come to promote liberalization in response to an improvement in our balance of payments and an increase in our foreign exchange reserves. The Japanese economy of the last few years, then, has achieved its high level of economic growth in an environment of stable domestic prices and a basically surplus position in the balance of payments; and it is judged that, if our economy is able to obtain appropriate policies henceforward as well, it will be able to further promote liberalization hand in hand with the continuation of rapid growth.

In view of such domestic and foreign conditions, we can expect many desirable effects on the national economy arising out of aggressive relaxation of trade and foreign exchange restrictions at this time and out of our attaching altogether more importance to the independent ingenuity and responsibility of enterprises in accordance with economic rationality. Liberalization makes possible a much more effective use of economic resources and promotes an overhauling of the economy by eliminating the inefficiency and irrationality that accompanied the former system of administered controls. As a result of liberalization, free access to such things as low-priced foreign raw materials becomes easier, industry's costs decline, and rationalization efforts on a par with the international standard are demanded of firms; along with this, liberalization contributes widely to improving the lives of the people and thereby promotes the interests of our national economy as a whole.

In its effort to project the solemnity of official governmentese, the Plan's prose is a bit old-fashioned; but the phrase "the ingenuity of enterprise" once again appears even here, and in that sense the document is liberal and forward-looking. Immediately following this passage, the Plan emphasizes some concern over a transitory effect on industry, the existence of disguised unemployment, the lack of a cooperative economic bloc, etc., but on the whole there are numerous places where it agrees with the proposals of the Research Institute for Economic Policy of Japan (Sōgō Seisaku Kenkyūkai). As a concrete schedule for liberalization, the Institute was considering virtually complete liberalization in approximately four years, while the government's plan aimed at 80% liberalization (90% if coal and oil were liberalized) after three years, from which it may be inferred that the government plan was quite aggressive on liberalization. From about this time, when there was much criticism that the government was implementing policy with its hands tied behind its back, one has the deep sense that rapid growth was at its zenith during this period and that it was an era of good fortune and amicability between government officials and ordinary citizens.

Further changes in this aggressive Outline Liberalization Plan ensued as the schedule for its implementation was moved still further ahead by the Ikeda Cabinet. On July 18, 1961, the Cabinet reached an understanding on a policy that would advance the goal of 90% liberalization by half a year to October 1962, and on September 26 it reached agreement on a "Plan for the Acceleration of Trade and Foreign

Table 8–3. Changes in the Rate of Import Liberalization

End of Aug.	1959	26%	End of Dec.	1961	70%
End of Sept.		33	End of Apr.	1962	83
End of Apr.	1960	40	End of Oct.		88
End of July		42	End of Apr.	1963	89
End of Oct.		44	End of Aug.		92
End of Apr.	1961	62	End of Feb.	1965	94
End of June		65	End of Oct.	1966	95
End of Oct.		68	End of Apr.	1967	97

Source: Economic Planning Agency, "Gendai Nihon keizai no tenkai" [Development of the Contemporary Japanese Economy].

Note: The data are for months in which there were changes in the rate of liberalization.

Exchange Liberalization," which gave substance to that policy. In actuality, import liberalization proceeded at a more considered tempo, attaining 88% in October of 1962 and 92% at the end of August 1963 (Table 8–3). Here the increase in the rate of liberalization stopped, and did not resume its rise until after the beginning of 1970, when the imbalance created by the international accounts surplus became an issue leading to friction with the United States.

At a press conference in early October 1960, the day after he took office, Prime Minister Ikeda stated that there would be 9% growth in three years and that the rural population would decline by one-third in ten years—statements which aroused some controversy.

Confidence in rapid growth and in the prospects for modernization was based on faith in free business activity. Should not the Income Doubling Plan and the Liberalization Plan be viewed as manifestations of liberalism as it occurred in Japan, rather than as policy statements of "Japan, Inc."? Economically, the emphasis on full employment made it possible to leave the allocation of resources to the market mechanism, which was seen as desirable.

Pattern Transition and Productivity Differential Inflation

The Period of Pattern Transition

Growth policies were not something begun by the Ikeda Cabinet, which did no more than simply affirm the rapid growth that was already a fact. However, this affirmation in itself was a matter of no small importance; in the same sense, one may say that, while there was a Keynesian revolution, it only ratified the already existing New Deal. The bewildered reaction of the leading opposition party, the Japan Socialist Party, to the failure of its doctrine of structural reform suggests how great a compensation is required when one is too late in perceiving the real situation.

Reality, however, is even more complex than any theory. Under the leadership of Ikeda, who combined vision with candor, the Japanese economy exhibited undreamed-of changes.

The Income Doubling Plan and the trade liberalization policy progressed still further during the final days of the Iwato boom. The financial austerity measures which had been expressly adopted for preventive purposes in the fall of 1959 were abolished in August of 1960. In addition, from the end of 1960 to the spring of 1961 a policy of lowering interest rates—including interest on corporate debentures and on deposits—was enforced. This led to a tremendous amount of activity in the securities market, and it was in such an atmosphere that the Bond Investment Trust (Kōshasai Tōshi Shintaku) entered the market in January of 1961. The trust was spectacularly popular, collecting over ¥100 billion by March. Firms were spurred to invest in plant and equipment in anticipation of growth and to strengthen their international competitiveness, but now they fell into the illusion that they had been promised an inexhaustible supply of funds. It was, once again, the balance of payments that placed a ceiling on this plant and equipment investment boom, like a bedevilled chase after pie in the sky. The Ikeda growth policies initiated in 1960 had to encounter a setback at the very outset, just as Finance Minister Ikeda's fiscal policies in the Ishibashi Cabinet had come to grief with the imposition (albeit reluctantly) of monetary stringency in mid-stream that marked the end of the Jimmu boom. This occurred in spite of the fact that the ¥100 billion fiscal spending policy and ¥100 billion tax-cut budget which Finance Minister Ikeda drew up for the Ishibashi Cabinet in 1956 are historically significant as a growth finance prototype rich in vision.

The Japanese economy made a sharp recovery from the recession following the 1957–58 Jimmu boom. This is interpreted as having been a drawing down and rebuilding of inventories which took place in the course of the upswing of the plant and equipment investment cycle. Things did not turn out that way following the 1960–62 Iwato boom, however, because plant and equipment investment itself came to a standstill. This was pointed out early on by Hori Hiroshi, who was at the time on loan to the Economic Planning Agency's Domestic Research Division, and, based on his views, the 1962 Economic White Paper diagnosed the Japanese economy as being in a period of pattern transition away from its plant-and-equipment-investment-biased growth—a process of bringing unbalanced growth into balance.[2]

As has been mentioned repeatedly, since the capital stock inherited from prewar days was large, the expansion of plant and equipment investment in the decade following the war was modest, and it constituted only a small proportion of gross national product. With the coming of the second postwar decade, however, plant and equipment investment had to expand rapidly, even if only in order to expand production capacity to match growth. In this process, the rate of investment rose to exceed the standard defined by the product of the growth rate and the capital coefficient. This was the configuration around 1960. However, once the imbalance of the initial period was

[2] See Hori, 1961; Shinohara, 1962; Shishido, 1967.

Table 8–4.   Adjustments in Economic Growth and the Capital Stock

	1960/1955	1965/1960	1965/1955
Economic Growth Rate (%)	8.7	9.7	9.2
Capital Stock Growth Rate (%)	7.9	10.9	9.4
Growth Rate of Plant & Equipment Investment (%)	22.5	8.7	15.4
Percentage Plant & Equipment Investment (beginning of period) (%)	7.7	14.0	(end of 13.3 period)
Capital Coefficient (average, beginning of period)	1.09	1.05	(end of 1.11 period)

Sources: "Kokumin shotoku tōkei" [National Income Statistics], etc.

eliminated, the expansion of plant and equipment investment fell off even though the growth rate of the economy as a whole was the same; the ratio of plant and equipment investment to GNP also had to decline. The essence of the theory of the period of pattern transition may be understood in this way (Table 8–4).

The pattern modification theory applied the acceleration principle to the special initial-period conditions of the postwar Japanese economy, and to that extent it was appropriate. In contrast to what one might have expected, the theory did not necessarily predict a sharp drop in the growth rate. The Japanese economy got through the first half of the 1960s with a continued high growth rate of nearly 10%. Perhaps it should be said that such changes in the demand structure correspond with the ideas in the Income Doubling Plan, which stresses investment in social capital. Notwithstanding the foregoing, however, the recovery during the period of plant and equipment investment adjustments was weak, and it was inevitable that a feeling of disillusionment with rapid growth lingered. In 1965, after the short-lived recovery of 1963, the bankruptcies of Sun Wave Cabinet Making, Sanyō Special Steel, and Yamaichi Securities took place in the worst recession of the postwar period. Another round of great prosperity began in the latter half of the 1960s, so in the 1970s the working of the acceleration principle was again experienced.

Productivity Differential Inflation
Another—and more basic—threat to the smooth functioning of the growth policies was the fact that in 1960 consumer prices began to rise at an annual rate of 5%. The National Income Doubling Plan assumed virtually static prices during the plan period; this is in keeping with the situation in the latter half of the 1960s, and also theoretically

Table 8–5. Labor Supply and Demand, and Price Trends

	Whole-sale Price	Consumer Price Increases	Percentage "Spring Offensive" Wage Increases	Effective Ratio of Job Openings to Applicants	Number of Persons Employed
1956	4.4%	0.3%	5.0%	0.38	98 (10,000s of
1957	3.0	3.0	8.4	0.48	82 persons)
1958	−6.5	−0.4	5.5	0.39	90
1959	0.9	0.9	6.9	0.48	98
1960	1.1	3.6	8.7	0.62	75
1961	1.0	5.3	13.8	0.73	66
1962	−1.7	6.8	10.7	0.71	59
1963	1.8	7.6	9.1	0.73	59
1964	0.2	3.9	12.4	0.79	54
1965	0.7	6.7	10.6	0.61	57
1960/1955	0.5	1.5	6.9	0.47	89
1965/1960	0.4	5.1	11.3	0.71	59

tallies with the assumption implicit in the plan that pressure on the labor supply and a genuine narrowing of income differentials would begin in 1968, when entrance into the labor market by the postwar baby boom generation would end and a labor shortage become pronounced. In fact, however, the rise in consumer prices had already begun when the plan was being formulated in 1960.

Reality stayed one or two steps ahead of the plan's assumptions. First, demand for labor, primarily that of young workers, began growing during the Iwato boom years. Just as the legendary eight million gods gathered at Takamagahara pushed away the boulder from the entrance to the heavenly cave where the Sun Goddess Amaterasu had hidden herself, the Iwato boom finally permeated the labor market, whose excess supply was considered the the traditional foundation of the Japanese economy. The tightening of the labor market occurred not, as the planners had expected, after the absorption of the postwar baby boom into the labor force, but even earlier, in the mid-1960s, when the new labor force which reflected the wartime drop in the birth rate was settling in.

At the same time, the overall ratio of job offers to applicants was still below one, primarily among new entrants into the labor force. Only in 1967 did this ratio rise above one. Perhaps it was still too early to declare the achievement of full employment in the full sense of the term. Notwithstanding that, however, full employment had only to loom into view for price increases to occur. Increases were limited to consumer prices, but all the same, the Keynesian proposition that the increased demand following the achievement of full employment produces price increases applies (Table 8–5).

The reason consumer prices rose while wholesale prices remained stable was that cost increases in fields with low rates of productivity increase pushed up prices in those fields while wage levels were being standardized as the supply and demand for labor improved. One interpretation of this relationship is "an increase in the value of human beings," but in a more subtle formulation it is called productivity differential inflation (Takasuga, 1972).

Since the early 1960s, consumer price increases have continued without letup. During the ten years extending into the first half of the 1970s, they coexisted with the rapid growth of the economy. They did not impede rapid growth, but they did serve to dampen enthusiasm for economic growth. The shadow of rising prices lay behind the substitution of a Medium-Term Economic Plan for the National Income Doubling Plan.

9

An Interlude in Rapid Growth

Plant and Equipment Investment Adjustments

In reaction to the brisk plant and equipment investment during the Iwato boom, the rate of expansion in that area dropped off in the first half of the 1960s, effectively cancelling out any sense of prosperity. Sustained by personal consumption and government expenditures, however, the economic growth rate remained high, as before. As Table 9.1 shows, from 1951 to 1970 periods of upsurge in plant and equipment investment and periods in which government expenditure and personal consumption increased alternated every five years. During 1962–64 the labor market continued to tighten, the rate at which wages were increasing rose, and consumer prices began to climb. These were the conditions responsible for the considerable acclaim accorded the theory of the pattern transition period.

A Brief Improvement in Business Conditions

The distinctive feature of this period with its economic fluctuations was the short-lived nature of the revival of prosperity. The business upturn of 1955–56 lasted for 31 months, and that of 1959–60 for 42 months, but the upturn in 1963 lasted only 24 months (Economic Planning Agency, "Keiki kijun hizuke" [Reference Dates of Business Cycles]).

Thus, the fact that the period of rising prosperity was brief corresponds to the fact that the first half of the 1960s was in a downswing of the plant and equipment investment cycle. According to business cycle theory, during the downswing of the major cycle (Juglar cycle), the minor cycle (Kitchin cycle) is short and lacks vitality. 1963 was a textbook example of this kind of development.

Of course, the realities of individual business cycles are complex and diverse, and they are not always amenable to categorization according to a formula. The business upturn of 1963 was no exception: a number

Table 9–1. Composition and Rate of Growth of Gross National
        Expenditure

(%)

	Component Ratio (Nominal)					Growth Rate (Real)			
	1951	55	60	65	70	55/51	60/55	65/60	70/65
Gross National Expenditure	100	100	100	100	100	8.2	8.7	9.7	11.6
Personal Consumption	60.2	63.7	55.9	56.8	51.4	10.0	7.7	8.9	9.2
Government Expenditure	16.6	16.5	16.3	18.5	16.8	2.6	6.0	10.5	7.9
Plant & Equipment Investment	11.4	10.8	19.6	15.3	19.8	8.7	22.5	8.7	21.1

Source: "Kokumin shotoku tōkei" [National Income Statistics].

of special conditions contributed to its early demise—for example, a low balance of payments ceiling and a pronounced increase in consumer prices. However, the impression that the business upturn at that time was an interim rally backed up by an easing of monetary conditions cannot be gainsaid, and it is certain that the business recovery itself was not very strong.

Actually, the monetary relaxation and money supply increase in 1963 were striking. After a 17% increase in 1962, bank lending expanded 27% in 1963. The discount rate was lowered four times, and the average contracted lending rate of interest for all banks dropped from 8.24% in October of 1962 to 7.67% in February of 1964. The money supply increased by 35% in 1963, and the Marshallian k rose at one stroke from its previously maintained level of around 27% to 32% in 1963 (Table 9–2).

Why did such an increase in the money supply occur? Supply-side conditions were such that banks' ratios of deposits to loans were less than healthy, and the fall of interest rates in the short-term money market was a limited phenomenon. One can only say that the phenomenal expansion in bank lending was a temporary change in bank behavior. In concrete terms, the fierce battle for market position among the leading banks competing to reach the level of about a trillion yen in deposits became linked with competition in lending after the abolition of Bank of Japan window guidance. Also at work here was the lack of experience directly following adoption of the New Monetary Adjustment System, which will be described below.

On the demand side, plant and equipment spending remained essentially constant among the large firms while there was, by contrast,

Table 9–2. Financial Trends in the First Half of the 1960s

End of Calendar Year	Money Supply		Bank Lending Nationwide		Corporate Inter-firm Credit (Credit Granted)		Marshallian k
	Money Stock (¥trillions)	Growth Rate (%)	Out-standing Balance (¥trillions)	Growth Rate (%)	Out-standing Balance (¥trillions)	Growth Rate (%)	(%)
1960	4.2	(20.6)	8.2	(20.3)	7.3	(19.2)	27.1
61	4.9	(17.9)	9.8	(19.4)	10.3	(40.4)	25.7
62	5.8	(11.8)	11.5	(17.7)	12.4	(20.7)	27.4
63	7.8	(34.9)	14.5	(26.7)	15.8	(27.5)	31.9
64	8.8	(12.9)	16.8	(15.6)	17.0	(8.2)	30.4

Sources: (1) From "Honpō keizai tōkei" [Economic Statistics for the Nation].

(2) Money stock figures employ data from money supply tables; figures on interfirm credit are taken from flow-of-funds tables.

Note: Off-the-record loans are unadjusted.

a striking demand for such funds among small and medium-sized firms and in the distribution sector. During the decade of rapid growth from 1955 to 1964, a backlog of unsatisfied demand had been accumulating in these sectors, which had been left short of funds by the large firms' voracious appetite for capital. Small firms' modernization and labor-saving investments consisted of housing and welfare benefits for employees (at least in part a response to a shortage of workers), reorganization of distribution channels, building and remodelling of stores, and so on.

However, lending did not grow in response to "real demand" alone. A look at business firms' overall finances in 1963 shows that (1) increases in firms' liquidity (funds on hand), (2) increases in inventories of manufactured goods and distributors' inventories, and (3) the expansion of interfirm credit were conspicuous. Interfirm credit for all corporations combined came to about ¥16 trillion, a figure whose size rivals total bank lending or total sales volume of all corporations. In expectation of a relaxation of monetary conditions, firms would themselves hold unsold inventories, or would engage in "high-pressure sales" to the financial groups using interfirm credit. (These sales would become the "unsold inventories" of those who had been the objects of the "hard sell.") The expansion of a credit network in this way gave rise to misgivings: although the practice supported the boom of the moment, an end to easy monetary conditions and a business downturn would completely transform the situation; there were fears that a chain reaction of bankruptcies would follow, exacerbating the psychology of economic contraction. These fears were partially realized in the course of the 1965 recession, which was accompanied by large-scale bankruptcies.

The economic fluctuations of the first half of the 1960s extended the technological revolution and modernization, until then limited to large firms, to small enterprises and the distribution sector as well, laying the groundwork for the growth that followed. At the same time, these fluctuations also elicited some short-term, artificial stopgaps in the process of adjusting to the decline in plant and equipment investment and prepared the way for deeper, more far-reaching adjustments, liquidations, and contractions in the next recession.[1]

A larger-scale example of the same thing can be observed in the period between the First World War and the Great Depression. More recently, fluctuations similar to those of 1963 are discernible for 1953, exactly ten years earlier, and in 1973 as well, ten years later. In 1973 the growth rate of the Japanese economy as a whole was already beginning to slow, but in response to the artificial stimulus of the "rebuilding the archipelago" boom, firms nevertheless expanded in such areas as plant and equipment investment and in hiring. The false start at that time protracted and intensified the subsequent adjustment process.

Monetary Adjustment and the Promotion of Designated Industries

The pause in rapid growth biased toward plant and equipment investment gave rise to some soul-searching by the industrial and financial "system" that had supported this growth. It is often said that Japan's rapid growth was supported by the "Japan, Inc." system: overborrowing; window guidance (restraints by the central bank on city bank lending); financial ties within the *keiretsu* groups of firms; discriminatory allocation of Treasury loans and investments; closeknit, hand-in-glove relationships between the major firms and the bureaucracy; and so on. The industrial and financial arrangements that gave substance to this "Japan, Inc." image had already taken shape during the period of take-off into economic growth in the first half of the 1950s. In the common view, Japan, Inc., in this form consistently dominated the rapid-growth period for its duration. In this author's view, however, "Japan Inc." was not all of a piece, and, moreover, it did not provide decisive support for rapid growth. Rather, this institutional structure

---

[1] See the analysis in the 1964 Economic White Paper (*Keizai hakusho*).

was forced to fundamentally transform itself in the process of rapid growth; if it had not, it would have lost its effectiveness as a mechanism for stimulating growth. In the reevaluation of the "system" during the first half of the 1960s, there were those who recognized this flexibility, there were those who did not, and there were also those who urged that use of the system be intensified. Thus, this process of self-examination was translated into reality as a tangible new system; but, sadly, it also miscarried.

In October 1962 the Bank of Japan Policy Committee decided to implement a "New Monetary Adjustment System" along with a lowering of the discount rate. In April 1963 the Monetary System Research Council put together its "Report on the Correction of Overloans." The overloan phenomenon began with efforts to offset, via Bank of Japan lending, the strain imposed on the raising of private capital by compulsory balancing of the budget as called for under the Dodge Plan. It became a problem when increases in lending exceeded increases in bank deposits. A long debate was subsequently conducted over the significance of overlending and a corrective policy for it. The details need not detain us here, but suffice it to say that agreement was achieved between the pro-overloan and anti-overloan factions on the two principles that (1) it is necessary for the Bank of Japan to provide currency for growth; but (2) since the distinction between this process and lending becomes lost when it is carried out as a part of Bank of Japan lending activities, it should instead be taken care of in market operations.[2] Overloans were not, as the popular "Japan, Inc." view held, beneficial for rapid growth and for monetary control by the Bank of Japan as well. Precisely because they were not, they had to be replaced by the New Monetary Adjustment System, which imposed ceilings on borrowing from the central bank.

However, the New Monetary Adjustment System was not smoothly managed from the start, either. After the system was adopted, the money supply increased sharply in 1963, cutting short the business upturn. Adding to the financial confusion during this period were the policy authorities' abolition of window guidance in their zealous overidealization of the functioning of the New Monetary Adjustment System; the fierce competition for deposits among banks that was opened by the end of window guidance; and premature expectations of monetary restraint and future balance of payments instability,

---

[2] Owing to the underdeveloped character of Japan's commercial paper and bond markets, Bank of Japan securities purchasing operations could not be termed "open-market" operations, but were conducted on the basis of administered prices in a managed market until 1972. See Suzuki, 1980: 32–33; Ch. 11.

ironically induced by the overhasty lowering of interest rates. Despite the many problems at the beginning, however, the New Monetary Adjustment System, which got off to a less than smooth start, ultimately became established as the primary channel for supplying currency, having weathered the national bond issue and the reopening of the bond circulation market in 1965.

With regard to the financing of business firms, many take the view, in accordance with the popular "Japan, Inc." stereotype, that firms' overborrowing strengthens the banks' control over industry, and that competition among banks is linked to excess competition in plant and equipment investment in industry. However, two aspects of the actual circumstances after the beginning of rapid growth argue for a revision of this popular image. First, during the process of rapid growth, firms' ability to finance out of retained profits was on the whole strengthened, to judge by the balance between savings and investment alone; in growth-sector firms in particular, the ratio of equity capital was rising. Second, during the period of rapid growth the *keiretsu* finance framework was relaxed, primarily for the growth firms, which exploited to the hilt a diversity of methods for elbowing their way into the *keiretsu* and raising funds, capitalizing on the competition among the banks (refer to Table 7–3). Miyazaki Yoshikazu (1977) has recently advanced the idea that the self-financed type of firm has also appeared in Japan; but it must be pointed out that a large gap exists between this assertion and Miyazaki's "one-settism" hypothesis of the financial groupings' workings. Would not self-financing have been impossible if the equity firms had attempted to seize upon rapid growth in the stereotypical finance capital fashion—not an undertaking to be achieved in a single day in any case? Moreover, contrary to the so-called excess competition theory of that time, Komiya Ryūtarō, Takenaka Kazuo, and others have assessed the performance of Japan's interfirm competition as generally good (Komiya, 1972; Takenaka, 1962).

However, the one-settism theory was widely supported in the 1960s. While on the one hand taking advantage of the *keiretsu* relationships between the banks and business firms, the government on the other hand intervened to correct the abuses of excess competition in industry arising therefrom, making repeated attempts to create a new industrial structure. Of these efforts, the one to stir the most controversy was the Draft Law for the Promotion of Designated Industries. The Designated Industries Law was inspired by the French concept of economic concert—government and businesses undertaking industrial regulation as equal partners. Japan's Designated Industries Law was rejected because it smacked too strongly of bureaucratic control. But what came afterward were the ideas embodied in the Economic and Social Development Plan (1967), which, under the threat of capital liberalization and in the shadow of the 1965 recession, promoted, on grounds of efficiency, business mergers, under business leadership but with the assistance of the government.

Growing Medium-Sized Firms, the Distribution Revolution, and the New Industrial Cities

Plant and equipment investment by the major firms stagnated, but personal consumption expanded and government expenditures increased; and, as rapid growth continued, demand for labor increased. The macro theory of supply and demand says that in such a situation there is continuous movement toward a dissolution of the dual structure, which is natural owing to the fact that the dual structure is more a result of supply and demand relationships than of systemic and structural factors. In the process of fulfilling this macro theory of supply and demand, individual entrepreneurs are required to innovate, and this infuses the economy and the society with dynamism.

If the heroes of the growth of the 1950s were the leaders of Japan's big businesses, the heroes of the 1960s were those who shouldered responsibility for innovation in the growing middle-tier firms and in the distribution sector. A common image of the dual structure is one in which, with a handful of giant corporations towering above them, a multitude of tiny firms swarm below; but the continuation of rapid growth spurred innovation in small firms and produced a layer of medium-sized companies that filled the gap between the giants and the midgets.

The 1957 Economic White Paper discussed the dual structure in the following terms: "In our non-modern sectors, we will see that it is made profitable to manage middle-sized companies, the proportion of which is especially low in our country; strengthening such companies should be stressed in making policy." The 1960 Economic White Paper stated, "It is time for the machinery industry, whose market is in the private sector, to lead the development of industry." Noting the strength of small enterprises in the parts industry, the White Paper pointed out: "Hundreds of small and medium-sized parts makers have been incorporated into *keiretsu* groupings with giant assembly plants at their apexes, forming a pyramid-shaped production system. The mass production of such things as automobiles and household electric appliances is swelling the number of small and medium producers, increasing their earnings, and, accordingly, promoting the rational-

Table 9–3.   Distribution of Firms by Rate of Growth

(%)

			Increase in Sales from 1956 to 1960				
			Less than doubled	1.0 –1.4 fold	1.5 –2.0 fold	2.5 –4.9 fold	More than 5-fold
Listed Companies	(247 firms)	100.0	2.4	26.3	48.6	22.3	0.4
Higher ranked	(61 firms)	100.0	0	39.4	44.2	16.4	0
Lower ranked	(61 firms)	100.0	3.3	19.7	52.4	23.0	1.6
Over-the-counter Companies (151 firms)		100.0	4.0	14.6	43.0	33.8	4.6

Source: From Kosai, 1961.

Notes: (1) Listed companies are those in the manufacturing industry at the March and September closings with capital of ¥8 billion or more.

(2) Higher (lower) ranked firms are an average of one-fourth of the higher (lower) ranking firms in each industry.

(3) Over-the-counter companies (later the second class of listed companies) excludes 31 firms for which data were ambiguous or unknown.

ization and modernization of production plant and equipment." Going a step further, the 1961 Economic White Paper went so far as to emphasize the existence and development of "independent specialist producers," who advanced beyond the confines of this type of *keiretsu* framework (Table 9–3).

In fact, the Tokyo Stock Exchange's opening of a secondary market in 1961 established a public route to raising capital for the middle-sized growth firms, and by the end of 1963 the number of companies on the Exchange came to 583. Besides the parts makers who had become independent specialist producers, these medium-sized companies included plant producers making efficient use of specialized technology and consumer goods producers who expanded markets in step with the growing diversity of consumer life. A high degree of manufacturing was the common technological feature of many of these firms. On the basis of a solid case study, Nakamura Shūichirō identified a category of "growing medium-sized firms" (*chūken kigyō*) that rose above the multitude of small and medium firms and called them "the concentrated expression of the transformation into a mass society" and "one of the bases for establishing postwar democratic society" (Nakamura, 1964).

In tandem with mass production and mass consumption, distribution channels must also be put on a mass basis. A distribution revolution

Table 9–4.   Business Conditions of Retail Firms

		1960	1966	1972
	Department Stores	309	364	508
Number of Stores	Supermarkets	—	1,633	5,274
	Small & Medium Retail Stores	1,288,292	1,373,397	1,427,182
Annual Sales	Department Stores	0.4	1.0	2.7
(¥ trillions)	Supermarkets	—	0.4	2.0
	Small & Medium Retail Stores	3.9	9.3	18.6
Area of Sales	Department Stores	1,525	2,256	4,363
Floor (1000s sq.	Supermarkets	—	998	3,243
meters)	Small & Medium Retail Stores	29,556	41,587	54,418

Source: From "Shōgyō tōkei hyō" [Table of Commercial Statistics].
Quoted in Hayashi, 1962.

theory along these lines flowered in the 1960s.[3] In addition to being
a period of instability for the distribution industry and of advances
in the provision of distribution channels for consumer durables such
as automobiles and electric machinery and appliances, the first half of
the 1960s was the take-off period for Japan's mass sales industry.
Japan's first self-service store is said to have been Kinokuniya, which
opened its doors in Tokyo's Aoyama district in 1953, but today's
representative mass distribution companies established their basic
strategies in the first half of the 1960s (Table 9–4).

With the coming of the first half of the 1960s, store managers were
moving on the basis of their own experience in the direction of
supermarkets, and as it became increasingly possible to go abroad
freely, they gained a grasp of the essence of discount stores overseas, which in essence is the process of transformation into a regular chain. Supermarkets already employed the technology of
self-service, but they came to realize the importance of chain stores
which had become awakened to consumer sovereignty (Nakauchi,
1969: 95).

Coming home from an overseas observation tour of distribution

___

[3] Hayashi Shūji's 1962 book *Ryūtsū kakumei* [The Distribution Revolution] which
had gone through 50 printings by 1977, aroused an extensive debate over the
author's theory that wholesalers would eventually disappear. Hayashi did not
consider distributors useless, however (Hayashi, 1962: 170).

systems in 1961, Itoh Masatoshi, President of the Itoh-Yōkadō Company, remodelled the Kita-Senjū store, in a Tokyo suburb, into a self-service discount department store; at the same time he opened a store in Akabane and set up a regular chain system. President Nakauchi Isao of Daiei Incorporated, moved by President Kennedy's message at the twenty-fifth anniversary celebration of the U.S. National Supermarket Association, determined to establish Daiei as "the homemaker's store." With the establishment of its Nishinomiya headquarters as a start, in 1963 Daiei began to emerge as a full-fledged self-service discount department store. The opening of Seibu Stores' Takadanobaba branch, "the first self-service discount department store in the capital city of Tokyo," took place in September 1962. The announcement that Seibu Stores would launch a chain of supermarkets and super stores came in April of 1963. In November of that year the four companies Serufuhatoya, Okamoto Stores, Yamato-Kobayashi Stores, and Erupisu merged to form Nichii. Already a considerable entity at its inception, with ¥70 million in capital and ¥2.8 billion in trade annually, and with 350 empoyees whose age averaged 19.9 years, Nichii planned to enlarge its sales in ten years to an annual ¥100 billion. In reading the success stories of these volume sales distribution companies, the most moving element is the image one gets of the managers as human beings. They seem to have been the flotsam and jetsam of society: former soldiers, elementary school teachers who resigned at the time of the defeat, veterans of the student movement; their numbers included followers of Mao Tse-Tung, of Uchimura Kanzō's idea of a churchless Christianity, of the old merchants' code, etc.

We saw earlier that the Income Doubling Plan was based on industrialization that centered primarily on the Pacific Coast belt, but the beginning of the 1960s saw the dispersion of industry to other regions. The designation of new industrial cities precipitated intense competition among regions. Passage of the Basic Agriculture Law, which sought to promote income equilibrium via broadening of production options, also took as its point of departure the perception that economic growth was continuing to permeate ever more broadly and deeply into every sector of the economy. (It is noteworthy, however, that the farmers' movement actually had the side effect of bolstering income demands.)

Thus, the path leading up from the foothills into the higher reaches of the mountain of economic growth broadened further still as the first half of the 1960s began, and became the base for the long-term prosperity of the latter half of that decade. Nevertheless, even with the middle-tier high-growth firms, and even with the help of the distribution revolution, the path was not a smooth and level one. From 1964 to

1965 a number of the growing medium-sized firms were driven to the wall by harsh circumstances and experienced hardships not encountered in the *keiretsu:* the bankruptcy of Sun Wave Cabinet Making was an example. Even distribution was swept by a stormy shakeout; it came to be said, "Here today and gone tomorrow—that's a supermarket for you." The mania for the new industrial cities suddenly cooled, and agriculture's dependence on price supports was growing. In all that, however, the high-growth sectors continued to grow, and became the force for changing the Japanese economy.

The Economic Superpower Emerges
The decade from 1955 to the mid-1960s was an era of phenomenally rapid growth for the Japanese economy, and historically it was a period in which Japan's international position was conspicuously enhanced. In 1963 Japan became one of the International Monetary Fund Article 8 countries,[4] and the following year it joined Organisation for Economic Cooperation and Development (OECD), in recognition of its status as an advanced nation. In the fall of 1964, when the growth decade that began in 1955 was drawing to an end, a swift and somewhat awesome succession of events occurred that gives an indication of the self-confidence of Japan the economic superpower.

On September 7 of that year, the Tokyo General Meeting of the IMF and the World Bank, with 1800 representatives from 102 nations participating, opened in the Heian and Chitose rooms of the Hotel Okura. Prime Minister Ikeda, who gave the keynote address, emphasized that "the Income Doubling Plan has given the nation self-awareness and self-confidence." "With the 19 postwar years of rapid growth," he said, "Japan's national income is approaching the Western European level; we are attempting to do in 20 postwar years what we were unable to do in the 80 years before the war, and what made this possible are the efforts of our people and international cooperation." He urged the developing nations to take heart from this experience and proposed that international assistance be increased. This turned out to be Prime Minister Ikeda's last public speech. His hoarse voice betrayed the progress of his illness, and two days later, on September 9, the Prime Minister entered the National Cancer Center.

---

[4] Nations that had, like Japan, joined the IMF under the postwar "transition period" conditions of Article 14 and then had decided to accept the obligations of Article 8 were encouraged in the early 1960s to convert to Article 8 status, which implied that they would assume full responsibility for, e.g., refraining from exchange controls and maintaining full convertibility, as would be expected of an advanced industrial nation. Refer to Horsefield (1969).

On October 1, 1964, the Japan National Railways' Tōkaidō Bullet Train—the Shinkansen—opened for business. The Hikari, which travels between Tokyo and Osaka in three hours at speeds up to 200 kilometers per hour, symbolizes the extent to which the Japanese economy had caught up with the advanced nations in the century since the coming of Japan's first steam locomotive. Plans for the Bullet Train had been announced in July 1958, at about the time the transportation bottleneck along the Tokyo-Osaka route began to be pronounced. Criticism was heard to the effect that investing in railroads in the age of the automobile was an anachronism like the Battleship *Yamato*, but, as the then Chief Accounting Officer of the Finance Ministry, Shikano Yoshio, later revealed to the author, the decision to adopt the plan had been taken on the basis of calculations of transport capacity per unit of land area used. JNR President Sōgō Shinji announced the adoption of wide-gauge tracks standing before the grave of Gotō Shimpei.[5]

During the six years from 1958 until the Shinkansen finally commenced operations, the JNR resolved a number of thorny technological problems involving the tracks and wheels, the wiring and the pantograph, control of the train, etc., as well as the political problems involved in buying up right of way from 50,000 different landowners (Kakumoto, 1964). At the front of the stairs to the Bullet Train platform in Tokyo Station is mounted a commemorative plaque on which is inscribed, in both English and Japanese, "The New Tōkaidō Line, a product of the wisdom and effort of the Japanese people." One is a bit embarrassed by the somewhat sentimental expression, but these were most likely the true feelings of the Japan National Railways, which had completed a great undertaking. The Bullet Train's success was responsible for making construction of a transportation network a pillar of the following year's Plan for Rebuilding the Archipelago. On the other hand, ironically enough, JNR went into the red for the first time in the year of the Shinkansen opening; moreover, opposition to the line arose over noise pollution.

Then on October 10, 1964, came the opening of the Tokyo Olympics, for which the the Bullet Train had been rushed to completion. The five Olympic rings inscribed in the sky over Tokyo by Air Self-Defense Force planes floated a long time as they faded away in the clear autumn sky. Just as with the Bullet Train, there were those who thought the

---

[5] Gotō Shimpei (1857-1929) had been president of the South Manchurian Railway, Home Minister, Foreign Minister, and Mayor of Tokyo. The decision to use wide-gauge tracks was a historic departure from Japan's longstanding policy of using only narrow gauge on the theory that such railroads could not be taken over and exploited by enemy powers that used wide gauge. —Trans.

Olympics a waste of energy, but as the opening of the Games approached, enthusiasm rose to fever pitch. The conformist instincts of the Japanese, their curiosity about foreigners and a desire to "put on appearances" were at work; at the same time, however, there was also undeniably a strong desire to show off at home and abroad the fruits of the postwar recovery. After the defeat it was, "Industrialization is a manifestation of the self-assertion of the Japanese people"; now, the feeling was: "The leap has been made from a backward agricultural society to a modern industrial society." It is precisely this way of thinking that made it a psychological necessity that at the end of the decade from 1955 to 1964 (the "Shōwa 30s") a climatic event like the Tokyo Olympics be held.

With militaristic ambitions cast aside, prosperity in peacetime became the refrain of the day. Was not this goal, however, pursued in a self-sacrificial spirit little different from that of wartime? Director Ichikawa Kon's splendid documentary film of the Tokyo Olympics begins with the rebuilding of old Tokyo and reaches its climax with the heartbeat and breathing of Sakai Yoshinori, the torchbearer, as he ascends that long, long flight of stairs. Do we not see captured and revealed here too, like it or not, the same Japanese character—*plus ça change, plus c'est la même chose.*

Aside from its value as symbol and spectacle, the Olympics also had an economic aspect. Expenses incurred in preparation for the Olympics totalled ¥970 billion, including ¥380 billion for construction of the Shinkansen. ¥175 billion for roads and ¥149.5 billion for subway construction changed the face of greater Tokyo; ¥15.7 billion went into facilities for the athletic competitions, and ¥11.1 billion into construction of the Tone aqueduct in order to alleviate the water shortage. In the private sector, a remarkable number of hotels were built. Demand related to the Olympics came to 0.9 % of gross national expenditure for the years from 1961 to 1964. This was considerably higher than the scale of demand incurred from 1967 to 1970 in connection with the Osaka World Exposition—0.5 % of gross national expenditure (Economic Planning Agency, 1970).

During the two weeks of the Olympics, conditions at home and abroad continued to change. The Soviet Union startled the world twice, sending a three-man satellite into space on October 12 and on the 15th relieving Premier Khrushchev of his post. On the 16th China successfully conducted nuclear weapons development tests, and the Labour Party was victorious in the general elections in England. On October 25, the day after the Olympics ended, Prime Minister Ikeda announced his intent to resign due to his illness, and Satō Eisaku, who advocated promoting social development, began forming the first of his three Cabinets.

Amid the clamor of the Olympic festivities, out of nowhere rumors of a post-Games recession began to circulate. As business bankruptcies continued to increase, the securities market did some very low-altitude hedge-hopping, with the Dow average at ¥1200. The heights of merriment dissolved into gloom. While the excitement over the Olympics had yet to cool, the 1965 recession was arriving on nearby street corners.

10

The Economic Superpower

Post-Recession Prosperity

The second half of the 1960s was a period of rapid growth without precedent, a time of record-setting long-term prosperity. The real economic growth rate was even higher than that of the decade from 1955 to 1964, which had been termed rapid growth, reaching an average of nearly 12%. The period of economic upturn lasted from the fall of 1965 to the summer of 1970, a total of 57 months. During that time the rate of consumer price increases, at 5.5%, was lower than that during the first half of the 1960s (6.3%). From 1966 to 1968 in particular, annual price advances were confined to the 4% level. The job market became a complete sellers' market. The ratio of effective job offers to applicants exceeded one in 1967, and the economy was thrust into a state of hyper-full employment. As balance of payments deficits became a thing of the past, the country began to enjoy a comfortable margin in its foreign exchange reserves (Table 10–1).

Why did rapid growth recur at this time? That it did seems strange, at least if one judges by conditions at the time the process began. Aware that the 1965 recession was viewed as the severest one in the postwar period, many people believed that it marked the conclusive downturn away from growth. Instead of rapid growth, the Satō Eisaku Cabinet which succeeded Ikeda's emphasized social development, stable economic growth, and welfare measures to help the less privileged in society. Under such conditions, how was the economy able to shift into ultra-rapid growth at rates exceeding 10%? In the explanation lies one key to explaining the economic trends of the latter half of the 1960s.

With the lowering of the discount rate early in July 1965, monetary austerity was lifted, and it was thought that the economy, which had not seemed much affected by the preceding monetary stringency, would without further vagaries turn toward recovery. However, the real

Table 10–1.   Main Economic Indicators for the Latter Half of the 1960s

Year	Real Growth Rate	Rate of Increase in Consumer Prices	Ratio of Effective Job Openings to Applicants	Balance of Payments (Current Transactions Balance)	Foreign Exchange Reserves
	(%)	(%)	(%)	($ millions)	($ 100 millions)
1960–65	9.7	6.3	0.66	−205	18.6
1965–70	11.6	5.5	0.96	1,310	29.7
65	5.7	6.4	0.64	1,019	21.0
66	11.1	4.7	0.73	996	20.7
67	13.1	4.2	1.00	−311	20.0
68	12.7	4.8	1.12	1,473	28.9
69	11.0	6.7	1.30	2,044	34.9
70	10.4	7.2	1.41	2,349	43.9

recession came afterwards. This is an example of a long-term and irregular monetary policy lag, one which manifested its unexpected influence at unexpected times. As more concrete advance warnings of the arrival of this recession, one may point to the bankruptcies of Sun Wave Cabinet Making (December 1964), Sanyō Special Steel (March 1965), and Yamaichi Securities (May 1965); these bankruptcies caused a contraction in interfirm credit, which had been expanding earlier, agitation in the stock market, and a withering of transactions in the goods and services economy, due to the uncertainty over credit. In this way the medium-term prosperity based on the monetary expansion of 1963 exacted severe reprisals.

Yet another tangible clue to the coming of this recession was that tax revenues were insufficient due to stagnating business conditions, and government spending was held down in order to balance the budget (Table 10–2). Typical of fiscal behavior at that time was a proposal to withhold 10 % of the budget from disbursement owing to inadequate revenues. A Cabinet council actually reached verbal agreement on such a scheme on June 1. Albeit on a smaller scale, this was the same type of blunder made by Herbert Hoover in 1931: increasing taxes in order to maintain a fiscal balance between revenues and expenditures during the Great Depression.

On the other hand, one may describe the eventual response to this unexpectedly severe recession as shrewd. Not only did the Bank of Japan provide financing to Kyodo Securities, which was supporting stock prices by a buying operation; it also provided special financing to Yamaichi Securities, preventing a credit crisis. At an economic policy meeting on July 17, 1965, after a decision to cancel the previous

Table 10–2. Fiscal and Monetary Indicators for the Latter Half of the 1960s

Year	Annual General Account Expenditures at Closing (¥ 100 millions)	Public Bonds Issued (closing figure) (¥ 100 millions)	Tax Reduction (for first year of reduction) (¥ 100 millions)	Money Supply (¥ trillions)	Discount Rate (month)	(%)	Nominal GNP (¥ trillions)
1965	37,230	1,972	4,647	25.6	Jan.	6.21	32.8
					Apr.	5.84	
					June	5.48	
66	44,591	6,655	1,190	29.7		—	38.4
67	51,130	7,093	7,353	34.1	Sept.	5.84	45.3
68	59,370	4,620	9,476	39.4	Jan.	6.21	53.3
					Aug.	5.84	
69	69,178	4,126	11,905	46.6	Sept.	6.25	62.3
70	81,876	3,471	13,771	55.0	Oct.	6.00	73.0
1965–70 Growth Rate	17.0%	—	—	16.5%		—	17.4%

Sources: "Nihon zaisei yōran" [Handbook of Japanese Public Finance], "Keizai yōran" [Economic Handbook], etc.

month's withholding of 10% of the budget from disbursement, the government decided to make preparations for issuing government bonds. Abandoning the Medium-Term Economic Plan, which declared that no public bonds would be issued, the Satō Cabinet began 1966 with a special issue of public bonds.

Thus ended the balanced budget finance that had been in effect for 15 years since the Dodge Plan. Call them shrewd, call them unprincipled, but Japan's conservative politics were conducted pragmatically and opportunistically.

The Satō Cabinet criticized rapid growth and emphasized social development and stable growth instead; but included in this concept was also a new policy mix of tax cuts and public spending. Public finance for 1966 turned out to consist of a large-scale, countercyclical budget that called for ¥4.3 trillion in general account expenditures for the year, ¥730 billion in public construction bonds, and a national tax cut of ¥310 billion. Amid the pessimistic economic forecasts at the time, it was thought that this would be just the thing to achieve stable growth, but what it actually evoked was the supergrowth of the latter half of the 1960s.

Even so, the initial doctrine of stable growth cannot be said to have come to nothing at all. Throughout the latter half of the 1960s money supply expansion was held to 16.4%, and the ratio of money stock to money national income (Marshallian k) showed a downward trend. The memory of the failure of money expansion in 1963 was still alive. This stabilization of the money supply coincided with the settling down of consumer prices and is presumed to have been the cause. On the fiscal side, in 1967 and 1968 there was pressure to do away with fiscal rigidity, and a policy of gradually reducing the national debt was adopted. When flourishing private plant and equipment investment demand is assumed along with prudent fiscal and monetary management rooted in the stable growth doctrine, the government's job is considered to be that of sustaining the business upturn. The other side of the coin was that all this exacted a price in the form of a lag induced in the public sector relative to the private sector in such things as social capital and social security—a lag which was contrary to the original goal of social development.

Thus, in the latter half of the 1960s, between the reality of the recession economy and its aftermath and the ideal of stable growth, the era of Japan as an economic superpower began.

Economic Power and Internationalization

The Riddle of the Acceleration of Growth

Apart from the policy factors sustaining prosperity, which we will set aside for the time being, the high growth of the latter half of the 1960s was also sustained by private demand, primarily plant and equipment for business firms (Table 10–3). Expansion of plant and equipment investment exceeded 20% annually, ranking with that from 1955 to 1960, and the expansion of exports and personal consumption expenditures exhibited a rising trend. What were the primary causes of this acceleration in growth?

The rapid growth during the ten years following the war can be explained by the economic recovery, and that of the next ten years in terms of the swift development of the technological revolution. Leaving aside the question of how they are supported quantitatively, these characterizations synthesize the impressions and direct perceptions of many people. We saw in Chapter 7 just how magnificent the technological revolution around 1960 was. New durables such as television and electric refrigerators, new producers' durables such as silicon steel plates and polyethylene, and new modes of production such as thermal

Table 10–3.   Fluctuations in Real Gross National Expenditure

(¥ trillions, %)

	Year	Personal Consumption Expenditure	Private Housing Investment	Private Plant & Equipment	Government Expenditure	Exports	Imports
	1965	23.8	2.5	5.5	8.4	4.1	−3.6
	66	25.9	2.7	6.7	9.0	4.7	−4.1
	67	28.6	3.3	8.6	9.8	5.0	−5.0
	68	31.3	3.7	10.6	10.6	6.2	−5.6
	69	34.3	4.4	13.1	11.0	7.4	−6.5
	70	36.9	4.8	14.4	12.0	8.6	−7.7
Component	1965	57.3	6.1	13.3	25.5	10.0	−8.6
Ratio	70	51.2	6.6	20.0	16.7	11.9	−10.7
Growth	1955–60	7.7	14.5	22.5	4.9	12.3	16.9
Rate	60–65	8.9	17.4	8.9	10.6	13.2	12.5
	65–70	9.2	13.5	21.1	7.5	15.8	16.7

electric power plants, strip mills, and transfer machines were developed by the truckload during this period.

By contrast, one has the inescapable impression that the technological revolution of the latter half of the 1960s somehow smacks of tea brewed from old leaves. Five-hundred-ton blast furnaces were turned into 5000-ton blast furnaces, and 50,000-ton ethylene plants became 300,000-ton ethylene plants. Although this was important, was it enough to sustain the rise in the annual rate of increase in economic productivity from 7.4% in 1955–60, to 10.4% in 1965–70? One can't help thinking that there is quite a gap between impressions and the figures, between macro and micro.

Careful scrutiny of both the macro data and the micro impressions should more or less fill this gap. Let us single out several points. First, the increase in productivity reflects not just technological progress, but labor-capital substitution and the advantages of scale as well. The years 1965 to 1970 were a period of phenomenal capital accumulation and market expansion in addition to being a period of technological progress.

Second, the weight of the growth sector was already increasing. In the Japanese economy productivity differentials by industrial sector were large. Because of this, the productivity of the economy as a whole rose, and economic growth was sustained as labor and capital shifted out of the low productivity sectors and into the high. This fact is well known; eventually the contribution to total growth made by this kind of shift decreases, but the industrial structure, with its differential sector weights, is an important condition in the initial stages of growth. Let us suppose that an economy consists of sectors A and B, with A growing at a rate of 10 % and B at 5 %. An economy in which the ratio of A to B is 1 to 4 is only growing at a rate of 6 %, but an economy in which this ratio is 4 to 1 is growing at 9 %. Since the weight of the high-growth sector increases, at a certain phase in the life cycle of growth, growth itself becomes the primary factor accelerating and thus continuing growth.

A third characteristic to be noted is the diffusion of the technological revolution. Whether it was a strip mill or a transfer machine, imported technology attracted the public's attention, and the introduction of each item was a spectacular affair. But what influenced average productivity was not just the efficiency of new products and brand-new plant and equipment, but the proportion they represented of all products and all production plant and equipment. The rate of productivity increase in the latter half of the 1960s was high in spite of the fact that technological innovations were less numerous than they had been in the past because the technological revolution was diffusing broadly and swiftly.

This diffusion of the technological revolution can be termed one primary factor in the shift noted above. However, there is also the velocity of the diffusion, an aspect depending on the diffusion's extent. Let us for a moment think of the technological revolution as having a path that can be traced by the same process as that used for contagious diseases. The appearance of new cases of a contagious disease depends on contact with the uninfected, so if we let n stand for the population and x for the number infected, the incidence of new cases dx/dt becomes $dx/dt = \beta x (n - x)$, where β is the rate of contact (a constant). This reaches a peak when $x = n/2$ (Bailey, 1964, Ch. 12). One may think of the tempo of diffusion of the technological revolution as being controlled by the same kind of mechanism.

Fourth, since the center of gravity of technological progress shifted away from hard areas and into soft, the presence or absence of a technological revolution probably became difficult for an outside observer to discern. For example, according to a productivity survey by the Labor Ministry, the heart of rationalization in the automobile industry from 1955 to 1964 was machining. During the decade from 1965 to 1974, rationalization shifted to the assembly process as a whole. In contrast to the productivity increases of the decade from 1955 to 1964 embodied in the introduction of such tangible items as giant presses and transfer machines, productivity increases in the decade from 1965 to 1974 are considered to have been produced by more impalpable changes like plant and equipment layout and process control (including the administration of subcontracting). Of course, such changes in systems and organizations were not inconsistent with plant and equipment investment on a massive scale, and in some aspects they were supported by it. Thus, this "soft" phase of the technological revolution brought to completion the move toward mass production.

Related to this is the swift rise in the quality of Japanese goods which was also a feature of the decade 1965–74. The reliability engineering developed in the U.S. in connection with military technology and space exploration was applied in Japan to machines and tools for private consumption. This process made itself felt as a strengthening of Japan's export competitiveness.

Mention must also be made in more concrete terms of something else that supported the economy's development in the latter half of the 1960s: development of the consumer durables industries, producing such universally desired products as automobiles, color television sets, and air conditioners. They were acknowledged as leading industries not only because of their relative importance in terms of output volume, but because they showcased the improved quality in industrial products. The "3-C" industries (named after the car, color TV, and air conditioner desired by every family) had a high relative weight in the economy. To tell the story of economic development in the latter half of the 1960s, however, one must not overlook the dramatic rise in agricultural productivity that took place against the background of a sudden 6% average annual decline in the farm population, the full-scale expansion of new distribution companies such as supermarkets; and so on.

One might summarize the foregoing more generally as follows. The main causes of economic growth were shifting away from exogenous, independent factors such as postwar reconstruction or the technological revolution toward the endogenous condition that growth occurs because growth is occurring; the growth rate was entering a stage in which its increases were autonomous and spontaneous. In the first half of the 1960s, although it was a time of "investment calling forth investment," investments were innovative, creating new industrial processes (thin steel sheets; the production of passenger cars). Investments in the latter half of the 1960s expanded these industrial conditions. The controlling factor here was the interaction with expansions in scale. This is the state of affairs that the inaccurate phrase "transformation into an economic superpower" attempted to convey.

The Impact of Internationalization

Internationalization is a dry word, but it was in vogue in the economic journalism and official documents (such as the Economic and Social Development Plan) of the latter half of the 1960s. Here we want to look at two international factors that were linked to the sustaining of economic growth: (1) changes in Japanese industry's rate of dependence on foreign trade, and (2) the way government and business dealt with capital liberalization.

The relationship between export trade and scale expansion has often been noted. The world market is obviously the largest there is, and it is in targeting this market that maximum advantages of scale are realized. When targeting only the domestic market, each industry must as it grows strike an internal balance based on the limits of demand. Export trade removes such constraints and facilitates a situation in which those industries capable of growth can grow to the limits of their capabilities. These are the conditions for strengthening export competitiveness in industries with increasing returns, in a large domestic market, and this competitiveness is still further fortified by entry into the world market. In growth industries economies of scale are easily realized, and expansions in scale increasingly strengthen international competitiveness, with the result that participation in the export market is expanded even more. High growth came to be sustained by this kind of cyclical interaction.

This analysis also applies to earlier periods, but it acquired decisive importance in the latter half of the 1960s. In terms of the national economic accounts, Japan's export dependence rose in the latter half of the 1960s, but this could not be termed particularly remarkable. In terms of export composition, however, export dependence on the part of the major firms and the heavy and chemical industries rose swiftly, while that of small firms and light industry was declining (Table 10–4). For the growth-led industries, the expansion of export markets had reached the point of being built into enterprise behavior. Inflation abroad due to the Vietnam War also reinforced Japan's international competitiveness. As firms faced the 1970s in such an environment, they were trying to raise their levels of export dependence ever higher (Economic Planning Agency, 1970).

If one considers export trade to have solved the problems of industries with increasing returns, then imports are what liberated these industries from raw materials constraints—that is, from the domination

Table 10–4. Changes in the Composition of Exports and Imports

(%)

	1965	1970
Proportion of exports consisting of light industrial products	31.9	22.4
Proportion of exports consisting of chemical and heavy industrial products	62.0	72.4
Rate of dependence on primary energy imports	66.2	83.5

of the law of diminishing returns. Alfred Marshall racked his brains over the problem of industries with increasing returns in the mature industrial economy, but it was David Ricardo who was concerned with constraints on the raw materials supply (the niggardliness of the land, the decline in its marginal productivity) in the process of industrialization. Ricardo's solution to this problem was the import trade. Let us recall that in the 1950s diminishing returns caused by high coal prices were real fetters on the Japanese economy. By contrast, Japan's rate of dependence on imports of raw materials and energy rose sharply in the latter half of the 1960s. Of the nation's primary energy, more than half was supplied domestically in 1960, and one-third was still so obtained in 1965. By 1970, however, the proportion domestically supplied had dropped to one-fifth (Table 10–4). In the 1960s, oil fields were discovered in rapid succession all over the world; synthetic chemistry also developed, and the terms of trade were favorable to the industrial nations (Japan's terms of trade index was 110.9 in 1960, 92.1 in 1965, and 100 in 1970). In 1960 OPEC (the Organization of Petroleum Exporting Countries) was formed with the intention of exercising cartel-like control over oil prices, but this effort, however successful it became later, was a failure at first.

The reappearance of rapid growth after the 1965 recession and the transformation into an economic superpower would have been unthinkable without the dramatic development of both export and import trade (and the attendant resolution of the problems of industries with increasing and with diminishing returns). With all that, however, as the 1960s drew to a close Japan's share of foreign markets in both exports and imports began to become controversial.

Inflation abroad due to the Vietnam War was also at work in the development of Japan's export trade. At the some time, the United States was coming under increasing pressure to defend the dollar following the introduction of the Interest Equalization Tax in 1963. Under these conditions, Japan–U.S. trade friction intensified. On the import side, there were negotiations on the expansion of imports of

Table 10–5. Particulars of the Liberalization of Capital

Date		Event
April	1964	Japan joins OECD.
July	67	First capital liberalization is implemented; Category 1 (50 % liberalization) consisting of 33 industrial categories, and Category 2 (100 % liberalization) consisting of 17 industrial categories (shipbuilding, iron & steel, etc.) approved.
March	69	Second capital liberalization implemented. Category 1 consisting of 160 industrial categories, and Category 2 consisting of 44 industrial categories approved.
September	70	Third capital liberalization implemented. Category 1 (447 industrial categories) and Category 2 (77 industrial categories) approved.
April	71	Capital liberalization of the automobile industry.
August	71	Fourth capital liberalization. Category 1, confirming to the exceptions-list formula (7 industrial categories), and Category 2 (151 industrial categories) approved.
August	74	Computers 50 % liberalized.
December	74	Real estate industry 100 % liberalized.
June	75	Small and medium-sized retailing 100 % liberalized.
December	75	Computers 100 % liberalized.
April	76	Data processing industry 100 % liberalized. (Exceptions list reduced to the four industrial categories: agriculture, forestry & fisheries; mining; petroleum; and leather & leather products.)

Source: Economic Planning Agency, "Gendai Nihon keizai no tenkai" [Development of the Contemporary Japanese Economy], Table 3–14.

passenger car engines and on the removal of residual import restrictions in 1968. With regard to exports, voluntary restrictions on steel were implemented in July of 1968 and textile negotiations began the following year (these would result in the adoption of voluntary restrictions in 1971). When all of this is added to the demands for capital liberalization, the impact of internationalization can be seen to have been reinforced still further.

Capital liberalization was not necessarily assumed in the postwar world order of IMF-GATT, etc., but as a result of the OECD (Organisation for Economic Cooperation and Development) capital liberalization principles, it came to be regarded as a duty of the advanced nations. When Japan joined OECD in 1964, it held back on capital liberalization, but implementation gradually became a matter of some urgency, and a basic policy on capital liberalization was formulated in June 1967 (Table 10–5). It so happened that this was the heyday of the multinational corporation, and there were apprehensions that Japan's growth industries (passenger cars, electric calculators, electrical parts, etc.) might become targets for absorption by the multinationals. While promoting price stabilization and social development, the Satō Cabinet's Economic and Social Development Plan (1967) at the same time pushed ahead with making the economy efficient—in the sense of counteracting excessive competition, via mergers and cooperation, as a means of coping with capital liberalization and strengthening firms' international competitiveness. The Plan's approach thus differs from that of the Law for the Promotion of Designated Industries with regard to the relationship between government and the private economy (see Chapter 9): under the Plan the government provided assistance while the private sector took the initiative.

The latter half of the 1960s was marked by waves of giant mergers, and the industry concentration ratio shifted out of its earlier decline into an upward climb (the Herfindahl index was 100.0 in 1960, 96.8 in 1965, and 110.1 in 1970). In the midst of a succession of mergers—three Mitsubishi heavy industries in 1964, Nissan Auto and Prince in 1965, Nisshō and Iwai in 1968, Ōji Paper and two other companies in 1969 (a planned merger that fell through), Daiichi Bank and Nihon Kangyō Bank in 1971—the greatest controversy arose when in 1969 the two steelmakers Yawata and Fuji signed a merger contract, obtained a consent decree from the Fair Trade Commission, and succeeded in launching the Japan Steel Corporation (Shin Nippon Seitetsu) in March of 1970. A number of economists—the "modern" economists, or structural reform faction of the Marxian economists, issued statements opposing the merger, and the Fair Trade Commission's review attracted great attention. This took place only three years before antibusiness sentiment erupted during the oil crisis and five years before the Anti-Monopoly Law was amended.

Thus, certainly, the extent of oligopoly in the Japanese economy grew somewhat. However it did not amount to a general upsetting of that special feature known as a flexible market system. The "disturbances" over capital liberalization and industrial reorganization, like others which often occur in the Japanese economy, did not leave many traces behind once they were over, and appear to have been no more than minor disturbances. However, perhaps they ended as simply incidents, not because the sense of crisis on which they were premised was necessarily mistaken, but because in dealing with the crises the Japanese economy displayed its superb capacity for turnarounds.

Although a great hue and cry was raised over the seeming concentration of economic power in the hands of a small elite, the economy did not move in accordance with every wish of these moguls, as is shown by the fact that the plan to consolidate the automobile producers at that time did not bear fruit. Productivity increases at a more grassroots level appear to have been the deciding factor in the economy. Be that as it may, the furor over mergers raises some interesting questions which still cannot be definitively answered: Are the inclination to create such commotions and the economy's superb adaptability somehow inseparably linked? Or do such overreactions themselves work in the direction of undermining the system's adaptability (do, for example, giant mergers before long produce price rigidity)?

As Rapid Growth Takes Root, the Seeds of Discontent Are Sown

The latter half of the 1960s was for the Japanese economy the period in which rapid growth took root.

As we have seen, the technological revolution which began in the mid-1950s now reached the peak of its diffusion and penetration. Firms, households, and the government had all come to behave as though economic growth were the natural course of things, and this further sustained economic growth. The boundless world market seemed to limitlessly guarantee continuation of the transformation into an economic superpower.

This means that, once the initial objective of overcoming poverty had been achieved, economic growth was made automatic, began to seem commonsensical, and was systematized. If the first decade after the war (1945–54) was the mythical era of the creation of heaven and earth, and if the following decade (1955–64) was the era of charismatic leaders who fought hard battles, then the decade from 1965–74 was the age of the masses, the era of technostructure. The process illustrated the words of the Meiji-era thinker Uchimura Kanzō: "The spirit, reduced to a system, dies; this is a law of history." As systematized economic growth gains its own momentum, its original goals are lost sight of. As a result it becomes difficult to maintain the enthusiasm or loyalty of the members of society. The latter half of the 1960s, with its long-term prosperity, was simultaneously a time of growth for the dreams of many reform-minded local municipalities, the time when the anti-pollution movement began, and, more symbolically, the years of large-scale student uprisings, whose participants included many young people who grew up in the culture of rapid growth. From another perspective, the empire of "automated growth" had become insensitive to signals announcing changes in public opinion, and the feedback mechanism for changes in the environment had begun to rust. The interlocking of rapid growth with the period of protest is probably due to this insensitivity and economic single-mindedness.

Part

III

The Changeover

11

From Yen Revaluation to Oil Crisis

The International Monetary Crisis

Once the 1970s had gotten underway, a number of international economic crises produced severe shocks in the domestic economy: the 1971 yen revaluation, the February 1973 shift to the floating exchange rate system, then the oil crisis in the fall of the same year.

On August 15, 1971, U.S. President Richard Nixon announced (1) suspension of the dollar's convertibility into gold, (2) the imposition of an import surcharge (10%), and (3) a domestic wage-price freeze, while at the same time he called for an upward revaluation of the currencies of all major nations (the New Economic Policy). After closing their foreign exchange markets for a short while, the nations of Europe reopened them under a system of floating exchange rates; Japan, too, which alone during that time had kept its market open and supported the dollar at 360 yen, switched to the float on August 26. Subsequent to the deliberations at meetings of the Finance Ministers of ten nations in September and November, a multilateral currency adjustment was effected at a series of Smithsonian meetings, where it was determined that the revaluation of the Japanese yen against the dollar would be the most extensive (16.88%) of all the revaluations among the advanced nations (US$1 = ¥308) (Table 11-1). President Nixon spoke of this meeting as follows:

> Bretton Woods came at a time when the United States immediately after World War II was predominant in the economic affairs of the world.
>
> Now we have a new world, fortunately a much better world economically, where instead of just one strong economic nation, the nations of Europe, Japan and Asia, Canada and North America—all these nations are strong competitors, and as a result it was necessary in these meetings for a negotiation to take place between

Table 11–1. Multinational Exchange Rate Adjustments (end of 1971)

Against the Dollar	Against Gold	% Change Against Dollar	Major Countries Involved
		16.88%	Japan
Upward Revaluation	Revaluation	13.58%	West Germany, Switzerland
		11.57%	Holland, Belgium, etc.
	Pegged at Gold Parity	8.57%	France, Great Britain, etc.
Pegged against the Dollar	Devaluation	8,57%	Italy, Sweden, Denmark, etc.
		0.00	U.S.A., Brazil, United Arab Republics, South Korea, etc.
Devaluation			Union of South Africa, etc.

Source: Economic Planning Agency, "Gendai Nihon keizai no tenkai" [Development of the Contemporary Japanese Economy].

equally strong nations insofar as currencies were concerned.

And the fact that these gentlemen ... have reached agreement on the realignment of exchange rates is indeed the most significant event that has occurred in world financial history. . . .

What has happened here is that the whole free world has won. . . .

We will have a world in which we can have more true prosperity than would be the case if we continued to have an alignment which was inevitably doomed to fail because of the instability. . . .

Congratulations ... to these men for their service ... to a more peaceful world. (*New York Times*, Dec. 19, 1971)

Here is the Japanese government's statement on the yen revaluation:

It may be said that there was an "end to the postwar system" in the background of implementation of the multilateral currency adjustment.

With the passage of the quarter of a century since the war, along with the progressive multipolarization of international relations through the expansion and strengthening of the European Community and our own nation's rapid development, in international society the system which was built around the dollar has come under pressure to change, and we are on the verge of welcoming an age of pluralistic international cooperation and competitive coexistence. This nation has recently achieved the status of the second largest economy in the free world; we have acquired a comfortable margin in our balance of payments position, and as a result the time has arrived when we should, domestically, further increase welfare and, abroad, make still greater contributions to international society.

The leaders of both countries referred grandiosely to the demise of the postwar system, probably because the event tempted them, as human beings, to indulge in historical generalization. However, this was only the "beginning of the end."

Saying that the Smithsonian meetings "would buy two or three years' breathing space," British Chancellor of the Exchequer Anthony Barber pronounced a realistic judgment more moderate than that of either the Japanese government or the American. Even this assessment was optimistic, however, particularly with regard to England: a mere half-year later, in June 1972, the pound had to quickly shift to the float. In another six months, in January 1973, Italy adopted a two-tiered float and Switzerland switched to the float as well. At about that time the international monetary situation began running into some very rough sledding. Faced with heavy speculation in February, the dollar was devalued by 10%; the yen was floated; and so on. When in March there was a recurrence of speculation against the mark, which was trying to hold its own at fixed parity, arrangements were made for an EC joint float. Thus, the advanced industrial nations all abandoned fixed parity and found themselves hailing the era of the float. So ended the Smithsonian system after its brief life of one year and two months.

When, on top of this, the oil crisis occurred in the autumn of 1973, it dealt a terrible blow to the world economy, Japan included. Before moving into that discussion, let us first ask why the Japanese economy, having come so far, was repeatedly buffeted by external shocks. Then let us see how the economy dealt with such shocks, as exemplified by the international monetary crisis.

The Shock

This was not the first time the Japanese economy had been tossed on the high seas of the international situation. We have already seen how much the economic recovery process after the Second World War was influenced by the development of the East-West confrontation. From the mid-1950s onward, however, the world political situation was moving in the direction of peaceful coexistence, and the international economy as well was entering an era in which the IMF-GATT system was able to function smoothly. In this setting rapid growth and liberalization advanced side by side in the Japanese economy, which substantially improved its international position. Small shocks were felt in the forms of the interest equalization tax, devaluation of the pound, textile negotiations, and the television dumping controversy, but these were all small in scale. The yen revaluation and the float necessitated major changes in the framework of the system (which had been based on fixed parity with the dollar as key currency), and the dimensions of their influence distinguish them from these clusters of small shocks. This was an event unparalleled since the U.S.$1: ¥360 rate had been established twenty years earlier. On August 16, 1971 (Japan time), the day Nixon's New Economic Policy was announced, the volume of transactions on the Tokyo foreign exchange market exceeded $600 million, ten times the volume on an average day, and stock prices fell sharply, by an average ¥215.50.

Why did the international monetary crisis grow increasingly severe with the beginning of the 1970s and expand in scale to include the yen as well as the dollar? First one must point to inflation in the U.S. and that country's cumulative balance of payments deficits, and the appearance of worldwide excess liquidity. Also in the background is the American efforts to build the Great Society at home and to bring to a successful conclusion the Vietnam War abroad, and the reversals it encountered in those efforts. In spite of its wealth, the U.S. could not afford both guns and butter. Furthermore, the Vietnam War revised America's global strategy, and the resulting U.S.-China rapprochement (announced one month before the New Economic Policy) over the heads of the Japanese became one more component of what came to be called the "Nixon shocks."

The primary factor that particularly deepened Japan's involvement in the monetary crisis was the generally improving international position of the Japanese economy. Breaking through the "dollar umbrella," the yen was growing powerful. The "small country hypothesis"—that Japan is influenced by the world situation but does not itself influence that situation by its behavior—no longer held. More specifically, when U.S. inflation was advancing in 1969, Japan adopted a policy of monetary restraint in order to avoid price increases. Thus, in terms of both prices and the balance of payments, the two countries were pursuing

Table 11–2.   Changes in the International Balance of Payments

($100 millions)

	Overall Balance	Current Transactions Balance	Trade Balance	Trade Balance with U.S.
1965	4	9	19	5
66	3	12	22	8
67	− 5	− 1	8	3
68	11	10	25	12
69	22	21	36	16
70	13	19	39	14
71	76	57	77	33
72	47	66	89	39
73	− 100	− 1	37	13

Source: Data from "Gendai Nihon keizai no tenkai" [Development of the Contemporary Japanese Economy].

Notes: Figures are rounded off.
      Trade balance with the U.S. is F.O.B.

policies that led in opposite directions. In contrast to the United States, Japan had a large balance of payments surplus (and a particularly large trade surplus with the U.S.), which made the Japanese economy a leading actor on the international monetary stage (Table 11–2).

There are generally two approaches to understanding the international monetary crisis and the foregoing material. One is to take the liquidity approach and to regard the sequence: U.S. inflation → surplus dollars → development of worldwide inflation, as the reason for the monetary crisis. The other approach is to set out from the standpoint of exchange rate adjustments and to view the causal sequence as: differing rates of price increases in the U.S., West Germany, and Japan → expansion of international payments imbalances. According to the former viewpoint, the monetary crisis will not end unless American inflation ends, but according to the latter, the monetary crisis will end if inflation can be isolated by means of exchange rate adjustments. The former censures the United States, which caused the inflation; the latter takes Japan to task for its failure to raise the exchange rate. In contrast to these approaches, the material presented above synthesizes—or compromises between—the two theories, and attempts a tentative explanation of the crisis as an expansion of disequilibria in the midst of inflation.

One's view of the extent of the crisis depends on which of these two theories one employs. According to the latter theory, a switch to the floating exchange rate system disposes of the problem, and one might venture to say that the matter could not be called a crisis. However, "monetary crisis" is a common expression here, and the psychological influence of the whole series of events was considerable at least in Japan, so the expression "crisis" has been adopted in this context.

The fact that these events were a shock—a crisis—for the Japanese economy suggests that there was also a problem in the way they were parried by that economy. In the latter half of the 1960s Japan's leading industries greatly increased their rates of export dependence, and they were trying to increase them still further as the 1970s began (see Chapter 10). There is no doubt that this heightened the degree of shock, the impact at home of worldwide monetary events. Japan's response to the crisis also had great influence on the subsequent course of the Japanese economy. One cannot avoid the conclusion that the government did not grapple with the crisis in an autonomous, *ex ante* manner, but instead overreacted in a passive, *ex post facto* fashion. In the following section let us examine this controversial question of crisis management.

Early Warnings, Actions, Explanations

The Nixon announcement in the summer of 1971 was a bolt from the blue for the majority of the Japanese people. The extent of the yen revaluation at the end of that year far exceeded everyone's expectations. The degree of upward revision subsided a bit with the float in February 1973, but only after the summer 1972 uproar over the revaluation had already quieted down somewhat by the year's end.

Were there really no early warnings of these events? One cannot say that there were none. When a view favoring establishment of a standing balance of payments surplus was advanced at the end of the 1960s, revaluation of the yen became an issue, and there were both international and domestic fears that the 1969 monetary restraint would expand the imbalance due to the international payments surplus. A sliding peg proposal by a group of economists was presented in July 1971. There were similar trends abroad. At the beginning of that year President Nixon claimed, "We are all Keynesians now," hinting at a switch in which the Republicans would appropriate the policies of the Democratic Party; and powerful U.S. Congressmen such as William Proxmire and William V. Roth, Jr., were clearly seeking an international monetary adjustment. In May of that year there was speculation against the mark, which switched to the float even before the Nixon announcement.

All such signals were ignored in Japan, however. Even after the

Nixon announcement, the foreign exchange market remained open, occasioning a massive monetary expansion due to heavy purchasing to support the dollar, which was termed "an act of madness" abroad. The Japanese government consistently did its best to avoid a revaluation and, even when revaluation became unavoidable, strove to keep it as small as possible. Is a "rational" explanation of such behavior possible? Or was this perhaps nothing more than the simple result of confusion?

There were several factors at work which, combined, may be considered a rational explanation. The Japanese economy was in a recession at that time, and there was anxiety over the deflationary effects of a revaluation. The government was anxious to avoid a revaluation prior to the return of Okinawa to Japanese rule, for political reasons. The move to support the dollar in the face of that unknown quantity the float amounted to a temporary underwriting of foreign exchange banks' and export trading companies' losses by the government and the Bank of Japan. While this step raised problems with respect to income distribution, it was an emergency measure that prevented the spread of panic.

In order for these factors to be considered a rational explanation, however, there must be grounds for believing that the government had a definite plan for autonomously revaluing the yen after its measures to revive business activity had succeeded and after the return of Okinawa. Whether or not this was the case cannot be ascertained. Nor is there much evidence of concern over the money supply's influence on prices.

The 1972 Economic White Paper says: "From the point of view of the improvement of social welfare, clinging to fixed parity while neglecting such things as price increases and distortions in resource allocation at home and abroad is something which [based on our experience with the revaluation] must be avoided." It also pointed out that "in times of necessity, the possibility of making practical use of foreign exchange policy should also be investigated." But these reflections were not put to good use. The foreign exchange coup engineered in France by De Gaulle and Pompidou—toppling expectations of the franc's inevitable revaluation in 1968 by supporting the exchange rate and then devaluing the franc during the summer vacation a year later, when everyone had almost forgotten the matter—was a performance not to be duplicated. The Japanese government, by contrast, repeatedly drew up plans for yen revaluation measures and participated in any number of talks on rectifying the U.S.-Japan trade imbalance by promoting imports of individual commodities: the Hawaii Conference, the Hakone Conference, and so on. The energy brought to bear on these efforts was amazing. These talks also became an issue in the Lockheed bribery scandal the following year.

Another hypothesis, therefore, is that the bureaucratic system determined Japan's handling of the international monetary crisis. A bureaucratic organization's principles of behavior are (1) sectionalism and (2) adherence in period t to standards established in period $t-1$. Such a venture into the unknown as a revaluation of the yen in anticipation of a monetary crisis is not included in this behavior code. Furthermore, when one considers the complexity of the positions advocated by each individual government organization, such a bold response would have been impossible in view just of the time and trouble required to achieve agreement on the measure. Thus, each organization anxiously attempted to grapple with yen countermeasures in its own bailiwick, but bureaucratic sectionalism insured that each organization's efforts were cancelled out by the efforts of those pursuing other objectives and the overall reaction ended by being inadequate or an overreaction. It is a fact that the succession of shocks of the 1970s and the way they were handled caused a great loss of confidence in the bureaucracy—Japan's "best and brightest."

Such tendencies cannot be denied. But the fact that the handling of the situation was inadequate before the fact and excessive afterwards can also be viewed as a result of the domestic political process. Avoiding the revaluation was the goal of powerful pressure groups made up of throngs of export companies. Nor did the opposition parties, the labor unions, or the newspapers offer many divergent views. On the foreign exchange market, which fluctuates on the strength of rumors alone, the vociferous discussions of revaluation brought on unanticipated disturbances, and everyone was afraid of being treated like a traitor for dissenting. A Cabinet member who had just taken office felt impelled, fielding a question in the Diet, to categorically deny the need for a revaluation of the yen. Once such a denial was made, however, it became a public commitment of the government. Aside from questions of propriety involving outright breach of promise, nothing more readily sows distrust in the government's statements. It is impossible to deny that open politics made it difficult to build a national strategy. Moreover, there were strong feelings in some quarters, even in those days, that the dollar, not the yen, should be revalued. Pride became more important than the effects of economic policy as such. And this is not to say that the government did not engage in strategic maneuvering of its own, exploiting external pressure prior to the revaluation to obtain approval of the strongest possible countermeasures, and similarly promoting liberalization and tariff reductions, which were strongly opposed domestically.

It is difficult to discern the essence of decisionmaking during a crisis. Following Allison's (1971) analysis, we have seen Japan's handling of the monetary crisis from three points of view: (1) as a rational action; (2) as a typical bureaucratic response; and (3) as the product of intra-governmental politics. However, if such an analysis discloses only responses originating in bureaucratic dissonance or intragovernmental politics, the locus of political leadership must necessarily be called into question.

Prime Minister Satō Eisaku continued to display understanding and tolerance toward America's policy switches, specifically the two Nixon "shocks" of Sino-American rapprochement and the demand for a yen revaluation. This was a stabilizing factor in the midst of the crisis, a fact which should be appreciated for its contrast with the frenzied response to subsequent events. Public opinion, however, did not support Satō's attitude. It is usually the mass media that compensate for their own inability to foresee the future with attacks on the government's lack of policies. When Prime Minister Satō retired in 1972 after presiding over the historical return of Okinawa, and when the new prime minister, Tanaka Kakuei, took the stage, public opinion welled up with excited media-fanned expectations of "decisive and active politics." No doubt they were expecting a hero.

Gropings and Setbacks

Merits and Demerits of the Yen Countermeasures

In June of 1971, when speculation against the mark was creating an uproar, the Japanese government, while approving an eight-point comprehensive external economic policy including (1) import liberalization, (2) tariff reductions, (3) removal of non-tariff barriers, and (4) promotion of economic cooperation, at the same time contrived to reduce the balance of payments surplus by expanding aggregate demand through supplements to Treasury loans and investments (Table 11-3). This became the prototype for the revaluation countermeasures that were subsequently repeated in May and October of 1972. These measures resulted in a renewed acceleration of import liberalization, which was brought up to the West German standard. In the area of tariffs, too, a 20% across-the-board reduction was effected on 1,865 items in 1972. Generally speaking, the international opening up of the Japanese economy progressed in tandem with the

Table 11–3.   Changes in Fiscal Policies

(¥ trillions)

	Government[a]					
	Fixed Capital Formation	Current Purchases	Transfers to Individuals	General Account[b]	*(Social Security Expenses)*	Income Tax Reductions[c]
1970	6.2	6.0	3.2	8.2	*1.2*	0.28
71	7.9	7.1	3.6	9.6	*1.5*	0.20
72	9.4	8.4	4.6	12.1	*1.9*	0.28
73	10.6	10.4	5.6	15.2	*2.5*	0.38
74	12.8	14.2	8.1	19.1	*3.5*	1.78

Notes: a From "Keizai yōran" [Economic Survey] (rounded up or down to nearest whole number).

b Figures are rounded down to the nearest whole unit.

c From "Zusetsu Nihon no zaisei" [Japanese Public Finance in Charts] (1964 edition).

reform of the system of favorable tax treatment and financing for exports, increased economic cooperation, and so on. This was the great achievement of the yen countermeasures.

It was unreasonable, however, to think that such measures could substitute for currency adjustments. They reinforced dependence on economic controls by making too imperative the goal of somehow reducing the balance of payments surplus, administrative interference in exports and imports, and so on.

The tendency toward greater control was also a worldwide trend. In the United States, a wage-price freeze was imposed. In West Germany, Economics Minister Walter Schiller, who was of the foreign exchange adjustment persuasion, was ousted and exchange controls were strengthened. Public opinion in Japan as well leaned strongly in the direction of controls. Government leaders studied application of the Foreign Trade Control Law to specific rapidly expanding export items, ordered the drafting of regulations for ship chartering, and sought to develop a list of items to be targeted for priority as imports. On the domestic front as well, the government singled out steel and lumber as the culprits responsible for price increases, sought to regulate imports and the shipping of freight through "administrative guidance," and tried to deal with the rising prices of stocks and land by tightening bank credit. Immersing themselves in such individual regulations and using their influence and their energy, the political leaders worked ably with the bureaucracy but they failed to develop a policy that would be a genuine solution.

Rebuilding the Archipelago
While all this was going on, a debate arose over the necessity of re-
directing the resources currently going to exports and plant and equipment investment into the building of a welfare society through a public-
sector-led economy in order to achieve a "genuine" internal and
external balance.

Rebuilding the Japanese Archipelago by Tanaka Kakuei, which was
published just before Tanaka took office as Prime Minister, attracted
a great deal of attention by presenting a definite prescription for the
excess concentration of population in urban areas and the simultaneous
underpopulation of the countryside. Tanaka proposed dispersing
population and industry to selected non-urban regions in accordance
with redirected flows of resources.

> The concentration of population and industry in the large cities
> was the prime mover that created today's prosperous Japan. How-
> ever, this massive flow at the same time resulted in crowding into
> these cities large numbers of people who called only a two-room
> urban apartment their family home; in denuding the provinces of
> young people; and in leaving behind in the countryside only house-
> wives and the elderly to do the heavy farm labor. The energy to
> cut a path for the people away from such a society cannot be
> produced in 100 years. So, I have determined to promote a "re-
> gional dispersion" that will reverse the flow of people, money and
> goods away from the huge cities to the provinces, using as a lever
> a redistribution of industry and the formation of a nationwide
> network for transportation and for information and communica-
> tions. (Tanaka, 1972, p. 216).

Rebuilding the Japanese Archipelago was distinguished by its ready
wit, elements of surprise, power of expression, ideas (for example,
new cities of 250,000 population; industrial parks), proposals rooted
in personal experience, and optimistic futurism; it was rich in charm
and persuasiveness; and it offered an expansive vision.
    However, when this discourse on rebuilding the archipelago shifted
into actual implementation, land speculation became rife in areas
earmarked for development, and people's feeling of being cramped for
housing space was further exacerbated as land prices soared nationwide. The initial acclaim in time changed to murmurs of complaint.
One can't help concluding that as a policy, this scheme ended in failure,
even if the vision it represented is still worthy of consideration today.
As reasons for its failure, one may offer such methodological factors

as the bad timing inherent in trying to implement the policy in the midst of the excess liquidity being created by the yen revaluation which occurred at that time and which was exacerbated by the oil crisis that followed; the major side effects arising from the fact that the scheme also became entwined with the policy of maintaining yen parity; the overhasty tempo of implementation; etc. Can one not say, however, that behind such methodological failures lay the "poverty of philosophy" of the rebuilding-the-archipelago concept itself? Its goal was to "restore serenity and prosperity," but it considered serenity and prosperity to be something which could only be obtained as a result of a materialistic rebuilding of the archipelago rather than something created subjectively. Moreover, the scheme was insufficiently cautious about the impact public sector expansion would have. That is to say, it lacked a sense of liberalism and individualism.

The failure of the rebuilding-the-archipelago program was also a failure to build a welfare society. Just as lavish social spending in connection with the scheme to rebuild the archipelago was criticized, reckless welfare spending has left behind a great deal of baggage to this day. The shift from growth to welfare is not easy. In America, too, after the achievement of full employment under President Kennedy, the Johnson administration had embarked upon the building of a Great Society. But in spite of advances in human rights legislation and social security, race riots, the crisis of the cities, and inflation knocked the props from beneath the very foundations of those hopes. This and Italy's "long hot summer," as well as Japan's failure at building a welfare society are included among the episodes of cultural and social chaos that beset the advanced nations after the golden 1960s.

If we were to seek a moral from this sequence of events, it would be that easy-going reliance on the public sector is dangerous, and that if that sector is going to expand, a stable outlook is required. Even more so today, the choice of how the public sector is to be handled holds the key to the fate of the Japanese economy; this choice is a question not only of economics, but also one of ethics, encompassing, for example, one's view of society and of the individual in broad terms.

Adjustment Inflation

In the presence of a balance of payments surplus, fiscal and monetary policy had gradually been more aggressive since the spring of 1970. But after the American announcement of the New Economic Policy in the summer of 1971, the Japanese government took action not only to buy up dollars on a large scale, but also to draw up an oversized budget, cut taxes, issue national bonds, lower interest rates, and so on,

Table 11–4. The Advance of Inflation

(%)

	Rate of Increase in Money Supply	Rate of Increase in Land Prices	Rate of Increase in Wholesale Prices	Rate of Increase in Consumer Prices	"Spring Offensive" Wage Increase (%)
1970	15.9	15.7	−0.8	6.0	18.5
71	**24.3**	13.2	0.8	4.6	16.9
72	**24.7**	**25.1**	**15.9**	**11.8**	15.3
73	16.8	**23.0**	31.3	**24.3**	20.1
74	11.5	−4.3	3.0	11.9	**32.9**

Source: From "Keizai yōran" [Economic Handbook].
Notes: (1) Land price increases are the ratio of prices in March of the previous year to prices in March of the current year.
(2) Figures in boldface type are those of striking magnitude.

under the banner of achieving international payments balance, rebuilding the archipelago, and expanding social programs. In this process an unprecedented level of welfare spending made medical care for the aged free of charge, increased family health insurance benefits (from 50% to 70% of costs), increased to 50,000 yen the national pension annuity, introduced a sliding-scale system for the national pension, and on on. These were historic advances, necessary steps. On the other hand, however, these aggressive policies also became the fire that ignored a hyper-inflation almost unexampled in peacetime. The upward trend in prices intensified around the autumn of 1972 (Table 11–4). Shortages appeared in textiles in the spring of 1973 and spread to steel products, cement, and chemical products that summer. Finally in the autumn a panic situation developed in which such things as toilet paper and detergent completely vanished from the stores. In the earlier, productivity-differential inflation, consumer prices had risen while wholesale prices remained stable as income distribution equalized. During the inflation of 1972–73, the prices of assets (land, stocks, works of art, golf club memberships) were the first to rise; then wholesale prices rose, ahead of consumer prices. In this process inequalities of income distribution—as exemplified at one extreme by land profiteers—were revealed; and as accounts of speculation, market-cornering in certain commodities, and hoarding came to light, public anti-business sentiment was sharply stimulated. Such signs as these suggest that this inflation was of the classical monetary type.

The price advances of this period are sometimes called "adjustment inflation." This term suggests both the policy of correcting the yen's relative cheapness abroad by means of domestic price increases and that of adjusting the balance of payments surplus. Should Japan's inflation of 1972–73 be called adjustment inflation or not?

The insistence on supporting fixed parity for the yen resulted in inviting an oversupply of currency and inflated fiscal spending, which were the sources of this inflation. If continual recourse is made to expanding aggregate demand with a fixed exchange rate in a situation in which a balance of payments surplus remains even under full employment, it is only natural that price increases will arise. This phenomenon is none other than the balance of payments equilibrium mechanism conceived of by Hume and Ricardo. The Japanese inflation of 1972–73 was a large-scale and moreover inevitable fulfillment of that theory.

Determining why such foolish policies were implemented, however, requires further thought. It is a fact that the adjustment inflation policies obtained the support of some influential people, and it is also a fact that there is no concern for price stability in the leading official documents of the time. However, it is also possible that adjustment inflation was reinforced by mistake. It is arguable that, misreading the extent of the supply and demand gap, the government thought that real demand would continue to expand without inflation occurring. Perhaps the effects of the aggregate demand policies or of time lags were miscalculated. Perhaps too much effort was invested in countermeasures for individual commodities. It is not easy to identify intensions and errors, because the human animal is prone to indulge in wishful thinking. Just as with the question of why fixed parity was tenaciously clung to at that time, here, too, ambiguity remains.

There are alternatives to the adjustment inflation interpretation. One theory holds that Japan's inflation was imported. The time period involved was the same as that during which worldwide inflation was in progress. International prices climbed steeply from the middle of 1972, and import prices for fiscal 1973 showed a 33% increase as well. Such an influence cannot be ignored. One major factor increasing international prices, however, was Japan's excess demand (negating the "small country hypothesis"); in addition, if Japan had switched to the float sooner, the effects of inflation would have taken a different form.

A second theory attaches great importance to changes in supply behavior. It views the origins of the inflation as having been not only on the demand side, but also due to the conservative turn in the behavior of firms and their lack of effort to increase supply. If one sees the behavior of firms as having changed from demand-leading to demand-following, then the influence of such a change would not be small. This would be a secondary explanation for hyperinflation, however. A third theory is that of "demand shift" inflation due to the expansion of fiscal spending. But this explanation does not contradict the concept of adjustment inflation.

In the fall of 1973 the Japanese economy was already entangled in price increases exceeding 20% per year. Just then the oil crisis occured, pummelling the already stricken Japan with yet another—and decisive—nflationary blow.

12

Reaching for Steady Growth

The Battle Against Inflation

From the latter half of 1972 to the first half of 1974 hyperinflation raged throughout Japan. In addition to the fundamental cause, the swelling of the money supply that had been under way since 1971, partly as a result of the policies aimed at avoiding a revaluation of the yen, speculative demand became brisk in anticipation of the Rebuilding the Archipelago project and its attendant large-scale government spending. Moreover, as recession cartels, pollution problems, drought, industrial accidents, labor shortages, and so on accumulated, the supply outlook for businesses grew less and less promising. In addition, prices overseas continued to skyrocket with the rapid progression of worldwide inflation due to the Vietnam War. The *coup de grace* after all of this was the oil crisis in the autumn of 1973. When word of the oil embargo brought on by war in the Middle East got out, the price of oil quadrupled at a single bound. From January to March of 1974 wholesale prices soared at an annual rate of 50%, while consumer prices climbed 40% (annual extrapolation). They were literally "crazy prices."

With panicky hoarding and market cornering adding to the confusion, the speculative behavior of firms was severely censured as "the root of all evil." As Keynes pointed out, if entrepreneurs become profiteers, capitalism cannot continue to exist. As adverse criticism of business firms continued during the classical inflation, symptoms of social dissolution were evident.

As methods of figuring inflation, (1) controls, the regulation of speculation, etc., and (2) orthodox fiscal and monetary stringency both came under consideration. For both prescriptions, how much and for how long became issues. As one might naturally expect in a democratic system, the government adopted both policies. Moves along the path to controls included approval of the Oil Demand and Supply Adjustment Law and Emergency Measures for the Stabilization of National Life,

Table 12–1. Government Intervention in the Prices of Individual
            Commodities

Form of Intervention	Target Items (Applicable Period)
Standard Prices Set	Kerosene (Jan.–June 1974), liquid petroleumgas (Jan.-May 1974), tissue/toilet paper (Jan.–May 1974)
Standard Amounts Set	Gasoline, naphtha, crude oil (Dec. 1975–May 1976)
Administrative Guidance	Small steel bars; aluminum items; low-density polyethylene, etc.; cement; plate glass; corrugated cardboard egg sheet; nylon filament; synthetic rubber; automobile tires; paint; housing facilities; prefab housing; light bulbs for home use; electric motors; cultivators; tractors; rice planting machines; agricultural polyethylene film; polyvinyl chloride film; fertilizers such as superphosphate of lime; agricultural chemicals; synthetic detergents; wheat flour; soy sauce; sugar, edible oils; instant noodles; beer; pharmaceuticals; dairy products such as butter; for a total of 59 items (specified in March and April 1974; cancelled between May and September of that year)

and adoption of a standard pricing system for petroleum products and a system of providing advance notice of price changes for key materials (Table 12–1). Rumors also circulated that the government was planning a price freeze. However, in spite of soaring prices, support for price controls was halfhearted at best: people had not forgotten the experience of wartime price controls, which, once undertaken, led to rationing of everything, right down to flowerpots. Controls were assuredly inadequate. In the end, the market economy won out, and fiscal and monetary policy came to play the leading roles in counterinflationary policy.

From one standpoint, it was politics that determined the battle stance against inflation. Three factors dominated policy choices: (1) the personalities and fortunes of political leaders; (2) sudden interventions of public pressure; and (3) scandals and horse-trading. Just prior to the oil crisis, the Tanaka Cabinet had lowered interest rates on deposits, had announced plans for the Shinkansen, and had directed a ¥2 trillion tax cut. The sudden death of Finance Minister Aichi Kiichi on November 23, 1973, created the powerful impression that an outstanding politician had died prematurely at his post while serving under the difficult circumstances of the time. For the Tanaka Cabinet, however, which was battling on two fronts to suppress inflation while supporting expansionary government policies, Aichi's death meant the loss of the staunchest supporter of its policies. When Tanaka rival Fukuda Takeo became the next Finance Minister, Tanaka's leadership retreated a step, further reinforcing the underlying tone of fiscal austerity and monetary stringency. In tandem with the two trillion yen tax cut, the axe was taken to the fiscal 1974 budget in such areas as public investments.

As a result of an unanticipated reversal for the Liberal Democratic Party in the May 1974 House of Councillors election, parity was achieved between the conservatives and the leftist opposition parties. This intervention of the popular will effectively dashed what had become virtually universal hopes for an early easing of the austerity; long-term suppression of aggregate demand became inevitable, and advance investments in inventory suddenly turned into unintentional overstocks. What dominated the situation at that time was the general public's deep-seated aversion to inflation. From there it was virtually a straight line from the Tanaka Cabinet's resignation over questions of financial probity (suspicions connected with the Lockheed bribery scandal) to the Miki Takeo Cabinet's appearance on center stage like a bolt from the blue. Also during this period, Bank of Japan Governor Sasaki Tadashi was succeeded by Governor Morinaga Tei'ichirō.

The Miki Cabinet was defeated in the 1976 session of the Diet in its efforts to obtain revision of Japan National Railways (JNR) fares and of telephone and telegraph rates; was damaged by an intraparty confrontation over the prime ministership; and brought on a situation in which the slowdown from prosperity had to be left to run its increasingly serious course. While these political events, coming at such a time, had the effect of prolonging the business recession, they also served to decisively suppress inflation.

The Dilemmas of Decelerating the Growth Process

Recession with Inflation

Monetary policy shifted toward austerity in 1973, and fiscal policy followed suit in fiscal 1974. At first, however, inflation was not easily subdued, and an unusual situation arose in which a recession was proceeding in the midst of this inflation. Expressed in terms of Fisher's equation of exchange, $MV = PT$ (volume of money × velocity = prices × transactions), since the expansion of the money supply M was very modest in 1974 and the rate of increase in prices P was high, the increase in the velocity of circulation of money V did not match the other increases; thus it turned out that the volume of goods transactions T bore the brunt of the strain and fell sharply (Table 12–2). 1974 became the first year since the early postwar days that the Japanese economy recorded negative growth.

When one examines the antithetical relationship between price increases and the decline in real transactions broken down by demand categories (Table 12–3), this contrast is striking not only in such categories as plant and equipment investment and inventory investment, but even in personal consumption, private housing, and fiscal spending, which had until that time expanded rapidly, even in periods of recession, and had come to be thought of as being stable demand categories. The fact that these areas actually experienced a large-scale collapse during the recession-with-inflation resulted in a systemic change with the development of personal loans that became sensitive to periods of feast and famine in the availability of finance. More fundamental, however, were changes in the budget behavior of households, which, caught between the two-pronged onslaught of inflation and recession, could not help but be increasingly apprehensive about the future. The fact that the personal savings rate rose sharply during this period might have reflected a decline in long-term expected income. Thus, the unexpected frailty of mass consumption society was exposed, and one of the myths of the modern economy was exploded.

The situation was the same for fiscal policy. In nominal terms fiscal outlays ballooned, but after correction for price rises, the increase in real expenditures was low. Moreover, there was considerable resistance to expanding the deficit in order to pursue stimulatory economic policies. Thus was that article of faith of the modern economy known as fiscal policy divested of its authority.

The decrease in real transactions had a great impact on employment (Table 12–4). Assiduous in their work force adjustments, firms strove

Table 12–2.   Money, Price, and Output Trends (by comparison with the previous recession period)

	Money M	Velocity of Circulation V	Wholesale Prices P	Mining & Mfg. Output T
1962	1.183	0.834	0.979	1.003
5	1.184	0.868	1.008	1.018
1	1.402	0.732	0.992	1.034
4	**1.152**	0.862	**1.305**	**0.701**

Note: Figures are ratios of the troughs to the preceding peaks of business conditions for each of the recession years indicated.
Boldface type indicates particularly striking ratios.

Table 12–3.   Nominal and Real Price Changes in the Period of Inflation

	1974			1975		
	Nom-inal	Defla-tor	Real	Nom-inal	Defla-tor	Real
Private Consumption	20.4	19.6	2.3	14.2	10.0	3.8
Private Housing	−2.3	16.9	−16.4	15.5	2.3	12.8
Businesses' Plant & Equipment Investment	8.4	20.0	−9.7	−2.4	2.0	−4.4
Government Consumption	35.7	29.5	−1.2	9.3	9.7	4.5
Government Fixed Investment	21.6	23.3	4.8	16.0	4.7	5.8
Private Inventories	−0.8	10.9	−35.9	−82.0	2.6	−80.2
GNE	18.7	18.7	−0.0	10.0	6.6	3.2

Source: "Kokumin shotoku tōkei" [National Income Statistics].
Figures shown are relative to previous year.

to reduce numbers of part-time workers, regulate overtime, reshuffle personnel assignments, transfer employees temporarily to other offices, and curb the hiring of replacements for retirees. As the number of the employed declined, primarily in manufacturing industries, unemployment continued to increase and the effective rate of job offers to applicants deteriorated persistently. Moreover, since data on hiring cutbacks and direct work force reductions did not take into account part-time female workers who withdrew from the labor force entirely and returned to the household, the apparent level of unemployment was still deceptively low during this period. It was not until 1977 and thereafter that it clearly increased. Nevertheless, even at the level already apparent in 1975, both the myth of full employment and the tradition of lifetime employment were undermined.

It may be concluded that a downward shift in the long-term expected rate of growth occurred, paralleling the monetary austerity and profoundly influencing consumption, investment, employment, and so on. The impact of the expected rate of growth on investment can be explained by the acceleration principle and its influence on consumption, by means of the permanent income hypothesis, as has been seen. The influence on employment is evident in view of the fact that lifetime employment is the firm's most important long-term investment.

During the process of monetary tightening following the oil crisis and the period of crazy prices, four myths of the modern economy were

Table 12-4.　Changes in Key Economic Indicators, 1975–78

	Supply/Demand Gap			Inflation/Deflation Gap		Employment Gap	Balance of Payments Gap	Fiscal Gap
	Mining & Mfg. Output (relative to previous year)	Inventory-Sales Ratio (1975 100)	Operating Rate for Mfg. Industries (1975 = 100)	Wholesale Prices (relative to previous year)	Consumer Prices (relative to previous year)	No. of Unemployed Persons (10,000s)	Current Transactions Balance ($100 millions)	Rate of Dependence on Government Bonds (%)
1975	4.4	95.1	101.9	2.0	10.2	104	1	25.3
76	10.8	83.3	109.1	5.0	9.4	107	46	29.9
77	3.2	89.9	107.6	1.9	6.8	113	139	29.7
78	7.0	82.3	107.8	−2.3	3.4	122	118	36.9
								(initial figures)

exploded: those having to do with (1) the mass consumption society, (2) fiscal policy, (3) full employment, and (4) economic growth. This was both the result of uncertain economic conditions and a primary factor contributing to the uncertainty of those conditions. Against a background of anti-inflationary popular feeling, and by means of sacrifices, aggregate demand was in the end restrained. As it turned out, this feat had the unanticipated effect of producing price stability. Economic Planning Agency Director Fukuda's public promise to hold consumer price increases for March 1975 to 15% less than those for the same period the previous year and to hold those for March of 1976 to 10% less, while it betrayed the expectations of many, was superbly kept. Faced with their employers' desires to reduce employment, the company unions exercised self-discipline in their wage demands, thus avoiding a vicious wage-price spiral. The argument that monetary stringency is ineffectual in combatting the cost-push effect of oil price increases lost currency as not only wholesale prices but also consumer prices steadied. One more item of dogma—that the final stage of state monopoly capitalism is always accompanied by inflation, ended up refuted by the miracles of the twentieth century. There can be no doubt that this was the brilliant result of the Fukuda economic policies.

The "Failure" of the Business Revival

The *quid pro quo* for the suppression of inflation from 1974 to 1975 was that economic growth was at a virtual standstill: mining and manufacturing output and the operating rate in the manufacturing industries dropped 20% from their 1973 peak, and the number of the completely unemployed exceeded one million. It is only natural that there was a rising desire for a restoration of prosperity. However, the economic growth rate for 1976 to 1978 came to no more than about 4%, producing no noticeable feeling of a business revival.

A look at the record from year to year shows that on numerous occasions during this period there were signs of a business revival, but these nascent recoveries were repeatedly stifled. Since inventory investment revived during the first half of 1975, business conditions bottomed out and increases in output and in prices were observed. The inventory restocking process had run its course after a single round, however. In the first half of 1976 exports expanded swiftly, and mining and manufacturing output also rose sharply, but business once again stagnated under the impact of slack worldwide business conditions from the summer onward. Recovery was further throttled by restrained public spending resulting from the postponement of fare and rate revisions for the National Railways and the telephone and telegraph monopoly. Again in 1977, a light spread over business conditions during the first half as appropriations for public investment were made in advance from the budget for the second half of the fiscal year. But with the coming of a short-winded second half, fluctuations in inventory adjustments arose instead.

Inventory investment, exports, and public investment, which had provided the motive power behind business recoveries in the past, did not succeed this time in mobilizing the principal forces of the economy—consumption and plant and equipment investment—toward a business upturn. The first stage of the rocket fired, but the second failed to ignite. In the background, the long-term expected rate of growth for the main constituents of the private economy declined. The government piped but the private sector failed to dance. The government made advance appropriations for public investments against the budget for the first half of the fiscal year, but the private sector was apprehensive over a certain shortness of breath in the economy in the latter half of 1977. The government's Economic Plan for 1976–80 aimed at a high rate of growth during the first half of the plan period (1976–78), but firms took this to mean slow growth during the latter half. In the face of such "rational expectations," the government's aspirations and policies were unavoidably betrayed by reality.

The difficulties that such a slow recovery produced domestically were businesses operating in the red, increased unemployment, and the appearance of "structurally depressed industries" (Kosai and Ogino, 1980). On the international front there were, in addition, balance of payments surpluses and sharp criticism thereof by various nations. The pressure of international opinion was also intensely felt in the area of policy. One view held that the problem at this time lay, not in a decline in the utility of effective demand policies, but rather in the fact that the government hoped for a business recovery but did not take adequate action: while loudly advocating recovery, it was always too late with too little in the way of action.

There is some truth in this criticism, but there is no simple explanation for this policy failure. Probably the simplest hypothesis is that the government, immersed in its optimistic economic forecasts, misperceived the real situation. From another point of view, however, the incongruousness of the government's assertions and actions may have been the result of sectionalism within the government bureaucracy. The Economic Planning Agency hoped for a high rate of growth, but those in charge of implementation had from the first no intention of adopting stimulatory policies. Their compromises in prose perhaps highlighted the discrepancy between words and deeds.

Skeptics may hold that perhaps the government was only paying lip service to the goal of an economic recovery while from the start actually aiming at 5–6% growth and just accumulating *faits accomplis.* (From the outset the government's revealed preference had been stable growth as the ultimate *desideratum.*) The fact that, in spite of the clamor of public opinion, active policies were not adopted until inflationary expectations had been dispelled may have been the greatest economic policy success of this period. This may well be contrasted with the experience of the United States, which adopted the "engine of growth" theory at that same time and thereby fell victim to serious inflation the following year.

Still another theory is that the blind and fortuitous intervention of the political process (in the form of the LDP's poor showing in the 1974 election) caused the loss of an opportunity to move toward monetary ease. But politics is not blind, and one may also argue that the correct instincts of the people forced the government to adopt the correct policy of making a top priority of stamping out inflationary expectations. It would be no simple matter to ascertain which of these hypotheses is correct, because public records cannot always provide evidence sufficient to gauge the government's "true intentions," and this is even more true of opinion in financial circles While privately realizing that slow growth was inevitable, the leaders of private industry loudly and ceaselessly importuned the government to make efforts to stimulate an economic recovery. The same contradiction was at work in opinion abroad, which warned against a build-up of Japan's economic strength in world markets while at the same time demanding rapid growth of Japan.

The economy itself was in a quandary. Although the long-term expected rate of growth (natural growth rate GGn) was declining, the growth that would satisfy entrepreneurs (warranted rate of growth GGw) was conspicuously rising. Would not raising the real rate of growth in pursuit of the warranted growth rate precipitate a crash into the barrier of the natural growth rate? This was the focal question in a debate over the desirability of a soft landing versus a breakthrough. The fiscal authorities were concerned that if the goal of a long-term growth rate were set too low, temporary deficit financing might impose a fiscal handicap that would make a recovery impossible. Out of this dilemma arose vacillation and wishful thinking. Both the private and the foreign sectors seem to have taken sometimes the natural growth rate and sometimes the warranted growth rate as the standard for their policy demands.

The leader in economic policy throughout this period was Fukuda Takeo in his capacities as, at various times, Finance Minister, Director of the Economic Planning Agency, and Prime Minister. Fukuda's original intention was to pursue stable growth, but he inevitably took the contradictory posture of stressing limited resources while at the same time publicly promising an economic recovery. While advocating price stability and stable growth for Japan, he faced a vast chorus of criticism for his beggar-my-neighbor policies as a result of Japan's huge balance of payments surpluses, and had no choice but to give lip service to a 7% growth rate in keeping with the industrialized nations' engine-of-growth doctrine.

Furthermore, there was a certain inconsistency between stable growth and promoting conservation, saving, and diligence. This is because thrift and saving are, unadorned and quite simply, the logical correlates of balance of payments surpluses and capital accumulation. If the rate of saving rises, the warranted growth rate rises still further, and the departure from the low natural rate of growth becomes pronounced. Fukuda's policy of making the suppression of inflation the first priority had quite outstanding merits. Even so, it should be noted that adquate solutions to the problems of managing an economic superpower apparently have yet to be found.

As 1978 began, fiscal policy had reached the scale befitting an economic superpower, domestic demand was reviving steadily. However, the yen's swift upward climb was proceeding apace, prices were remarkably stable, and export volume was declining. The belated rise of the yen at least eliminated a source of international friction. After the oil crisis, women workers entered the job market in large numbers, and unemployment accordingly reached a high level. In the background firms were adapting to a 5% growth rate, which appeared to have taken root as of 1975. The scaled-down activities of individual firms reduced the general level of economic activity through the economy, in many instances cancelling out scale-down efforts at the micro level. During 1978, however, firms' profit rates revived as a result of Operation Scale-down, and it seemed as though the adaptation to stable growth had succeeded. Even 5% growth had come to be seen as "no longer a recession" (Kosai and Ogino, 1980). Also contributing to the situation were the support afforded by increased public spending and an improvement in the terms of trade due to the favorable exchange rate. From the latter half of that year and into 1979, the long-awaited rise in private plant and equipment investment at last became marked. For the time being the first oil crisis had been surmounted by the achieving of price stability and a revival of business investment.

The Curtain Rings Down on Rapid Growth

During the generation following the defeat in World War II, the Japanese economy achieved remarkable growth, and national life took on a completely different aspect. The defeat sowed the seeds of this "growth revolution" in a time of trouble for the existing economic order: land reform, dissolution of the zaibatsu, liberation of the labor movement, and so on. Interfirm competition became vigorous, and as technology was introduced from abroad, plant and equipment investment rekindled into a blaze. That this was a revolution and not a *coup d'état* can be seen from the fact that the masses were mobilized and took part in it. The people participated in this process via their work, their voluntary job changes, their high rate of saving, and—perhaps most important—their considerable expenditures on durable consumer goods over the long term. As a result they achieved full employment and income equalization for the first time since the beginning of modernization. The success of the revolution at home became tied to exports, and high-quality, inexpensive Japanese goods flooded world markets. Thus, the course of the growth revolution resembles that of a political revolution in its sequence of events: (1) fragmentation and confrontation within the ruling order, (2) the elbowing in of the masses, and (3) foreign revolutionary wars.

The starting point for the growth revolution was the difference between the Japanese and American standards of living, of which the Japanese were forcefully made aware by military defeat and occupation. This consciousness had existed since the Meiji era, but traditionalism and a belief in austerity, which caused reluctance to close this gap, were also deep-rooted. Before the war, the ultimate values were traditional: they could be summarized as *wakon*, Japanese spirit; modernization was no more than a means of protecting what was traditional. After the war, however, modernization itself became a value, a goal. It became the ideology of the growth revolution.

Japan's traditional values were banished from consciousness into the world of the unconscious, but they survived in Japanese groupism as methods of goal attainment. Modernization made full use of the wisdom of Japanese traditional life (consensus, intragroup competition, selfless devotion to country), but conscious affirmation of this came only after rapid growth had continued for quite some time and the Japanese people had regained their self-confidence.

From about 1970 onward circumstances made the continuation of rapid growth difficult. To draw analogies with the French Revolution, the rebuilding-the-archipelago boom corresponds to the Jacobin

Reign of Terror, and the suppression of aggregate demand following the period of crazy prices surely resembles the reaction of Thermidor. The conditions that brought a halt to rapid growth are known to have been (1) the limits that external dependence placed on economic growth, as attested to by the oil crisis, trade friction, and fluctuations in the yen exchange rate; and (2) internal limits to economic growth as well, in the form of environmental problems, price increases, labor shortages, and so on. In the midst of all this, growth was no longer a simple consensual goal, and growthmanship itself was on the decline in Japan's already affluent middle-class society. When accelerating growth became impossible, the long-term expected rate of growth declined, the decelerated growth became a reality instead. The ideology of modernization that had sustained growth lost its power, its popularity displaced in the final phases of rapid growth by Japanese social theories such as the vertical society and the society of familism (*ie*). In place of stages-of-development theories such as the theory of modernization, comparative cultural approaches placing greater stress on individuality than on development became influential. For popular feeling, this was a real coming home to the Japanese traditions once suppressed as inferior, and it was a natural outgrowth of the revived self-confidence of the Japanese people, now that they had caught up with the advanced nations in terms of economic power.

Thus, the rapid-growth revolution that characterized the generation after the war appears to have breathed its last. Through rapid growth, however, affluence and an equitable middle-class society have been achieved. During rapid growth and the ensuing adjustment period, the vitality of firms has been further bolstered, and the market mechanism is showing greater flexibillty than ever. In order for the Japanese economy to reach a new maturity on such a base, and to achieve harmony with the international community while contributing to world security and development, Japan must reform its financial and tax systems, its public corporations and its social security system. It must also strive to improve the urban and residential environments and to create an industrial structure with low natural resource requirements. Decelerating growth is meaningful if and only if in the people's judgment moderate growth is preferable to super-rapid growth in resolving economic and social problems. It should be based on the intent to create an independent Japanese culture that will, with the passage of time, transcend the era of economic growth. The world situation today may be harsh, but with the oil crisis and inflation conquered for the time being, the future is bright for the Japanese economy.

Epilogue: Looking Back on the Rapid Growth Era

The rapid growth era came to an end around 1970. Having weathered the transitional adjustment period that ensued, the Japanese economy of the 1980s is setting out on a new path of development.

This does not mean, however, that rapid growth has become a matter of indifference to us. On the contrary, our lives today are incomprehensible apart from the experience of rapid growth. Rapid growth has ended, it is true, but in another sense it still survives after the chaos of the 1970s.

First of all, whether one talks of the people's affluent material life, of the brisk industrial and business activity that supports it, of the high level of employment opportunity and the equalized distribution of income, or of the nation's enhanced international status, the constituents of our world today all arose either from the process of rapid growth or from its results. Neither the hyperinflation of the 1970s, the oil crisis and other external shocks, nor the long recession seriously disturbed these fundamental conditions of national life.

Secondly, having completed the series of adjustments entailed by the retreat from rapid growth, the Japanese economy is embarking upon a new growth process that hinges on swift advances in energy conservation, on development of the electronics, chemical refining, and service industries, and on a renewed flourishing of investment in basic industries. Even if high growth rates such as those hovering around 10% in the 1960s will not be seen again, it appears entirely likely that Japan's economic growth rate in the 1980s will be relatively high compared to that of the other advanced industrial nations. Although it will differ in degree and scope, some portion of the experience of the era of high-speed growth will be repeated. This process, too, may be termed the legacy of rapid growth.

When we take a look at our lives, they are brimming with the legacy of economic growth. How did rapid growth begin and how did it end?

What is its legacy to the future? Finding answers to these questions remains important today.

Before drawing some conclusions about the high-speed growth era and its implications for the future, as a way of summarizing the discussion in the twelve preceding chapters, I would like to discuss five statements, or theses, about rapid growth.

> *Rapid growth was a series of technological innovations in the modernization of the Japanese economy, the process of catching up with the advanced nations.*

Rapid growth was the Japanese economy's way of modernizing and catching up with the world's leading economies. This fact is widely recognized; and in this book, too, we have looked back in retrospect on the growth era from this standpoint.

The theory that rapid growth equals modernization is itself a product of rapid growth. The Ishibashi and Ikeda Cabinets adopted growth-promoting policies in order to break up the dual structure, a traditional proclivity of the Japanese economy, and to achieve modern full employment. During the early postwar years the Marxist interpretation that rapid growth in fact depended on the dual structure was influential among intellectuals. It was around 1960 that the modernization hypothesis gained sway over the Marxist view. Thus, the breakup of the dual economic structure as a result of rapid growth contributed to the ascendancy of the modernization hypothesis.

When one speaks of rapid growth as the modernization process, it is easy to imagine a great leap forward or a take-off which leaves backwardness behind. And in some ways the Japanese economy's development in the 1950s did resemble this type of process. However, Japan had a history of industrialization preceding rapid growth that extended back to the Meiji era, not to mention a level of technology that had been equal to the demands of modern warfare. Moreover, the growth rate of the Japanese economy increased the most during the latter half of the 1960s, when the dual structure was broken up. These facts suggest that the primary factors in rapid growth were not uniform but varied, depending on the time period. At the same time they also suggest that we cannot simply view Japan's rapid growth as a linear progression from backwardness so long as this growth is considered to include the latter half of the 1960s. Accordingly, here modernization should not be taken only in the narrow sense of "take-off," but should be thought of as including the entire process of advancing toward maturity, achieving a mass consumption society, and so on. In this sense modernization covers catching up with the advanced nations and also economic development as an advanced nation. Perhaps that makes our target a moving one. With that in mind, I use the term "innovation" here to indicate that modernization proceeded rapidly. Since "big push" and "great leap forward" are phrases used in the sense of escape from the so-called vicious circle of poverty at the beginning of modernization, they cannot be employed meaningfully in the present context.

Modernization as the achievement of an affluent life by catching up with the advanced nations was a goal that captivated many people from the time of the defeat in World War II to the oil crisis of the 1970s.

Seen from the present point in time, however, the simple theory that rapid growth equals modernization does not offer a sufficiently broad field of vision. In the first place, while the scope and standards of the Japanese economy are catching up with or overtaking those of the advanced nations, in those same advanced nations the "disease of industrial society" is becoming evident. Interpreting rapid growth as merely a matter of "catching up with the advanced nations" precludes assessing the legacy of rapid growth or offering an outlook on post-rapid-growth trends. Even granting that the Japanese economy's scale and standard of industrial technology have attained levels that compare favorably with those of the advanced nations, its systemic features—its style of group behavior—have not been completely Europeanized or Americanized. Instead the features of Japanese society appear to be promoting the economy's development, preventing the appearance of the "disease of industrial society," and insuring good performance. A renewed inquiry must be launched into the relationship between modernization and the special characteristics of Japanese society's system and behavioral style.

> *The Japanese economy's rapid growth was achieved through reliance on the market mechanism.*

Rapid growth was not simply the result of growth policies; still less was it the result of a "plot" on the part of a segment of the elite. Rather, it was the cumulation of prompt responses to market conditions by firms and households at the grassroots level that was decisively important. A thriving entrepreneurial spirit, the high morale and discipline of the workers, the high saving rate of households, the high rate of college entrance, all were manifestations of this phenomenon. This does not mean there were no heroes in rapid growth, but (to put it in terms of *War and Peace*), instead of Napoleons they were Kutu-zovs or, better, Tushins, or even Dolokhofs.

Nor does the above-mentioned proposition simply mean that the price mechanism was dominant. Japan's market mechanism and the conditions surrounding it fulfilled the classical assumptions. Unlike Korea and Brazil during their years of rapid growth, Japan avoided hyperinflation. Moreover, in contrast to the situation in the other advanced countries, price controls were not adopted, either. As the economy grew, the level of interest rates declined, finance was "normalized," fiscal balance was maintained over a long period of time, "small government" was preserved, fixed exchange rate parity was maintained, and balance of payments deficits were overcome, even at considerable sacrifice. The source of capital accumulation was the frugality of the people, not exploitation by the nation. During rapid growth the Japanese economy operated to a surprising extent according to the game rules of classical capitalism. From the viewpoint of the late twentieth century, when big government is the rule in many countries, this was a miraculous phenomenon.

Writing as he does in basic agreement with the foregoing thesis, the author cannot entirely agree with a number of hypotheses that have been presented about rapid growth. In addition to the theory of excess competition and the oligopoly theory, which have been refuted by Komiya and Takenaka, some other popular hypotheses include the following:

• *The "Japan, Incorporated" hypothesis, the Ministry of Finance/Bank of Japan dynasty hypothesis, and other similar elitist historical views.* Perhaps the government-business relationship at the beginning of the 1950s, when the rationalization plans were launched, conforms with these theories. However, it must not be overlooked that those plans were from the beginning fraught with excesses. And even during that period, the initiative of private firms was decisive, as Kawasaki Steel's opening of an integrated plant in Chiba shows. One might add in passing that this type of dynastic-historical view is inconsistent with rational expectations theory, which has gained popularity of late.

• *The one-settism hypothesis.* The one-settism hypothesis, which focuses primarily on the financial groupings (*kin'yu keiretsu*), under-rates the fact that the rapid growth process strengthened the equity finance position of business firms, and the financial groupings as a result became more liquid.

• *The artificially low interest rate theory.* There is a theory that a policy keeping interest rates low was a primary cause of high growth, but a great number of facts are incompatible with the low interest rate theory: the sharp drop in the city banks' share of lending, changes in the financial composition of Treasury loans and investments (increases in the relative share of agricultural and small business finance), the rapidly declining trend in the lending rate of interest for small and medium-sized financial institutions, and so on.

• *The theory of the effects of micro planning.* This theory holds that the government's macro-economic planning is window-dressing, and that what has been effective is micro planning such as administrative guidance on an industry-by-industry basis. There are certainly examples of successful micro planning, but its overall validity is doubtful. Government intervention did not necessarily produce the anticipated results on all occasions, and negative assessments of such efforts do exist. The effectiveness of some macro-economic planning, on the other hand, is recognized for providing a national consensus and hastening adaptation to an open market.

• *The theory of the bloating of the intermediate goods sector.* When one views Japan's industrial structure as having an artificially bloated intermediate goods sector, it becomes easy to overlook the fact that high value-added also characterizes industries considered to be in the materials sector, and that the role of intermediate goods can also be seen in the development of the processing and assembly industries. Moreover, underrating the fact that Japan's industrial structure arose as an adaptation to the market easily results in damage to a fair assessment of Japanese industries' capacities for adaptation to changes in market conditions.

• *The corporatism hypothesis.* The view that economic management decisions during the rapid growth period were made in centralized negotiations among government agencies, business enterprises, labor unions, and other bodies is not adopted in this book. Such central organization was not very powerful. Inter-firm competition was fierce, and new entries into various industries were numerous. The labor unions were first organized at the business firm level; there was no national center at a united federation level or higher. Appearances to the contrary notwithstanding, the annual spring wage negotiations have always ended with results indicating that wage determination in Japan is flexible and subject to market pressure. Farmers' groups are powerful, but when there have been rice surpluses, the producers' price of rice has not increased. Power relationships among the political parties, the bureaucrats, and the politicians normally give priority to the politicians and the political parties. Japan's political-economic system can best be characterized as pluralism for the collective advantage, rather than as groupism.

Furthermore, when one focuses on adaptation to market conditions, one can see that the growth of the Japanese economy as a whole was not an unbalanced growth process but a balanced one. Nakamura Takafusa, who has analyzed Japan's prewar economic growth, distinguishes between a balanced period (from the Meiji era to the First World War) when traditional industries and industries of foreign origin coexisted harmoniously, and a period of imbalance (the interwar period), when contradictions and confrontations between the two became exacerbated and monopoly and the dual structure were reinforced (Nakamura, 1983). During the period of rapid growth, the dual structure broke up as the development of big business and the development of agriculture and small business paralleled each other. This shows that, in Nakamura's sense as well, the rapid growth period can be referred to as one of balanced growth.

Rapid growth was achieved on the basis of the special system, customs, and behavioral style of Japanese society.

The process of writing this retrospective enabled me in my own way to confirm my convictions with regard to the first two theses outlined above. Concerning the hypothesis that attributes rapid growth in any major sense to "special" factors in Japanese society, however, I remain skeptical.

Japan's economic society changed greatly as "rapid growth *cum* modernization" proceeded. Nevertheless, a distinctive system, customs, and behavioral style have been maintained in Japanese society. Moreover, the realization appears to have dawned that these distinctive features are making an unexpectedly positive contribution to rapid growth. After the discrediting of both the Marxist and modernist varieties of stages-of-development theory, works on Japanese society and social characteristics like those of Ben-Dasan (1972) and Nakane (1970) became very popular. These successes signalled the ascendancy of comparative culture theories in place of stages of development theories. In the field of economics, Takeuchi Hiroshi persuasively contended that Japan's behavioral style, differing as it does from that of Europe and the United States, was in fact becoming one of Japan's assets.

Now, where does this Japanese behavioral style stand relative to modernization and to the market mechanism? Iida Tsuneo has pointed out that the constituent members of close-knit groups respond to such shocks as growth, liberalization, industrial conversion, and so on as if they were their own problems; and it was precisely the Japanese behavioral style of contriving adaptations through tacit understanding and unified cooperation that displayed to the fullest the information efficiency of the market mechanism. According to Iida, this was without doubt a "synthesis of the old and new classical schools," of the market mechanism and the Japanese behavioral style. This results in the paradox that what is Japanese is universal, and what is universal is Japanese. The Takeuchi and Iida theories skillfully explain the Japanese economy's superb performance. This explanation is the most effective antidote for the complex toward the advanced nations that frequently afflicts intellectuals. Undiluted, however, the approach that emphasizes' social factors can take us to such lengths as the revival of theories of the superiority of the Japanese people and a halt to analytical thinking.

Several additional comments on this subject are in order. Of primary importance, the Japanese behavioral style did not in and of itself increase efficiency; freedom, democracy and the market mechanism provided a universalistic framework within which efficiency could be enhanced. In the period prior to the Second World War, the goal was to preserve traditional values (*wakon*, Japanese spirit), and the means of achieving this was European technology (*yōsai*, Western learning). After the war, however, modern democratism set the goal, and Japanese modes of behavior were banished to the realm of the subconscious, where they survived as a process or means, so to speak. It was as a result of all this that efficiency rose. The tension and balance among universal values and particularistic values are themselves important, and a one-sided view is dangerous.

Opinion is divided on the origins of Japanese customs. For example, one special characteristic of the labor force is that there is very little difference between white- and blue-collar workers; several different factors, which are difficult to separate, probably contribute to this characteristic: (1) egalitarian consciousness within the traditional community, (2) the experience and structure of the wartime Patriotic Industrial Associations, (3) modern egalitarianism, and (4) the equalizing influence of the absolute poverty following the war. The historical experience of the Pacific War and Japan's defeat had a major effect on the ethos of a generation of Japanese. Included in this war experience were (1) group discipline, which was built up prior to and during the war, (2) a common fighting experience, which stressed friendship and equality, (3) starvation and abject poverty, (4) the difference people keenly felt between the technological level and living standard of the advanced nations and their own, (5) the awareness of a common fate as a people, which was reinforced by military defeat, and (6) contact with American culture at the level of the masses. There is a theory that the primary carriers of the modernization ethos in England and America were the independent peasants. Moreover, it is said that the same role was played in the Meiji Restoration by the lower-class samurai. By analogy, the answer to the question of who supplied the principal support for the rapid growth ethos would be the skilled workers who were the mainstays of factories and offices. This situation is thought to be directly linked to the government's work during the demobilization. (On this point, Namiki Nobuyoshi's theory of the control of middle managers is worthy of close attention. See Namiki, 1980.) Rapid growth was achieved atop a delicate balance between reinforced traditional group discipline and an ethic of self-denial on the one hand, and on the other, an ethic of liberation in which freedom and equality were granted anew. While this increased the efficiency of the market mechanism, it also eased and compensated for the psychological tension produced by rapid growth.

The strength of the Japanese behavioral style is that it is well suited to minor situations, but its general effectiveness has, at the least, yet to be tested. A felicitous choice for Japan, and one leading to success, was postwar Japanese society's failure to take the path of political revolution advocated by the intellectuals, and its selection, instead, of the path to economic revolution via rapid growth, with the masses assimilating modernization and the technological revolution in a setting of traditional human relations.

A rapid growth ethos inevitably ages with time. The very results of "modernization equals rapid growth" create a new ethos. Of course there is nothing inherently bad about this. The merits of Japanese society (like its demerits) are still its own. The decline of the ethos of the rapid growth period does not inevitably mean economic chaos and the waning of international competitiveness. On the contrary: the propensity toward labor discipline, high morale, and technological refinement is alive and well even now. But the urgency of the growth period was replaced by a margin of complacency; humility and a touch of an inferiority complex will probably be replaced by a bit of self-confidence and even feelings of superiority. No one knows what the future may hold, but social change in Japan will be followed with great interest.

The Japanese economy pursued rapid growth *cum* modernization while leaving its traditional system, customs, and behavioral style intact. This configuration of customs, system, and behavioral style continues to retain its high efficiency even now. However, there are also thought to have been some conditions which made this socio-cultural combination especially effective in the rapid growth process.

Rapid growth was a process of reconciling external de-
pendence on raw materials and a high level of domestic con-
sumption with the development of exports and a technolog-
ical revolution in the processing industries.

The fact that the Japanese economy combined basic raw materials
imports with processing industries was a matter of being faithful to the
laws of a market economy. The question is, how much potential did
these industries have?

Rapid growth was sustained by the worldwide technological revolution, one current of which was the energy revolution. The blockading
of raw materials imports during the war and, in contrast to it, the 1947
and 1948 experiments with the priority production system; high iron
and coal prices at the beginning of 1950; and initial gropings toward
rationalization all show that one historical keynote throughout the
decade from 1946 to 1955 was the problem of raw materials constraints.
Not surprisingly, economists at that time engaged in a controversy over
trade-ism versus developmentalism—a discussion on a scale compar-
able with its epoch-making historical antecedent, the debate over the
Corn Laws in Britain. Faced with a deterioration in both natural and
labor conditions for domestic coal production and with the fact that the
development of hydroelectric power had reached the point of diminishing returns in terms of natural resources, Japan's industries were
making a major shift to bulk transport and bulk use of the foreign oil
which was being rapidly brought into production. This route took advantage of large-scale drops in transportation costs and of the coastal
locations with which Japan was well endowed by any standard.

It is well to recognize that liberation in this way from the shackles
of a meager domestic raw materials base was one of the conditions for
Japan's rapid growth. The oil crisis at the beginning of the 1970s testi-
fied to this fact in a backhanded way. The sudden leaps in the price of
oil neither sank the Japanese economy nor halted growth, but they
made it difficult to maintain the high growth rate of about 10% per
year.

The technological revolution of the rapid growth period, moreover,
was accompanied by the improvement of consumer durables such as
automobiles and television sets, as well as new products and processes
in the petrochemicals and steel industries. Since the development of the
inter-relationships among these industries was described in Chapter
7, it will not be discussed here. What I would like to emphasize here is
the triple and quadruple role the workers in these industries played in
the rapid growth process. First, they digested the new technology and

guaranteed high-quality production by making further refinements and improvements, using painstaking management and discipline. Second, these workers loosened the dual structure of the labor market by means of their mass relocations in response to the new employment opportunities that opened up in these industries, and they were the ones who promoted the equalization of incomes. Third, they (along with countless other individiuals) bought and used the new consumer durables they themselves had produced. Rapid growth brought about full employment, and a new middle-class society emerged. Its mainstay was the employees of modern industry. Fourth, the working class exemplified the Japanese system, customs, and behavioral style that worked to such good advantage during rapid growth.

Turning on the development of processing industries and foreign trade, an economic structure was produced which made dependence on raw materials from abroad compatible with a high level of domestic consumption. It may be criticized as a fragile structure, but by means of the efforts of working people, it achieved the highest possible standard of living, given Japan's territory and population.

Japan achieved rapid growth as a small country enjoying the benefits of world peace, free trade, and technology transfer.

There is no particular need to explain this statement. We all know that rapid growth was basically sustained by world peace. There were occasions when the Japanese economy appeared to benefit from local wars, but these were temporary, and a none-too-modest price had to be paid in the form of domestic inflation (in the case of the Korean War) or disruption of the global economy by worldwide inflation (the Vietnam War). The evident fact that having a very small defense burden contributed to rapid growth does not square with the argument of the Marxists that militarization sustained growth.

It is clear that free trade and the free transfer of technology were conditions of major importance for Japan's rapid growth. Also undeniable is the fact that the Japanese economy came to enjoy the advantages of being a small latecomer. Thus, the question of the form in which Japan-turned-economic-superpower will participate in the new international economic order has now become an issue.

The Outlook for the Post-Rapid-Growth Era

During the 1970s the Japanese economy departed from the rapid growth path, passed through a difficult period of adjustment, and greeted the eighties by embarking upon a more moderate growth path and taking the first steps toward new development. Since conditions during that period and my own views on the subject are related elsewhere (see Kosai and Ogino, 1984), I will not discuss this matter in detail here.

Instead, let us consider how the five points outlined above apply under current conditions. Once we have finished with that, let us venture something of an outlook for the post-rapid-growth era.

Clearly, the Japanese economy (which is not, needless to say, synonymous with Japanese society) has modernized and caught up with the advanced nations. While the nation's self-confidence is growing as a result of this success, however, at the same time a sense of a loss of goals is apparent—a loss which can lead to apathy, selfishness, and social disintegration. As a result, while it is to be hoped that liberation from the feeling of privation, a sense of serenity, and the diversification of values will continue, we must give some thought to the danger that self-confidence will turn into arrogance and an exaggerated awareness of the nation's superpower status.

Another danger for Japan is that imitation of successful models and dependence upon a soulless machine for unlimited growth could become a habit. The advantages that Japan was once able to enjoy as a small and backward country have been lost, and it is becoming difficult to rely on others to establish the technological frontier. The question now is whether the Japanese economy will be able to maintain its position and attitude both technologically and in spirit. The Japanese economy's achievements to date have been truly superb. Our task henceforward will be to make cultural progress that keeps pace with the technological.

Adapting to market conditions and making the most of its resources and the world environment, the Japanese economy performed superbly in the rapid-growth period. The energy crisis, however, posed a challenge to the manufacturing-oriented industrial structure. The experience of the adjustment process in the 1970s demonstrated that Japan's market mechanism and industrial structure had the capacity to survive such a crisis. It became the occasion for damping rapid growth and arousing a healthy new sense of tension.

The Japanese behavioral style will continue to pose a problem in the future as well. Are the Japanese people changing, or are they staying the same? Which would be better?

Above and beyond these specific questions, we Japanese have no choice but to risk all in our efforts to obtain the raw materials that will secure tomorrow's prosperity for the Japanese economy. That fact alone is certain.

The record of the era of rapid growth gives us courage. "The memorable events of history lift the spirit, and if one reads them discerningly, they are useful in nurturing one's critical faculties" (Descartes, *Discourse on Method*). It is my hope that this book, too, will prove helpful in that regard.

Bibliography

Allison, Graham T. 1971. *The Essence of Decision: Explaining the Cuban Missile Crisis.* Boston: Little, Brown.

Arahata Kanson. 1965. *Kanson jiden* [Autobiography]. Tokyo: Iwanami Shoten.

Arisawa Hiromi. 1948. *Infureshon to shakaika* [Inflation and Socialization]. Tokyo: Nihon Hyōron Sha; reprinted 1957.

Bailey, Norman T. J. 1964. *The Elements of Stochastic Processes.* New York: Wiley.

Ben-Dasan, Isaiah [pseudonym; the real author of the book is Japanese writer and critic Yamamoto Shichihei]. 1972. *The Japanese and the Jews* (translated by Richard Gage). Tokyo: John Weatherhill, Inc.

Cohen, J. B. 1949. *Japan's Economy in War and Reconstruction.* Minneapolis: University of Minnesota Press.

Dore, Ronald P. 1959. *Land Reform in Japan.* Oxford: Oxford University Press.

Economic Planning Agency. 1970. *Kigyō kōdō chōsa* [Survey of the Behavior of Firms]. February.

Economic Planning Agency, Research Division. 1970. "Bankokuhaku no keizaiteki eikyō" [On the Economic Influence of the World Exposition].

Ekonomisuto, ed. 1960. *Nihon keizai no seichō* [The Growth of the Japanese Economy].

Gardner, Richard N. 1980. *Sterling-Dollar Diplomacy in Current Perspective.* New York: Columbia University Press.

Gayn, Mark J. 1948. *Japan Diary.* New York: Sloan. Reprinted Tokyo: Charles E. Tuttle, 1981.

Gould, J. D. 1972. *Economic Growth in History.* London: Methuen.

Hansen, A.H. 1957. *The American Economy.* New York: McGraw-Hill.

Hata Ikuhiko. 1976. *Amerika no tainichi senryō seisaku* [The U.S. Occupation Policy for Japan], Vol. 3 of the 20-volume series *Shōwa zaisei shi* [Financial History of Modern Japan]. Tokyo: Tōyō Keizai Shimpō Sha.

Hayashi Shūji. 1962. *Ryūtsū kakumei* [Distribution Revolution]. Tokyo: Chūō Kōron Sha.

Hayashi Yūjirō. 1957. *Nihon no keizai keikaku* [Japan's Economic Plans]. Tokyo: Tōyō Keizai Shimpō Sha.

Hirschman, Albert O. 1958. *The Strategy of Economic Development.* New York: Norton.

Hori Hiroshi. 1961. "Tōshi ga tōshi o yobu mekanizumu" [The Investment-Calls-Forth-Investment Mechanism], *Keizai Geppō* [Monthly Economic Report], Economic Planning Agency Research Division, September.

Horsefield, Keith. 1969. *The International Monetary Fund, 1945–1965*, 3 vols. Geneva: International Monetary Fund.

Iida Tsuneo et al. 1976. *Gendai Nihon keizai shi* [Contemporary Japanese Economic History]. Tokyo: Chikuma Shobo.

Iron and Steel Federation. 1959. *Sengo tekkō shi* [The Postwar History of Iron and Steel]. Tokyo.

Johnson, Chalmers. 1982. *MITI and the Japanese Miracle.* Stanford: Stanford University Press.

Kakumoto Ryohei. 1964. *Tōkaidō Shinkansen* [The Tōkaidō Bullet Train]. Tokyo: Chūō Kōron Sha.

Kin'yū Zaisei Jijō Kenkyūkai, ed. 1959. *Nihon keizai no seichōryoku* [The Growth Capacity of the Japanese Economy].

Kojima Nobuo. 1954. *Amerikan Sukuru* [The American School]. Two translations have been published: by Bernard Susser and Genkawa Tomoyoshi (*Japan Interpreter*, Vol. 11 No. 4, 1977, pp. 467–82) and by William F. Sibley (in *Contemporary Japanese Literature*, ed. Howard Hibbett; New York: Knopf, 1977, pp. 120–44).

Kokumin Keizai Kenkyū Kyōkai. 1961. *Kikai kōygō nt okeru setsubi tōshi no kenkyū* [A Study of Plant and Equipment Investment in the Machinery Industry]. Tokyo.

Komiya Ryūtarō. 1970. "Nihon ni okeru dokusen to kigyō rijun" [Monopoly and Profit in Japan], in Baba Masao, ed., *Sangyō soshiki* Industrial Organization]. Tokyo: Nihon Keizai Shimbun Sha.

Kosai Yutaka. 1961. "Chūkibo kigyō no seichō to sono shihon chōtatsu" [The Growth of Medium-sized Firms and Their Capital Procurement]. *Keizai Geppō* [Monthly Economic Bulletin], Economic Planning Agency Research Division, April 28.

Kosai Yutaka and Ogino Yoshitarō. 1980. *Nihon keizai tenbō* [Outlook for the Japanese Economy]. Tokyo: Nihon Hyōron Sha. Adapted and translated as *The Contemporary Japanese Economy*, London: Macmillan, 1984.

Kosai Yutaka and Toshida Sei'ichi. 1981. *Keizai seichō* [Economic Growth]. Tokyo: Nihon Keizai Shimbun Sha, Nikkei Bunko.

Masuda Yoneji. 1965. *Sengo narikin no botsuraku* [The Ruin of the Postwar Nouveaux Riches]. Tokyo: Kōbun Sha..

Maxcy, C., and A. Silberston. 1959. *The Motor Industry.* Cambridge: Cambridge University Press.

Miyazaki Isamu. 1977. *Ningen no kao o shita keizai seisaku* [Economic Policy with a Human Face]. Tokyo: Chūō Kōron Sha.

Miyazaki Yoshikazu. 1977. "Sengo kigyō taisei no magarikado" [The Postwar Business System], *Sekai*, June.

Murakami Yasusuke, ed. 1971. *Keizai seichō* [Economic Growth]. Tokyo: Nihon Keizai Shimbun Sha.

Nakamura Takafusa. 1981. *The Postwar Japanese Economy.* Translation (by Jacqueline Kaminski) of *Nihon keizai: Sono seichō to kōzō* [The Japanese Economy: Its Growth and Structure]. Tokyo: University of Tokyo Press.

Nakamura Takafusa. 1983. *Economic Growth in Prewar Japan.* Translation (by Robert A. Feldman) of *Senzenki Nihon keizai seichō no bunseki* (Iwanami Shoten). New Haven: Yale University Press.

Nakamura Shūichirō. 1964. *Chūken kigyōron* [On Medium-sized Firms]. Tokyo: Tōyō Keizai Shimpō Sha.

Nakane Chie. 1970. *Japanese Society.* Translation of *Tateshakai no ningen kankei.* Berkeley: University of California Press.

Nakauchi Isao. 1969. *Waga yasuuri tetsugaku* [Our Philosophy of Discount Selling]. Tokyo: Nihon Keizai Shimbun Sha.

Nakayama Ichirō. 1954. *Nihon keizai no kao* [The Face of the Japanese Economy]. Tokyo: Nihon Hyōron Sha.

Namiki Nobuyoshi. 1980. *Nihon keizai ittō ryōdan* [Cutting the Gordian Knot of the Japanese Economy]. Tokyo: Nihon Keizai Shimbun Sha.

Nurkse, Ragnar. 1961. *Equilibrium and Growth in the World Economy.* Cambridge: Harvard University Press.

Ohki Yoichi. 1960. *Sekitan kōgyō* [Structure of the Coal Mining Industry], Vol. III of *Gendai Nihon sangyō kōza* [Lectures on Contemporary Japanese Industries], ed. Arisawa Hiromi. Tokyo: Iwanami Shoten.

Rostow, W. W. 1971. *The Stages of Economic Growth*, 2nd ed. New York: Columbia University Press.

Shinohara Miyohei. 1962. "Nihon keizai wa tenkeiki ni aru ka" [Is the Japanese Economy in a Pattern Transition Period?], *Chūō Kōron*, special issue on management, January.

Shishido Hisao. 1967. "Tenkeiki wa owatta" [The Pattern Transition Period Has Ended], *Ekonomisuto*, January 17.

Strachey, John. 1956. *Contemporary Capitalism.* New York: Random House.

Sumiya, Mikio, and Koji Taira, eds. 1979. *An Outline of Japanese Economic History 1603–1940: Major Works and Research Findings.* Tokyo: University of Tokyo Press.

Suzuki Takeo. 1952. *Gendai Nihon zaiseishi* [Financial History of Modern Japan], Vol. 1. Tokyo: University of Tokyo Press.

Suzuki Yoshio. 1980. *Money and Banking in Contemporary Japan* (translated by John G. Greenwood). New Haven: Yale University Press.

Takasuga Yoshihiro. 1972. *Gendai Nippon no bukka mondai* [Japan's Inflation Problem]. Tokyo: Shin Hyōron Sha.

Takenaka Kazuo. 1962. "Nihon sangyō no kōdō seichō to shin sangyō taisei" [Rapid Industrial Growth and the New Industrial System in Japan], *Kikan Nihon Keizai Bunseki* [Japanese Economic Analysis Quarterly], No. 4.

Tanaka Kakuei. 1972. *Nihon rettō kaiso ron.* Tokyo: Simul Press. Translated and published in English as *Rebuilding the Japanese Archipelago.* Tokyo: Simul International, 1973.

Tohata Sei'ichi. 1954. *Nihon nōgyō no sugata* [The State of Japanese Agriculture]. Tokyo: Nihon Hyōron Sha.

Tsuchiya Takao. 1939. *Nihon shihonshugi shi ronshū* [Collected Essays on the History of Japanese Capitalism]. Tokyo: Yūsei Sha; reprinted 1981, Shozan Sha.

U.S. Strategic Bombing Survey. 1946. "The Effects of of Strategic Bombing on Japan's War Economy." Washington, D.C.: U.S. Government Printing Office.

Index

acceleration principle, 108, 111, 139, 193
administrative guidance, 182, 205
Agricultural Land Reform Bills, 19
agriculture: population employed in, 39, 41, 163; productivity in, 23, 33, 34, 98, 163
Aichi Kiichi, 190
Allied Policy for Japan (1948), 54, 55-56
Anti-Monopoly Law, 167
Antitrust Law (1947), 25
Aoki Takayoshi, 59
Arahata Kanson, 29
Arisawa Hiromi, 42, 56, 80
Arisawa-Kimura Debate, 56
Ashida Cabinet, 47, 59, 62
Ashida Hitoshi, 58
automobile industry, 85, 168; growth of, 118-120
automobiles, imports of, 75

balance of payments, 3, 11, 138; deficit, 99; fluctuations in, 71-72, 78; stabilized, 97, 102, 157; surpluses, 11, 135, 157, 177, 178, 196
Ball, MacMahon, 19
Bank of Japan, 100-101, 104; and inflation at the end of war, 35-36; lending activities, 63, 89, 98, 144, 147
bankruptcies, in 1960's, 139, 146, 153, 156, 158
banks: at center of *keiretsu* financial groupings, 27, 121, 148; competition among, 144, 148; lending by, 143, 144
Basic Agriculture Law, 152

Bond Investment Trust (Kōshasai Tōshi Shintaku), 138
bonds, 60, 90, 98, 159
boom periods, 102, 106, 111; consumption boom, 74, 75, 76; investment boom, 77, 78, 112, 138; Iwato boom, 102-105, 111, 136, 137, 140, 143; Jimmu boom, 99-102, 104, 111, 138; "Rebuilding the Archipelago" boom, 146, 199; special procurement boom, 70-74, 77; "*sūryō*" (quantitative prosperity) boom, 97, 99
Bretton Woods system, 80, 173
budget (national): balanced, 11, 59-60, 158, 159; "one trillion yen," 78, 97, 101; "super"-balanced, 61, 62
Bullet Train (*Shinkansen*), 154, 155, 190
business cycle theory, 143
business cycles, 106-107, 143-144

capital accumulation, 8, 45, 49, 161, 204
capital coefficients, 5, 6, 37, 91, 92, 112
capital equipment ratio, 6
capital formation, 8-9
capital liberalization, 166-167
capital stock, 5, 37, 40, 49, 108, 111, 112, 138
carbide industry, 116-117
chemical industries, 120; export dependence of, 164; investment in, 85, 92, 117; plant and equipment capacity of, 37; raw materials for, 118

217

chūken kigyō (high-growth medium-sized firms), 149-153
coal, displaced by oil as energy source, 83, 116, 123
coal industry, 41-42, 49, 80, 82-83, 123; financing for, 45, 46-47; inventories in, 61; labor-management relations, 41, 82, 129; operating costs, 80, 92; production levels in, 33, 41-42
coastal industrial zones, 123, 209
Cold War, 54-55, 65, 66, 95, 96
Communist Party, 49; Occupation purge of, 65
computer industry, 120
constitution, provisions of, 29-30
consumer durables industry, 163
consumption, levels of, 8, 9, 74, 91
consumption patterns, 9, 48, 74, 76, 92, 99-100, 104, 120, 149, 202-203
Counterpart Fund, 61, 63
culture, American: impact on Japanese 17, 29, 208
culture, Japanese, 17, 31, 68, 199, 200, 206, 207-208
currency, stabilization of, 56

Daiei Incorporated, 152
Daiichi Bank, 167
democratization, under Occupation, 11, 17, 29-32, 53
depreciation, 89
Designated Industries Law, 148, 167
discount rate, lowered in 1960s, 144, 157
distribution system, 107, 150-152
Dodge Plan, 33, 47, 55, 56-65, 66, 67-68, 79, 89
Dodge, Joseph, 55, 59-60, 66
Dore, Ronald, 19
dual structure, 11, 76-77, 92, 96, 149-150, 202, 206; breakdown of, 125, 133, 210
Dulles, John Foster, 55, 69

Economic and Social Development Plan, 149, 167
Economic Planning Agency, 196
Economic Recovery Planning Commission, 58-59

Economic Stabilization Board, 56, 59
Economic Stabilization Plan (1949), 36
education, liberalization of, 27
Edwards, Corwin L., 23
Electric Power Industry Workers' Union (Densan), 84
electric appliances industry, 120
electric machinery industry, 116, 120
electric power industry, 34, 83, 116-117; labor-management relations, 84; reorganization of, 87
Emergency Financial Measures (1946), 36, 43, 44
employment: decline in, 193, 195, 198; increases in, 6, 156
energy, importation of, 165
Engel coefficient, 33, 75, 99
Enterprise Rationalization Promotion Law (1952), 88-89
equity/capital ratio, 89
exchange rate (yen/dollar): set at ¥308/$1, 173; set at ¥360/$1, 61-62, 67, 71, 176
exchange rates, floating, 68, 80, 173, 178
Export-Import Bank of Japan, 89, 98
Export-Import Transactions Law (1952), 88
exports: blockade of, 40-41; dependence on, 164, 178; expansion of, 8, 9, 64, 74, 78, 160, 195; promotion of, 88; volume of, 73

Farmers' Liberation Decree, 19
Fearey, Robert, 19
Federation of Electric Workers' Unions (Denrōren), 84
financial institutions, establishment of, 89
financial system, reorganization of, 89, 98, 146-147
fiscal policy, 43, 77, 90, 97, 101-102, 105, 184, 185, 192, 195, 197, 198
Fisher's equation of exchange, 191-192
Five-year Plan for Electric Power

Development (1956), 116
floating exchange rate system, 68, 80, 173, 178
foreign exchange: allocations, 88, 116; controls, 88, 182; liberalization of restrictions, 132, 133-137; reserves, 135, 157
Foreign Investment Law (Gaishi Hō) (1950), 88
Foreign Trade Control Law, 182
Fuji Steel Company, 86-87, 121, 167
Fukuda Takeo, 191, 195, 198
full employment, 3, 101, 104 131, 137, 140, 157, 193, 195, 202, 210

General Council of Trade Unions (Sōhyō), 65, 67, 96
General Strike (Feb. 1, 1947), stop order for, 28, 49-50
government: economic policies, 35-36, 56-59, 63, 89-90, 97, 98, 100-101, 130-132, 133-137, 178-181, 186, 195-197, 205; industrial policies, 42, 88-90, 148-149; investment, 77, 78, 196
growth: conditions for rapid, 3, 7, 8-11, 107-109, 112-113, 121, 160-163, 201-210; rapid, end of, 3, 11-12, 168, 199-200, 201; rapid, in 1960's, 157, 163; rates of, 3, 5, 96, 121, 139, 143, 157, 195

Harrod-Domar model, 3
Hatoyama Ichirō, 96
heavy industries, 120; export dependence of, 164; investment in, 92; plant and equipment capacity in, 37
Herfindahl index, 167
Holding Company Dissolution Commission, 24, 25
Hori Hiroshi, 138
housing investment, 9
hydroelectric power, 34, 83, 84, 116, 209; switch to steam power, 116-117

Iida Tsuneo, 206, 207
Ikeda Cabinet, 105, 128, 129, 130, 136, 137, 202

Ikeda Hayato, 62, 63, 89, 90, 130, 137, 138, 153, 155
imports: blockade of, 40-41; increase in, 74-75, 100, 107; liberalization of, 133, 136-137, 181; of food, 98; of oil, 116; of passenger cars, 75; of raw materials, 82, 91, 165, 209; of technology, 84, 85
income, distribution of, 9-10, 11, 31, 35, 36, 76, 185
Income Doubling Plan, 105, 130-133, 137, 139, 152, 153
industrial structure, 162, 205; changes in, 6-7, 86-88, 117, 118, 121, 123, 146-147
inflation, 48-49; and Reconstruction Bank, 47; at end of WWII, 3, 35-37, 71, 96; during Korean War, 71; in 1970's, 185-187, 191-195; overseas, due to Vietnam War, 164, 165, 189; principal factors in, 47; under Yoshida Cabinet, 43-44
interest rates, 97, 105, 137-138, 148, 204-205
interfirm credit, 145-146, 158
International Monetary Fund (IMF), 153, 166, 176
international money crisis, 173-187
international trade, entry into, 79-80
inventory: investment in, 107, 195, 196; management of, 138, 146
investment. *See* housing investment; inventory, investment in; plant and equipment investment; private investment; rationalization investment
investment ratio, 5-6
Investment Trust, 89
Iron and Steel Rationalization Plans, 81, 82, 87, 92, 113-114
Ishibashi Cabinet, 138, 202
Ishibashi Tanzan, 43, 44, 89, 101-102
Ishida Hirohide, 128
Itō Masutomi, 78
Itoh Masatoshi, 152
Iwai Akira, 96
Iwasaki Koyata, 24
Iwato boom, 102-105, 111, 137, 140, 143

Japan Development Bank, 89, 98
Japan Electric Power Generation
  and Transmission Company, 87
"Japan, Inc.," 90, 137, 146-147, 204
Japan National Railways (JNR), 64,
  65, 154, 191, 196
Japan Socialist Party (JSP), 96, 137
Japan Steel Corporation, 167
Japan Tobacco and Salt Corpora-
  tion, 64
Jimmu boom, 99-102, 104, 111, 138
Juglar cycle, 143. *See also* business
  cycles
just-in-time system, 120

Kawakami Hajime, 31
Kawasaki Steel Corporation, 82, 87,
  92, 121, 204
keiretsu (financial groupings), 27,
  121, 148, 149-150
Keynesian theory, 43, 137, 140-141,
  178, 189
Kimura Kihachirō, 56
Kishi Cabinet, 128-129, 130, 133
Kishi Nobusuke, 127, 129
Kitchin cycle, 143. *See also* business
  cycles
Kiuchi Nobutane, 89
Komiya Ryūtarō, 148
Korean War, and the Japanese eco-
  nomy, 65-67, 70-75, 80, 210
"kōzaha" theory, 20
Kurusu Takeo, 58

labor federations, 65
labor force: rate of increase, 6; special characteristics of, 207, 209-
  210
labor market, 140, 143, 149, 157,
  198
labor supply, 6, 11, 40, 140, 198
labor unions: enterprise-based, 29,
  205; legislation, 27-28, 64-65;
  Occupation policies for, 27, 64
labor-management relations: in coal
  industry, 129; in electric power industry, 84
land reform, under Occupation, 18,
  19-23, 31, 98
Liberal Democratic Party (LDP),

62, 95-96, 191
liberalization: of capital, 166-167; of
  education, 27, 105; of trade, 133-
  137, 180, 181
lifetime employment system, 193
Loan Trust (Kashitsuke Shintaku),
  89
Lockheed scandal, 180, 191
Long-Term Credit Bank Law
  (1952), 89

MacArthur, Gen. Douglas (SCAP),
  16, 19, 27, 60, 71
machine tool industry, 119, 120
manufacturing industry: production
  levels of, 33, 34, 41, 64, 74
Margaut, William F., 73
marginal capital coefficient, 5, 6,
  376, 91
marine transport, 84
market mechanism, 203-204, 207
mass production, 81, 118-119, 120,
  163
Matsumura Kenzō, 19
Matsunaga Plan (1955), 116
mergers, in 1960's, 167, 168
middle class, development of, 23,
  29, 120, 200, 210
Mihoro Dam, construction of, 84
Miike strike, 128-129
Miki (Takeo) Cabinet, 191
Miki Takashi, 86
Mindō, 65
mining industry: production levels
  of, 33, 34, 41, 64, 74
Ministry of Agriculture and Forestry, 19
Mitsubishi Shōji, 24-25
Mitsubishi zaibatsu, 24
Mitsui Bussan, 24-25
Mitsui Mining Company, 128, 129
Miyazaki Yoshikazu, 121, 148
Mizutani Chōzaburō, 42
monetary policy, 35-36, 56-57, 78,
  90, 97, 147-148, 157, 184, 186,
  187. *See also* tight money policy
money supply, 11, 63, 67, 144, 160

Nagai Kafū, 30
Nakamura Shuichiro, 150

Nakamura Takafusa, 206
Nakayama Ichirō, 74, 75, 79, 128, 130
Nambara Shigeru, 30
Namiki Nobuyoshi, 208
national wealth, wartime damages to, 37
New Economic Policy (U.S.), 68, 173, 176, 184
New Monetary Adjustment System, 143, 147-148
New Public Finance Law (Shin Zaisei Hō), 47
Nichii Company, 152
Nihon Kangyō Bank, 167
Nine-Point Economic Stabilization Plan (1948), 59
Nishiyama Yatarō, 87
Nissan, 119, 167
Nissho-Iwai, 167
"Nixon Shocks," 68, 173-174, 178, 181

Occupation, 16, 17; democratization polices of, 17, 29-30, 53; dissolution of zaibatsu under, 18, 23-27; economic policies of, 18, 43, 53-56, 58, 59; labor policies of, 27, 28-29, 49, 64; land reform policies of, 18, 19; powers of, 16, 21; purges of leaders, 16, 25
Oda Sakunosuke, 30
Ohta Kaoru, 96
oil: displaces coal as energy source, 83, 116, 123; price of, 116
oil crisis, 3, 116, 173, 175, 189, 198
Ōji Paper Company, 87, 167
Okita Saburō, 131
Olympics, 154-156
"one-settism" hypothesis, 121, 148, 204
Operation Scale-Down, 198
Organisation for Economic Cooperation and Development (OECD), 153
Organization of Petroleum Exporting Countries (OPEC), 165
Outline Plan for Trade and Foreign Exchange Liberalization (1960), 133-136

"overloan" phenomenon, 63, 67, 147

paper manufacturing industry, 87
Patriotic Industrial Associations (Sangyō Hōkoku Kai), 29, 207
pattern modification theory, 139, 143
Peace Treaty of San Francisco, 69, 70, 77
petrochemical industry, 117-118
plant and equipment investment, 8, 81, 85, 92, 100, 107, 108-109, 111-113, 138-139, 160; cycles of, 8, 9, 107, 143
plastics industry, 117
political system, stabilized, 95
population: increases in, 39, 40, 50, 58, 123; rural, 22, 123, 137, 163, 183; urban, 123-125, 183
Potsdam Declaration, 15-16, 18
Price Control Ordinance (1946), 36
price controls, 35, 45, 46, 59, 64, 190, 204
price increases, 48, 56, 71, 99, 138-141, 157, 185-186
price-differential subsidies, 44, 45, 47, 71
priority production system (keisha seisan hōshiki), 41-43, 44, 47, 49, 80, 209
private investment, 131
production capacity, 3, 33, 34, 35, 37, 41, 48, 74, 91
productivity: in agriculture, 23, 163; of labor, 6, 161, 168
productivity differential inflation, 139-141
Public Finance Law (1947), 60
public corporations (kōsha), 64, 67

quality control, 82, 163

railroads, 34
rationalization investment, 84-85, 86, 97
rationalization of industry, 64, 77, 108, 119, 209
raw materials: and shifts in technology, 116, 117, 118; dependence

on foreign, 123; high cost of, 92; importation of, 82, 91, 165, 209; shortages of, 40-41, 44, 91, 108, 164, 165, 209
Rebuilding the Japanese Archipelago, 183-184
Rebuilding the Japanese Archipelago Project, 154, 183-184, 189
recession: of 1953, 95; of 1965, 156, 157, 158-159; of 1970's, 179, 191-195
Reconstruction Bank, 44-45, 46-47, 61, 63, 89
reserve deposit system, 104
revaluation, 3, 173-180
"reverse course," 28, 54
Ricardo Effect, 48
Ricardo, David, 165
rice production, 33, 35, 98
"rōnōha" theory, 20
Rostow, W. W., 114, 129
Royall, Kenneth C., 53, 66
Rural Land Reform , Memorandum Concerning (1949), 19

Sakuma Dam, construction of, 83
Satō Cabinet, 157, 159, 167
Satō Eisaku, 155-156, 181
savings, rate of, 9-10, 37, 75, 91, 92, 99, 198
securities market, 138
Seibu Stores, 152
Shibusawa Keizō, 24, 36
Shikano Yoshio, 154
Shimomura Osamu, 107, 111, 131
Shimoyama Sadanori, 65
Shinkansen (Bullet Train), 154, 155, 190
Shinohara Miyohei, 131
shipbuilding industry, 90, 98
Shoup Report, 67
Shōwa Denkō Company, 47, 62
Small Business Finance Corporation, 89
"small country hypothesis," 176, 186, 210
Smithsonian Agreement (1971), 173-175
social progams, 157, 183, 184, 185, 200

Socialist Party, 49, 70
Sōhyō (General Council of Trade Unions), 65, 67, 96
special procurement *(tokuju)* income, 72, 74, 77, 79, 92, 96
stabilization: single-stroke theory, 56, 67; stopgap theory, 56-58, 63, 64, 68
standard of living, 3, 29, 58, 76, 96, 99; improvements in, 76
steam power, takes priority over hydroelectric power, 116-117
Steel Rationalization Plans, 81, 82, 87, 92, 113-114
steel industry, 41-42, 49, 114; operating costs, 80; plant and equipment investment in, 81-82, 113-114; production levels of, 41-42; subsidies to, 45-46, 80
strikes, 22, 28, 49-50, 84, 127. *See also* Miike strike
subcontracting, 119-120
Suez crisis, 101
superpower, Japan as economic, 31, 153-156, 160, 165, 210
Supreme Commander for the Allied Powers (SCAP), 16, 19
Suzuki Mosaburō, 70
Suzuki Takeo, 28, 39, 56
synthetic fibers industry, 84, 85, 118

Tadami River, development of, 83
Takano Minoru, 96
Takenaka Kazuo, 148
Takeuchi Hiroshi, 206, 207
Tanaka Cabinet, 190-191
Tanaka Kakukei, 181, 183
tariff reductions, 180, 181
tax collections, 59, 60, 62, 64
tax cuts, 101, 102
tax system, 67
technology: advances in, 3, 5, 85, 107, 111-125, 160-163, 202-203, 209; importation of, 84, 85, 88, 116, 117, 162
tenant-farmer system, 20-21
tight money policy, 97, 100-101, 104, 105, 107
Tokyo Olympics, 154-156
Toyota Company, 119-120

trade liberalization, 105, 133-137, 180, 181
Trust Fund Bureau banks, 63
Tsuru Shigetō, 80

unemployment, 3, 39-40, 101, 193, 195, 198
United Nations, entry into, 96
United States: trade with, 165-166
U.S. Initial Post-Surrender Policy (1945), 17, 18, 54
U.S.-Japan Security Treaty (Anpo), 69, 127; revision of, 105, 127-129

Vietnam War, 164, 165, 176, 189

wage differentials, 10-11, 76-77

welfare society, 157, 183, 184, 185, 200
West Germany, comparisons with, 41, 48, 56, 58, 65, 98
World War II, effects of, 11, 33, 35, 37, 40-41, 49, 51, 207

Yawata Steel Company, 86, 121, 167
yen: exchange value of, 61-62, 68, 71, 173; revaluation of, 3, 173-180
Yoshida Cabinet, 43, 44, 59, 90
Yoshida Shigeru, 59, 62, 68, 70
Yoshino Toshihiko, 131

zaibatsu, dissolution of, 18, 23-27, 31, 121